Walking Inside Out

Place, Memory, Affect
Series editors: Neil Campbell, Professor of American Studies at the University of Derby, and Christine Berberich, School of Social, Historical and Literary Studies at the University of Portsmouth

The *Place, Memory, Affect* series seeks to extend and deepen debates around the intersections of place, memory, and affect in innovative and challenging ways. The series will forge an agenda for new approaches to the edgy relations of people and place within the transnational global cultures of the twenty-first century and beyond.

Titles in the Series

Walking Inside Out edited by Tina Richardson

Walking Inside Out

Contemporary British Psychogeography

Edited by Tina Richardson

ROWMAN &
LITTLEFIELD
INTERNATIONAL

London • New York

Published by Rowman & Littlefield International, Ltd.
Unit A, Whitacre Mews, 26-34 Stannary Street, London SE11 4AB
www.rowmaninternational.com

Rowman & Littlefield International, Ltd. is an affiliate of Rowman & Littlefield
4501 Forbes Boulevard, Suite 200, Lanham, Maryland 20706, USA
With additional offices in Boulder, New York, Toronto (Canada), and London (UK)
www.rowman.com

British Library Cataloguing in Publication Information Available
A catalogue record for this book is available from the British Library

ISBN: HB 978-1-78348-085-2
ISBN: PB 978-1-78348-086-9

Library of Congress Cataloging-in-Publication Data

Walking inside out : contemporary British psychogeography / edited by Tina Richardson.
pages cm. — (Place, memory, affect)
Includes bibliographical references and index.
ISBN 978-1-78348-085-2 (cloth : alk. paper) — ISBN 978-1-78348-086-9 (pbk. : alk. paper) —
ISBN 978-1-78348-087-6 (electronic)
1. Geographical perception—Great Britain. 2. Human geography—Great Britain. 3. Walking—Great
Britain. 4. City and town life—Great Britain. 5. Sociology, Urban—Great Britain. I. Richardson,
Tina, 1960–
G71.5.W35 2015
914.1001'9—dc23
2015002561

Printed in the United States of America

This book is dedicated to the memory of Victoria Henshaw, who died during the making of this book. She was a kind, generous person, and her knowledge has contributed much to the fields of urban aesthetics and psychogeography.

Contents

Part IV: Practicing Psychogeography/Psychogeographical Practices

Part V: Outsider Psychogeography

Introduction

A Wander through the Scene of British Urban Walking

Tina Richardson

WHAT IS PSYCHOGEOGRAPHY?

Get a map of your local area and spread it out on the floor. Study the map, imagine the terrain, find your preferred route—perhaps a bridleway or a towpath—and trace it on the map. Grab your coat off the hook in the hallway and put on your sturdy shoes. Leave the house and dump the map in the wheelie bin. Forget the map. Go to the nearest bus stop and get on the first bus that comes along. Get off when you feel you are far enough away from home that the area is unfamiliar. Begin your walk here.

Psychogeography does not have to be complicated. Anyone can do it. You do not need a map, Gore-Tex, rucksack, or companion. All you need is a curious nature and a comfortable pair of shoes. There are no rules to doing psychogeography—this is its beauty. However, it is this that makes it hard to pin down in any formalized way. It is also this 'unruly' character (disruptive, unsystematic, random) that makes for much discussion about its meaning and purpose, today more than at any other time.

This volume does not pretend to have a definitive answer to what psychogeography is, but it does propose to open up the space that can be defined as psychogeography, providing examples and encouraging debate. In his introduction to *Psychogeography*, Merlin Coverley asks, 'Are we talking about a predominantly literary movement or a political strategy, a series of new age ideas or a set of avant-garde practices?' and goes on to say that it is all the above (2006, 9–10). In just a couple of sentences, we have opened up a can of nebulous worms on the ambulatory behemoth that psychogeography (or urban walking) is. What this volume does is present the state of play as it is for psychogeography in the United Kingdom in the twenty-first century.

As most texts covering the subject of psychogeography state, the origins of the term stem from the work of the avant-garde Situationist International (SI) (1957–1972), a fluid group of revolutionaries made up of artists and writers. For the SI, psychogeography was the 'study of the

1

specific effects of the geographical environment, consciously organized or not, on the emotions and behavior of individuals' (Andreotti and Costa 1996, 69). The *dérive* was a walking strategy used by the SI. Abdelhafid Khatib, a member, described the dérive thus: 'At the same time as being a form of action, it is a means of knowledge' (1996, 73). For the SI, it was important that the walks included in the dérive could not be considered a 'journey' or a 'stroll' (Debord 1996, 22). Despite the fact that a playful element was deemed essential, those taking part were expected to be conscious of the environment, especially in the way it tied in with a critique of capitalism. Walkers were encouraged to be aware of 'fissures in the urban network . . . microclimates . . . administrative districts, and above all the dominating action of centers of attraction' (ibid.). This book does not focus solely on the SI because there is ample material already available on and by them. Their work is referenced where relevant to the topic at hand, and there are two chapters that discuss their work in the context of practice and theory (see chapters 8 and 14).

While this volume concentrates on British psychogeography, dividing international and home-grown psychogeography into clearly delineated groups is not representative of the lineage of contemporary urban walking. Psychogeography is about crossing established boundaries, whether metaphorically or physically, locally or globally. The Situationists did not limit their psychogeography to their own location (Paris). They walked other cities, such as Venice and Amsterdam, and incorporated existing maps of cities (for instance, of the New York and London transport networks) into their own maps. Recent projects in the United Kingdom have involved international cities working together. One example was the Leeds-Dortmund Project (part of Superimposed City Tours 2002–2003) and incorporated a simultaneous psychogeographical mapping of both cities and their accompanying narratives. The newly created superimpositions were then seen as a virtual city, this third city resulting from the overlap of the other two. So, too, British psychogeographers often do not limit themselves to just British towns and cities. Will Self's *Psychogeography* (2007) includes walks in Liverpool and London, alongside those in Istanbul and New York. And Phil Wood, in chapter 5 of this volume, discusses two places he has explored abroad—Lviv and Odessa—demonstrating the peripatetic migration of walking across international lines.

Many see the origins of British psychogeography in the work of the SI. As Duncan Hay explained in his paper to the Literary London Conference in 2008, the methods of the SI can readily be translated to that of the contemporary London psychogeographer and writer Iain Sinclair:

> The technique of drifting, navigating the city on foot, the reading of the city in terms of the psychological effect that it has upon the individual that are present in the Situationist definition of psychogeography are all present in Sinclair's understanding of it. However, if one examines

the development of the concept from its emergence in 1950s Paris to its contemporary London usage, whilst the methodological foundations of psychogeography remain more or less constant, its teleological assumptions have shifted radically. (Hay 2008)

Hay goes on to explain that for Sinclair the method of walking itself might be similar to that of the SI. However, for the Situationists it was a revolutionary and utopian act, while Sinclair 'finds its expression as a literary mode, a position that would have appeared paradoxical to its original practitioners' (ibid.).[1]

The *flâneur* of nineteenth-century Paris is also considered an influence on urban walking today. Charles Baudelaire created the term, which referred to the male stroller of the city who took the position of a passive and detached observer of urban phenomena. While it is a rather nebulous term and still remains so, the flâneur was usually considered bourgeois, or at least independently wealthy, most likely a writer of sorts, and often a dandy. The first description of this character appeared in Baudelaire's 1836 text *The Painter of Modern Life*, which provided Walter Benjamin with material for *The Arcades Project*, his unfinished project on the Parisian arcades.

To a degree the surrealists have also been influential on contemporary urban walking. Translating the unconscious act of automatic writing into moving about urban space, the surrealists encouraged a form of walking influenced by subliminal desires. In 2013 the Museum of Modern Art (New York) put on a series of walks organized by Todd Shalom of the group Elastic City that was influenced by the surrealists' approach to urban walking. And a summer solstice walk was organized in June 2014 in London by Southwark Council and CoolTan Arts Largactyl Shuffles, which was a surrealist-influenced five-hour nighttime walk.

While these examples demonstrate the historic influence of European traditions of urban walking on those taking place today in Britain and elsewhere, what adds to the complexity of psychogeography is its heterogeneity. Rather, when using the term *psychogeography*, one should always be thinking of psychogeograph*ies*. The bricolage nature of psychogeography means that its influence for a specific group or individual will be vastly different from that of another. Even if two psychogeographers define what they do in, say, Situationist terms, this will result in a different practice and result for each of them. It might be better to think of the historic influences of urban walking practices as being a kind of toolbox for contemporary psychogeographers.

This volume sets out to demonstrate the diversity of urban walking in Britain today through the numerous factors that make up the walk itself: the individual walker(s), the space of the walk (town/city, rural/urban/suburban and so on), the 'method' (if there is a defined method being utilized, and, in fact, if there is no method, this is also a type of method for carrying out psychogeography) and the phenomena under observation or critique (urban decor, surface textures, prohibitive signs, other people, buildings, cars and so on). These are just a few of the factors that influence the walk itself. One could look further at such factors as night- versus daytime walking, as this also greatly changes the experience, and also the weather, especially in somewhere like Britain where it can change from moment to moment. The city looks hugely different on a bright sunny day than when it is overcast. These features of the walk change the subjective nature of the walk in the same way the intentions of the individual walker do.

Ultimately, people's motivations to walk are multifarious, and along- side psychogeography there exist many different terms for alternative forms of walking: rambling, perambulation, strolling, stalking, trekking, hiking, streetwalking, yomping, cruising and so on. I am discussing psychogeography as a method of walking that responds to and critiques the terrain. Nevertheless, I would like to add that in the instances it is used in this book, the forms of walking discussed are to be distinguished from a casual 'Sunday stroll.'

The authors in this book all practice or study urban walking as a way of responding to the environment, and it is carried out in an active rather than passive way, even though their methods differ. There are many different approaches to psychogeography. This might be in the way the paths are chosen (for example, by creating chance routes through space, as it would have been for the SI) or in the way the practical work is analysed or written up (for instance, in a prosaic or fictional account or with accompanying theoretical analysis [or the two combined, as some of the chapters in this volume show]). This book illustrates the variety of approaches and outputs of the walking practice. Significantly, what it sets out to do is bring together the work of the contemporary psycho- geographer, who comes from a creative and literary background, with academics also working in the field. I appreciate that this might engender the criticism of the academization of psychogeography. However, be- cause I am oriented in academia and my field is psychogeography, it is impossible to do the work itself without being caught in this trap. I would prefer to see it as an acknowledgement that, as academics, we do not have sole knowledge on this subject.[2] Academics might be able to philosophize, theorize and critique walking-based practices—while ob- serving them from the outside—but it is the walking itself that is psycho- geography. It is the psychogeographer who makes psychogeography happen. And, most of the time, these bipedal critics of urban space are not located in academia, nor are the product of their explorations. This means that psychogeographical texts have a tendency to be classified and indexed separately from academic texts. This is because it is the profes- sional location of the psychogeographer that influences where his or her work is published. Not only are they filed under different book categories outside of the institutional library (in the high street or on the online bookshop) but, even within higher education, the books on walking are a disparate set. They can be indexed under anything from philosophy to English literature, art to sociology.[3]

The biggest concern, as it pertains to the vagueness of the term *psychogeography* and to the task at hand, is that the texts by urban walkers that do not emanate from academia might be considered to have less 'value' in an academic setting. Not 'high-profile' published texts on the subject— such as the work by Sinclair or Self—but other forms of published content, such as blogs or small-production hard-copy zines. This can be seen as a value judgement on the material itself, although it has little to do with the quality of the actual work, in regards to both the practice of walking and the quality of writing. It is often these types of outputs, like blogs, that demonstrate the creative expression that language takes in psychogeographical accounts.

In *Cityscapes*, Ben Highmore uses the term *thickness* to describe a depth of description attached to cultural spaces (2005, 17) and says that it can be found in nonacademic texts about the city (30). These 'invented' terms bring something to descriptions of the city that acknowledge its complexity and at the same time focus on the subjective responses to its spaces. Psychogeography's modus operandi is this very subjective response, as is clear in the style of a number of the chapters contained here and their acknowledgement of terms like *affect* and *aesthetics*. These terms deal directly with psychological and individual reactions to objects, spaces and environments and feed into such concepts as mood and feelings. In a way they are the 'bread and butter' of psychogeography, the matter that enables its output (for example, in the form of the written word or in filmic images). It is this that means psychogeographical accounts can sometimes appear to be at odds with academic writing. The reflexive and subjective nature of responding to space in a psychogeographical way involves not only the negotiation of the terrain under exploration but also sometimes the negotiation of the site of writing itself. At times a space has to be carved out within academia to accommodate new types of writing and enable disruptive 'situations' to arise, challenging well-established conventions and provoking discussion.

It is apparent in this introduction, and the following chapters, how complex the term *psychogeography* is. There are no doubt readers who disagree with whom I have classified as a psychogeographer, and I accept this. However, this text is designed to reflect the broad field of urban (also suburban and at times rural) walking in Britain today and to promote discussion on whatever it is we might see psychogeography as being and becoming. I encourage readers to define their own form of *psychogeography* or use one of the many definitions included herein and to debate the merits of psychogeography and how we might put it to use in the twenty-first century. Indeed, this is the intention of the book: to spark discussion as much as to provide a representative sample of the work of some of the contemporary psychogeographers in the United Kingdom.

So far I have mostly used the term *urban walking* synonymously with *psychogeography*; however, this is an oversimplification. Because historically psychogeography is often associated with the SI and was one of their methods for critiquing the spectacle, it tends to be associated with urban space, as this is where the spectacle is most clearly expressed (in the images that mediate capital, the high street being a good example). But some psychogeographers do countertourist activities, which stray into more rural areas. Also, one might do a walk that crosses urban, suburban, or rural boundaries, so can we fairly say that we are not doing psychogeography at the point we cross these nebulous lines? Nick Papadimitriou's geographic concentration is the English county that used to be called Middlesex, and his book on the region, *Scarp* (2012), expresses the musings of someone who has walked and studied the area at length.[4] This region is urban and suburban but also contains Greater London's green belt. Papadimitriou was inspired by Gordon S. Maxwell's *The Fringe of London: Being Some Ventures and Adventures in Topography* (1925), where the author walked the outskirts of London, including the area containing Papadimitriou's geographical formation, the scarp itself. In 1925 these parts of what later became the peripheries of Greater London would have been much more rural than they are now when walked by Papadimitriou.

And what about areas that could be classified as completely rural? Can one be considered to be carrying out psychogeography in this terrain? There was a type of psychogeography that was developed by Howard F. Stein and quite likely preceded that of the SI. In his book *Developmental Time, Cultural Space: Studies in Psychogeography* (1987), Stein did not see psychogeography as an indefinable or cryptic response to space at all but something that is ever present in the individual. Approaching it from a psychoanalytical angle, Stein saw psychogeography as referring to 'people's shared psychological representation or "map" of the natural and social world' (1987, 3). In his edited text with William G. Niederland, *Maps from the Mind: Readings in Psychogeography*, Stein describes it thus: 'Psychogeography is the study of how issues, experiences, and processes that result from growing up in a male or female body . . . become symbolized and played out in the wider social and natural worlds, which serve as "screens" for these inner dramas' (1989, xvii). For Niederland and Stein, psychogeography took a Freudian look at space, which considered the inner life of the individual and, therefore, also his or her gender. This psychogeographic study aimed to look at what connected someone to place and how geography (whether urban or rural) made a person who he or she was.

There is little left of what might be described as 'natural' land when we look at rural space. What we see as 'nature' today is often what geographers would call second nature; it is land that has already been worked on (e.g., rural 'beauty spots' that have public access but can also be used for sheep grazing). W. G. Sebald's *The Rings of Saturn (Die Ringe des Saturn)* (1995) is a psychogeographical book covering the county of Suffolk. Sebald's protagonist (considered to be Sebald himself) walks urban, rural and coastal Suffolk (and parts of Norfolk). This region is also covered by Self in *Psychogeography*, where he acknowledges Sebald's walks. Chapter 2 in this book, by Ian Marchant, covers a regular walk he takes in Presteigne in Powys, Wales. The town sits at the edge of the countryside on the river Lugg, demonstrating that delineating psychogeography as a purely urban act is not representative of the practice. While the term *psychogeography* has generally been applied to urbia and can be a convenient way to differentiate the walking from that carried out in the countryside, its urban and rural deconstruction is just one of the qualities that adds to its indefinable character.

This volume is not a history of psychogeography, as Coverley has skilfully and more than adequately already written. Instead, it looks at the nuances between different types of critical urban walking. Psychogeography has its problems and its detractors, not least because of its vague label, although this vagueness could be seen as being positive as much as it is negative. I am sure that, in part, it is its undefinable quality that has led to its endurance. It can be utilized in a critical, creative and productive way and enable us to turn psychogeography into a micropolitical act, giving us a sense of autonomy when moving through the urban landscape. While the philosophical theories of Michel Foucault, or even Gilles Deleuze and Félix Guattari, do not deal specifically with walking in regard to power, their theories on micro- and biopolitics enable a useful critique of the body in space, which anyone interested in walking and power might find helpful in applying to walking practices, especially if one is a student or researcher in the field. Undertaking walking, while being cognizant of the urban decor around you, draws your attention to the power structures that are laid down in urban topography. These authoritarian schemas are not necessarily apparent on a casual walk, nor on the well-trodden routes that one might take daily: it is easy not to question the homogenizing effect of urban planning, where everything looks comfortably in its place and, in a sense, like it has been that way 'forever.'

The interdisciplinary nature of psychogeography enables a crossover with many broad academic fields (for example, art, performance studies, cultural studies, geography, social history and politics).[5] Four recently issued books reflect not only the current resurgence of walking-based practices but also the diverse nature of the authors' backgrounds: *Explore Everything: Place-Hacking the City* (2013) by Bradley Garrett (a human geographer), *A Philosophy of Walking* (2014) by Frédéric Gros (a philosopher), *The Psychogeography of Urban Architecture* (2013) by David Prescott-

Steed (a sound artist and urban walker) and *On Walking . . . and Stalking Sebald* (2014) by Phil Smith (an academic from a performance background who also wrote chapter 10 in this volume).

There are many texts on the subject of walking that are often applied theoretically to urban space. An example of this would be Michel de Certeau's 'Walking in the City' (2006; first published in 1980). It offers us a method of walking as a 'space of enunciation,' which he opens with his observation of New York's Manhattan from the 110th floor of the World Trade Center (de Certeau 2006, 98). His text provides us with a new character in the urban story, the city itself: the '*universal* and anonymous *subject*' (2006, 94; italics in the original). De Certeau makes useful semantic comparisons with the city and language, explaining that below the dominant discourse of the city lie alternative stories. This provides an opportunity for the city to be examined at the micro level through what he describes as 'spatial practices,' which take the form of modes of resistance (2006, 96). What de Certeau calls 'pedestrian speech acts' enable connections to come into being through a type of social contract (2006, 97–98). Thus, the 'act of walking is to the urban system what the speech act is to language or to statements uttered' (2006, 97).

Rebecca Solnit opens her introduction to *Wanderlust: A History of Walking* (2002) with the example of Doris Haddock, who in 1999 at the age of eighty-eight set off to walk across America because of her dislike of hostile financial corporate interests and to campaign for finance reform. Solnit explains, 'It was no coincidence that she chose an activity that required openness, engagement and few expenses to make her protest against the hidden corrosion of big money' (2002, xi). Solnit's concise study of walking—from Rousseau to Wordsworth, the Boy Scouts to the Situationists—provides us with every possible way of looking at walking, beginning in the first chapter with the physiological movement itself and finishing with one of her own walks in Nevada. At times Solnit also describes the city as a language; however, referring to de Certeau, she adds a caveat: 'If the city is a language spoken by walkers, then a pedestrian city not only has fallen silent but risks becoming a dead language' (2002, 213). Solnit also discusses the lack of theory on walking, something that this volume proposes to work towards addressing.

There are also many texts that deal with the city and urban space that can be applied to the practice of walking. And because these fields of theory are so broad, it is possible to find texts that deal with the specific type of psychogeographical enquiry one might wish to explore. Henri Lefebvre's *The Production of Space* (1991) supplies us with terms that enable us to analyse urban space and the practices that are involved in it. Also, in his homage to Raymond Williams, the geographer David Harvey offers us another approach to looking at space. In 'Space as a Keyword' (2006), Harvey breaks down space into absolute, relative and relational. Both Lefebvre's and Harvey's frameworks allow for methods of categorizing space that highlight a place that can appear at once dominant or rigid but also subjective or fluid, allowing room for negotiation or even appropriation. And one of the ways these challenges to space can take place is through the performative act of walking.

The zine-style format of Laura Oldfield Ford's *Savage Messiah* (2011) demonstrates the flexibility of the output of a walking-based critique of urban space that takes an activist approach. There is also a vast selection of psychogeographically oriented blogs available online. Most of the writers included in this volume have their own blogs, but other British walking blogs and bloggers include *Liminal City* (Matt Barnes), *The Lost Byway* (John Rogers), *The Psychogeographic Review* (Bobby Seal) and *The Fife Psychogeographical Collective*. As is the case with these blogs, the chapters in this book reflect the diversity of practice and context for British psychogeography today. And, so as not to duplicate the work by others on the lineage of British psychogeography, I shall include a short and selective history of contemporary psychogeography in the United Kingdom so as to orient the content of this volume. Coverley has written extensively about the British psychogeographical writers (primarily) of the late twentieth century, so I am not repeating that history here (see chapter 6, 'The Art of Wandering: Arthur Machen's London Science,' by Coverley, in this volume). But I briefly summarize some of the characters of the recent urban landscape so as to orient the current cohort within its relevant ancestry. I look in more depth from the point where Coverley's *Psychogeography* leaves off and introduce some of the recurring motifs that are redolent of current British psychogeography. This introduction should not be considered an extensive history of the past ten years (which would require its own book), but rather more a wander through the winding passageways of the topography of today's urban walking.

PERSONALITIES AND PERMUTATIONS

Arguably the most high-profile British psychogeographer is Sinclair, who is often labelled as being one of the 'London psychogeographers,' although this grouping tends to imply that all their approaches are the same when not even the geographical concentration is, it being so vast an area. Sinclair's influence and expertise in the field should not be understated. And while he describes William Blake as the godfather of psychogeography, the godfather of contemporary psychogeography is really Sinclair himself. Originally a filmmaker, Sinclair's books on London include *Lights Out for the Territory: 9 Excursions in the Secret History of London* (1997) and *Hackney, That Rose-Red Empire: A Confidential Report* (2009), in addition to such films as *Swandown* (2012), made with Andrew Kotting (which took a critical look at the impact of the London Olympics on the region).[6]

Coverley describes Sinclair's view of London as being one that 'views the present from the prism of the past' (2006, 14), which means he is often criticized for taking a nostalgic perspective of the landscape. British psychogeography, in particular, is often highlighted for its nostalgic bent, with Sinclair being cited as one of the main proponents of an approach where 'loss and redemption are explored and negotiated' (Bonnett 2009, 54). Alistair Bonnett's article 'The Dilemmas of Radical Nostalgia in British Psychogeography' explores these notions alongside a consideration that this strand frequently sits next to a radical activist lineage of psychogeography in Britain. Bonnett's question centres on how walkers can 're-enchant and de-mythologize prosaic geographies' (ibid., 46), and while this could be considered a positive thing, he sees it as not being constructive to contemporary political situations because it can sometimes be 'inadequate' and 'eccentric' (ibid., 48).

Nostalgia was recognized by the Situationists, who attempted to use old ruined buildings as sites that represented a historic mythical narrative—what they called the 'charms of ruins'—in order to critique the use of these buildings as spectacle. An example of this is their interest in the paintings of Claude Lorrain, a French baroque artist known for his romantic approach to landscapes and ruined architecture. In their map *Axis of Exploration and Failure in the Search for a Situationist Great Passage*, the SI used Lorrain's *Seaport with the Embarkation of Saint Ursula* (1641). This reappropriation by the SI was, as Thomas F. McDonough explains, a recognition by them 'that these "norms of abstract space" that construct the public domain as evacuated were not "charming at all"' (1994, 77). Nevertheless, Bonnett's recent work with Catherine Alexander demonstrates that nostalgia can be a positive reaction to postmodern space: nostalgia can be seen as a '"productive" and "living" disposition' (2012, 391; see his 'Walking through Memory: Critical Nostalgia and the City,' chapter 4 in this volume).

The criticism of nostalgia is often attributed to the occult aspect of psychogeographical texts that are written, in particular, about London. These books reveal hidden histories and forgotten characters and attract disapproval from some critics. It could be related to a 'harking back' to a 'rose-tinted' past that probably did not really exist. It might even be that the critique is levelled more at the reader, who can consume the rediscovered histories from the comfort of home without needing to do the actual 'legwork.' The reader of the book is then seen as viewing history at a distance, in a way as if it is not history at all but just a story about a mythical place.

Sinclair is considered part of the 'earth mysteries' strand of psychogeography, which looks at the more historic and hidden aspect of the landscape and contrasts with the activist psychogeographic tradition of the groups, such as the SI (although Hay states that Debord's walking style can be transposed onto that of Sinclair in *Lights Out for the Territory*).

Included within the earth mysteries strand is the theory of ley lines, a phrase coined by Alfred Watkins to explain the ancient paths that connected monuments and places of cultural and spiritual importance (often connected with paganism). Papadimitriou is also interested in ley lines, although he would not describe himself as a psychogeographer, but rather as a deep topographer. In *Scarp*, deep topography is described as the 'land's very structure and memory unfurling in the mind' (Papadimitriou 2012, 255). Papadimitriou has risen to prominence in recent times and had a film made about him, *London Perambulator* (2009), directed by his friend and long-term collaborator, the psychogeographer John Rogers (see Rogers's 2013 book *This Other London: Adventures in the Overlooked City* for an example of his work).

Self's aforementioned text and his *Psycho Too* (2009) reflect his caustic wit, and it is this type of subjective response to place that seems to be acceptable in textual representations of psychogeographic walks that come from a contemporary literary tradition. In an interview with Lee Rourke in 2007, Coverley states that the term *psychogeography* has now become a 'post-modern buzzword' as a direct result of Self's column in the *Independent*, which later became the book *Psychogeography*: 'When a column in a national broadsheet uses Psychogeography as its title you know the game's up' he says (cited in Rourke 2007). However, he believes this is also what has enabled its endurance, taking it out of the somewhat inaccessible field of the avant-garde (ibid.). It is this moment in psychogeography that Coverley says reflects the shift of its perspective and its accessibility to those who might not have an interest in the more activist Situationist approach. Coverley says it is writers like Peter Ackroyd who reflect this strand. Although not necessarily a psychogeographer in the way we might describe Sinclair, Ackroyd's books on London, such as *London: The Biography* (2000), alongside his connection to what has been termed *urban exploration*, have drawn psychogeographers to his work. Phil Baker says of Ackroyd that his 'almost Platonic worship of continuity is a neo-conservative attempt to change, and to reinscribe the city that threatens to become illegible' (2003, 328). More recently, Ackroyd published *London Under* (2011) which looks at the hidden London concealed beneath the concrete surface of the city, like sewers and underground stations. This idea of the unseen and often unreachable spaces that exist beyond the Londoners' gazes is in keeping with an interest expressed in such pursuits as bunkerology (the exploration of disused military bunkers). The urban walker Luke Bennett (originally a lawyer and also known for bunkerology) contributes chapter 3, 'Incongruous Steps toward a Legal Psychogeography,' in this book.

The current place-hacking work carried out by urban explorers (also known as UrbEx groups) and such individuals as Garrett responds to the city in a very specific way. Garrett illegally climbed the Shard in London in 2012 and was arrested for his efforts, to much media attention (see also

Mount London: Ascents in the Vertical City [2013], edited by Joe Dunthorne and Bradley Garrett, for similar studies). While there is a crossover with UrbEx and psychogeography, in order not to divert this introduction into other fields of urban exploration, I return to the literary tradition of psychogeography-oriented texts by briefly talking about J. G. Ballard, who, like Garrett, often responded to the vertical nature of the expanding city, although in a way much less threatening to his own life.

Ballard's dystopic novels on the encroaching nature of the effects of urban space on identity are reflective of a postmodern moment of a sense of loss that can provoke strange behaviour in the city dweller. His novel *High Rise* (1975) is about the residents of a tower block who, following a long-term power cut, organize themselves hierarchically (vertically by social class within the building itself) and devolve to a basic level of human development in order to survive (*High Rise* is currently being turned into a film). Ballard's books, while looking at the extremes of maladaptation to city living, bring to our attention the affective response of people to space.

Chris Petit's film *London Orbital* (2002), made with Sinclair, provides a Ballardian journey (and actually includes Ballard) around London's largest ringroad cum motorway, the M25. Patrick Keiller's films also reflect the idea of loss, but one rather more couched in mourning than in dystopia (although they do deal with what could be termed *societal decline*). Keiller's 'Robinson' films—*London* (1994), *Robinson in Space* (1997) and *Robinson in Ruins* (2011)—chart how the economic climate has played out in the London landscape during this period (the last of these films moving from the urban to the more suburban and rural). Owen Hatherley, regarding whether Keiller is a psychogeographer, says that he is 'occasionally welcomed into this zone, which is curious, given how it represents the precise opposite—a concretely politico-economic interrogation of landscape and its production, leavened with a flirtatious humour far from London literary laddishness' (2012). Keiller's protagonist Robinson—a part-time lecturer who in *Robinson in Ruins* has just been released from an open prison for a white-collar crime—haunts the spaces of his past. The concept of haunting (hauntology) is a key theme in some psychogeographical writings (see Phil Wood's chapter 5 herein). This is often reflected in the complexity of the palimpsest terrain of postmodernity, whereby psychogeography opens up the layers of space to reveal the ghosts of the past.

Keiller's essay films cum mockumentaries exemplify the subjective and aesthetic responses individuals have to space. They 'contain an instructive story on the relationship between cultural research and aesthetic practice, on the one hand, and the encroaching reach of neoliberalism as it has reshaped public bodies responsible for culture and the arts, on the other' (Dave 2011, 19). This neoliberalist approach to space is discussed further in my 'Developing Schizocartography: Formulating a Theoretical Methodology for a Walking Practice' (chapter 11).

Keiller's *Robinson in Ruins* also reflects the current interest in what could be termed *ruinology* or *ruin lust* (a polite term for what is often called *ruin porn*). In 2014 the Tate Britain held an exhibition on art and the ruin. The exhibition, and its supporting book by Brian Dillon, coincided with Geoff Nicholson's book *Walking in Ruins* (2013), although Tim Edensor's book *Industrial Ruins: Space, Aesthetics and Materiality* (2005) predates this example. Ruin lust is a subject in its own right, and many texts are available, depending on the angle one chooses to take to it. Edensor is also a walker, and industrial ruins are a common interest for contemporary psychogeographers. Nicholson is a walker, too, but, though British, he is based in Los Angeles.

Artists (both performance and visual), while not always describing themselves as psychogeographers, might call themselves 'walking artists.' There is a Walking Artists Network, which was set up in 2007 (www.walkingartistsnetwork.org). It enables artists to connect with each other, share ideas and further explore their art practices. Richard Long's *A Line Made by Walking* (1967) is a good example of a walking-based art project. It was a track left in the grass from walking backward and forward over the same trail. A discussion on the walking collective Wrights and Sites is included in Phil Smith's 'Psychogeography and Mythogeography: Currents in Radical Walking' (chapter 10 in this book). But I provide an example of another performance-oriented walking collective so as to situate this area within a contemporary interventionist approach to space.

C. Cred is a fluid arts collective that works on collaborative projects that attempt to connect to politics by opening dialogue, forming networks and encouraging learning. *Counter.Cartographies* is the title they have given a series of walks. Mostly based in London, they also worked in conjunction with the 16Beavergroup in New York on the aforementioned cartography project. They describe the motivation behind their walks as follows: 'Using the simple medium of collective walking, we wanted to explore and intervene in the historical, cultural and sociopolitical contexts of artistic practice and challenge what we felt were a set of often normative and authoritarian structures put into place by the various cultural and academic industries that seemed to us to govern the parameters of artistic production' (Cred 2007, 119). They explain that the walks created spaces for dialogue in the 'nomadic structures' that were made available, with the walking becoming a way to take apart dominant narratives that are invested geographically (ibid.). The walks were archived through images and texts, which were accessible to anyone and could be altered in any way or even totally destroyed. While the members of C. Cred might not describe themselves as a 'psychogeography group,' there are commonalities between such art-activist collectives and some psychogeography and urban-walking groups.

Many British psychogeography groups have appeared since the resurgence of interest in the field in the 1990s that came about with the London Psychogeographical Association (LPA; 1992–2000). These include the Loiterers Resistance Movement (LRM; a Manchester group run by Morag Rose, who wrote chapter 9 in this volume) and the Leeds Psychogeography Group (set up and run by myself from 2009 to 2013). In Scotland there is the Fife Psychogeographical Collective, which organizes field trips in the liminal spaces of Fife, and also the Psychogeographical Commission in Glasgow. At the time of the LPA, there also existed groups like the Nottingham Psychogeographical Unit and the Manchester Area Psychogeographic.[7]

Baker describes the LPA as a 'far-left post-Situationist group with a penchant for pranksterism and disinformation' (2003, 327). They were strongly influenced by the avant-garde artist Stewart Home, who produced a number of newsletters, pamphlets and journals under the fluid collective that was the LPA. Coverley says of Home that his 'flair for self-publicity has led him to be equated with the group and to be regarded as the author of its newsletter, yet, in reality, he appears not to have been a member' (2006, 129). Coming from the radical left and often representing antiestablishment ideals (rather like the Merry Pranksters of the hippy movement), Home presented the philosophical concepts that interested him in an ironic fashion. An LPA article titled 'Why Psychogeography?' appears in Home's own book *Mind Invaders: A Reader in Psychic Warfare, Cultural Sabotage and Semiotic Terrorism* (1997) and describes the LPA's principles along these lines: 'Psychogeography places itself beyond democracy. There is no process of sifting through everyone's experience of daily life to reproduce it as a soap opera, a political programme or college doctorate' (London Psychogeographical Association 1997, 136). *Transgressions: A Journal of Urban Exploration* was associated with the LPA and produced for four editions from 1995 to 2000. The final issue includes an editorial by Bonnett, an essay by the lecturer in architecture Thom Gorst and a report by Luther Blissett (a pseudonym that is also associated with the group).

Connected with the LPA were Fabian Tompsett (a.k.a. Richard Essex) and Tom Vague. Vague produced postpunk fanzines and psychogeographical reports. One pamphlet entitled *Wild West II* includes a large poster of Trellick Tower, the brutalist public housing project in London designed by Ernő Goldfinger (1972). Vague's booklet *London Psychogeography: Rachman Riots and Rillington Place* has an article in diarized format of the Christie murders at 10 Rillington Place, and another on the scandal and myths surrounding the 'slum landlord' Peter Rachman, who owned properties in Notting Hill. These types of short-run, low-cost production magazines are representative of the LPA (and psychogeography zines in general) and are an important part of British psychogeography heritage.

THE OTHER OF AND IN PSYCHOGEOGRAPHY

In the film *London Perambulator*, Papadimitriou acknowledges the issue of the other of psychogeography in regard to 'the gaze': 'It's about getting a very, very dangerous balance between finding the overlooked, and showing it to the other people who have an eye for the overlooked and not making the overlooked into something that is gazed at . . . like people looking through the bars of a monkey house while some baboon plays with his penis or picks his arse' (cited in Rogers 2009). In defining *deep topography*, Papadimitriou makes it clear that he does not want it to become 'touristic.' While this concept highlights the political dialectic of the other as being outside, located in urban space, it should also be noted that the other is also an issue for the inside of psychogeography, both from the perspective of the gender bias toward male psychogeographers and in the imposition of power in space itself as it is directed at the urban walker, whatever his or her gender.

Psychogeography has been oriented in a masculine tradition. This may have something to do with the historical exploration and colonization of space and the discovery of the New World, a domination of space that creates an order out of a chaos that is oriented in the lack of an anthropological understanding of other cultures. I am not suggesting that today's male psychogeographers are simply living though some evolutionary governing of geographical space via the phallus, but one should look at the stereotype of a psychogeographer. In the past this field has often been considered the pursuit of middle-aged men who are fortunate enough to have the luxury of time and money in order to wander through urban space formulating a commentary on it, as was the case with the flâneur. Today we might imagine a stereotype of a middle-aged, middle-class man with a rucksack and an Ordnance Survey map.

Ford dislikes her work being described as psychogeography for that very reason: 'I think a lot of what is called psychogeography now is just middle-class men acting like colonial explorers, showing us their discoveries and guarding their plot. . . . I think my understanding and negotiation of the city is very different to theirs' (2011, xiv). While this stereotype might describe a good percentage of psychogeographers, it nevertheless is not completely representative, and Ford demonstrates this by proffering herself as an example of the contrary, as do I with my own form of urban walking and as you will also see from the contributions included herein by female psychogeographers: Andrea Capstick (chapter 13), Victoria Henshaw (chapter 12) and Morag Rose (chapter 9).

Michèle Bernstein was a rare female member of the SI (and wife of Debord) and undertook some interesting psychogeographical work, specifically on places in Paris that she thought were being destroyed, such as the Square des Missions Étrangères. There are many more female psychogeographers (and urban walkers or critics of urban space) now than there were only a few years ago. There is even a branch of specifically feminist psychogeography that has developed in recent times. An example of this is the work that Judith Burnett, Erika Cudworth and Maria Tamboukou have done with women and dériving. Groups that carry out feminist walking practices include Precarias a la Deriva ('precarious women workers adrift'), a Spanish collective of activists interested in labour issues. One could also look at the work of the academics Dee Heddon and Cathy Turner in this field. Regarding this unrepresentative aspect of psychogeography, Smith states, 'I think it may be time to make a very clear distinction between what the dominant narratives and values tell us that walking women do and what those women, in the face of both real physical challenges and tales of their absence, actually do' (2014, 163). I direct you to chapter 9 by Rose and chapter 14 by Bridger in this volume for a discussion on feminist psychogeography.

While this feminist perspective alludes to the power located in historically gendered professions in general, there are also power structures that both female and male urban walkers are subjected to. Sinclair provides an example of how individuals who do not fit the model of a certain type of citizen can become a *persona non grata* in urban space:

> And so it was, on the fine and pleasant afternoon of Saturday 8th April, 1995, that I found myself trying to walk in through the front entrance of the Barbican Arts Complex and being treated like a bogside bomb-carrier. The sensation is not uncommon in the new City. It's how they want you to feel, uncomfortable: the stranger in town. They want you to carry a card, with a photograph and a number, that defines you as some sort of non-person lowlife. (2003, 99)

The Barbican Exhibition Hall is located in the heart of the finance district in London, and during the 1990s British security became very constricted because of the IRA bombings in the capital at that time. The reaction that Sinclair was subjected to is a common side-effect of being a psychogeographer (and also an urban photographer). Anecdotes abound of psychogeographers' 'run-ins' with security staff. This is a by-product of the paranoia inherent in surveillance society which has increased since 2001.

The elements of urban decor that reflect this phenomena, such as prohibitive signs that appear in the environment, can be intriguing to psychogeographers; however, they often represent the authoritarian approach of organizations in 'guarding their plot.' In his essay on walking around Bromley-by-Bow in London, Dougald Hine (a specialist in urban space and community living) explains how the signs that forbid action are the ones that predominate: 'Spaces are defined by the games we can't play, the activities which won't be tolerated' (2011, 4). He then remarks, 'Where are the suggestive signs, I wonder—the signs which invite you to try something you might not otherwise have thought of? . . . Even the sign at Prospect Park which reads "Play Here" feels like a command, rather than an invitation' (2011, 5).

Psychogeographers have to decide what boundaries they are prepared to cross, legal or physical, in order to find their 'story.' Maxwell states, 'The true rambler must never be afraid of committing the crime of trespass; fair words are a better help than fast legs' (1925, 22). However, in 1925, society was far simpler in structure, and such crimes as trespass might have not even been reported. Maxwell goes on to say, 'On the whole, people are courteous, when they know your errand is harmless. . . . I have known an Ordnance Survey map works wonders if prominently displayed. You are sometimes then mistaken for a Government surveyor by a farm labourer—a mistake which is often useful' (ibid.). This innocent comment is starkly contrasted to Sinclair's experience outside the Barbican. Nowadays a map in the hands of someone whose appearance might be deemed suspicious could be seen as a sign of a potential 'terrorist threat.'

THE PHENOMENOLOGY OF PSYCHOGEOGRAPHY

Coverley describes psychogeography as 'cutting across established routes and exploring those marginal and forgotten areas often overlooked by the city's inhabitants' (2006, 12), and I think this would be a good way of describing why many contemporary psychogeographers walk. It would at least be partly correct to say psychogeographers 'seek to reveal the true nature that lies beneath the flux of the everyday' (ibid., 13), although I would extend that to 'truths' in order to reflect the multiplicity of histories captured in the postmodern terrain. And, if individuals have a problem with labelling themselves, or others, as psychogeographers, then we can remain cognizant of Coverley's earlier quote and ask, 'Is this what I do?' If the answer is 'yes,' then we can call ourselves psychogeographers in the vein of one of the myriad versions of what that urban character represents, if we choose to.

To provide an aphorism of what psychogeographers do and why they walk assumes they are a generic group, which is not the case. It is as difficult as trying to provide a pithy sentence to describe what a writer or artist does and why they do it. Nevertheless, there are some universal qualities that are representative of many psychogeographers and that can help explain their intentions. For instance, they attempt to connect with the terrain in a way different from that of a casual stroll, bringing a focus to the walk that takes it beyond both a 'Sunday walk' in the country (where the landscape almost appears to be placed there in order to be admired) and a Saturday shopping expedition in the local high street. It is neither of these. Nor is it about getting from A to B—it is absolutely about the process itself, however clichéd that may sound. The walker connects with the terrain in a way that sets her- or himself up as a critic of the space under observation, but at the same time, they unite with it through the sensorial acknowledgement of its omnipresence. The space becomes momentarily transformed through this relationship. The psychogeographer recognizes that they are part of this process, and it is their presence that enables this recognition to occur.

The form and purpose behind the critique of the topology and topography will be very dependent on the individual walker. It might involve making mental connections with the space through a song or piece of literature, or it might involve a philosophical or theoretical analysis of particular objects under scrutiny. It could also be an overtly political process that applies an assessment of the power structures in play in a given situation or even a physical act of challenging those very structures directly in the moment. This could be thought of as a kind of traversing, whereby the walker sees this as a negotiation of the space that questions established routes and draws attention to the possibility of approaching the territory in a different way.

One thing that unites all these approaches is the concept of viewing anew what is often manifest as seemingly 'natural.' I do not mean natural in the sense of nature but in the sense of 'naturalness.' Louis Althusser used the term in relation to subjectivity and ideology, and this would lend itself to the way that urban space (especially) has the appearance of being 'perfectly natural' when in fact it is imposed through the process of an ideological effect. Psychogeographers want to see beyond this ideological effect and challenge the conventional discourse of a particular space through their practice.

Practitioners are continually reworking psychogeography and renaming it to suit their requirements and to differentiate what they do from each other. These nuances are very important to psychogeographers (psychogeophysics and cryptoforestry, to provide just two examples). Smith's chapter on mythogeography (chapter 10) and my own on schizocartography (chapter 11) reflect the need for practitioners to name their own approach and formulate it into a more clearly defined methodology. Both of these forms of psychogeography are politically oriented, and it could be argued that, without this disruptive emphasis, an investigation into the palimpsest postmodern urban space we occupy is absent. If a psychogeographer is not revealing the hidden topographical layers of social history or questioning the physical manifestation of some capitalist edifice or other, is psychogeography actually taking place?

Are we any closer to understanding why psychogeographers do what they do? If one looks at this as an ontological dichotomy between 'doing' and 'being,' we might get closer to the answer. For instance, if we make the assumption that 'one is a psychogeographer because one walks,' we are looking at the object of the walking process (we know that, just because one walks, it does not make one a psychogeographer). If, however, we reverse this and assume 'one walks because one is a psychogeographer,' then we are closer to the truth because it looks at the psychogeographer's subjectivity—his or her being-ness—and not what she or he does, but rather the 'why.'

THE STRUCTURE OF THE BOOK

Part I, 'The Walker and the Urban Landscape,' looks at visual urban phenomena from public sculptures to pavements. Concentrating on the appearance of the urban landscape and how walking with a critical eye opens up the spaces in which we live and move, these chapters draw our attention to both the aesthetics of spatial manifestation and the minutiae that can be easily overlooked on a casual stroll.

Roy Bayfield's reflective walk, taken in the company of a colleague, is set in Merseyside. His account in chapter 1, 'Longshore Drift: Approaching Liverpool from Another Place,' provides an excellent example of a walking-based narrative. Bayfield responds subjectively to the landscape, including affective cues alongside contemporary politico-cultural references sparked by the phenomena encountered. He weaves filmic, literary and geographical references together, producing a firsthand description of his walk from Crosby Beach to Edge Hill University.

Chapter 2, by Ian Marchant, 'Walking the Dog (For Those Who Don't Know How to Do It),' comes from the field of creative writing and covers a walk in his hometown of Presteigne. Marchant ruminates on walking literature and questions the label of 'psychogeographer' while making observations on the town he knows so well. The chapter includes personal references to the author's life, historical information on Presteigne and commentary on his fellow townfolk. In a writerly way, Marchant brings to life a walk that he takes with his dog every day and demonstrates how urban walking can becomes a reflexive tool but also how creative writing can bring a place to life.

Luke Bennett's 'Incongruous Steps toward a Legal Psychogeography,' chapter 3, takes an analytical view of the work of the deep topographer Nick Papadimitriou. By highlighting passages from Papadimitrou's *Scarp*, Bennett teases out conjunctions that arise in relation to the law and the built environment. Originally from a legal background, he uses his knowledge to bring a different perspective to urban walking (for example, by looking at public policy and geography in connection to Papadimitriou's descriptions of the Middlesex landscape). Bennett's chapter references theorists from the fields of geography, psychogeography and cultural studies, foregrounding both the landscape and the text of Papadimitriou's from the perspective of someone who can see beyond the surface of space to the policy decision making that lies beneath.

One of the ways past psychogeographical accounts have been used is to understand the aesthetics of a particular city at a specific moment in time. In part II, 'Memory, Historicity, Time,' the chapters deal with explorations and knowledge of the cityscape (in the past and today) by examining personalized accounts and histories. They reflect on how space is mapped out and how it is connected to memory, nostalgia, culture and geography.

In chapter 4, 'Walking through Memory: Critical Nostalgia and the City,' Alastair Bonnett introduces the Situationists and the way nostalgia influenced the creative aspect of their critique of the spectacle in order to explore the memory of place for ex-residents of Tyneside. He discusses his interviews with the group and their issues with the modernization of urban space in the way it affects them. Bonnett's text includes qualitative research in the form of individual testaments and discussion on memory map making. Situated within a psychogeographical framework, his chapter also references Sinclair and the magico-Marxist work of Home, demonstrating that nostalgia is not necessarily a negative response.

Phil Wood uses the walks he has taken in Lviv and Odessa to explore the concepts of memory, trauma and loss in chapter 5, 'Selective Amnesia and Spectral Recollection in the Bloodlands.' Drawing on his relationships with people from the region and the friendships he has developed, he introduces fictional characters in order to explore the concept of amnesia and spectrality in urban space. The author uses deconstruction to highlight concepts around haunting and the visible and invisible. The historical and contemporary politics of the region is woven into the account to produce a chapter that is both creative nonfiction and theoretical in its form.

Merlin Coverley situates the work of the Welsh author Arthur Machen within contemporary psychogeographical debate in chapter 6, 'The Art of Wandering: Arthur Machen's London Science.' By introducing the work of Sinclair and Self, Coverley fleshes out how the act of wandering was for Machen and reveals some of the tensions that psychogeography incorporates. He discusses Machen's walks in London, his purpose for walking and the influence of the flâneurs, making reference to specific regions of London in regards to Machen's texts. The chapter elucidates two 'fields' of psychogeography: the Situationist strand and that of earth mystery. Coverley situates Machen within a psychogeographical lineage, particularly that of De Quincey and the Northwest Passage, bringing a historical element to the volume.

Gareth E. Rees uses the urban phenomenon of memorial benches as a way of exploring the themes of memory, memorabilia and the landscape in chapter 7, 'Wooden Stones.' The author includes fictional dialogue and a storyline to fill in the gaps in what he perceives might be the lives of the people memorialized on the benches. Rees adds moments from his own life, which are sparked by the aesthetics of the terrain, particularly the protagonist of the chapter, his childhood friend Mike. This poignant and witty chapter reflects the creative aspect of urban walking, and the author demonstrates how the affective response to space can be used to produce a literary text.

Looking at psychogeography from the differing perspectives of a community artist and an academic researcher, the two chapters in part III, 'Power and Place,' discuss how urban walking can be used in an activist way through the insertion of the body into sociopolitical space. By demonstrating how psychogeography can become an intervention once applied to the objectives of a specific group, these authors explore and critique the way collectives of individuals can challenge dominant power structures through the act of walking. Analysing the more anarchic nature of psychogeography, today and in the past, these texts offer specific case studies so as to critique their efficacy as a means of radical political engagement and social change.

Christopher Collier's 'Psychogeography Adrift: Negotiating Critical Inheritance in a Changed Context,' chapter 8, foregrounds this section by providing the historic background of the Situationist's project of psychogeography within a framework of ontology and deconstruction. This academic chapter examines the literary heritage of psychogeography and the problem of seeing its critical origins as being solely located in 1950s Europe. The chapter discusses the problematic term *psychogeography*, introducing contemporary psychogeographers to explore some of the ideas related to its (mis)use, appropriation and circulation. It discusses both the 1990s and the current resurgence of the practice and includes many useful examples and practitioners.

As the organizer of the LRM, Morag Rose provides a personal overview of the origins and aims of the group within the context of her own experience as an anarcho-flâneuse in chapter 9, 'Confessions of an Anarcho-Flâneuse, or Psychogeography the Mancunian Way.' The author discusses such concepts as diversity and democracy within the LRM, offering her chapter in a journal format in order to introduce the practice of walking as it is for the group. Rose demonstrates the passion some individuals have for city life and how this can be expressed through engaging with it on a very concrete level. She believes psychogeographical practices should be made accessible to anyone who is interested and that engaging with your city can be ludic and political at the same time.

By examining the walking and spatial practices of individuals who specialize in psychogeography as a critical methodology, the chapters in part IV, 'Practicing Psychogeography/Psychogeographical Practices,' look at how it can be used as a tool and developed in particular ways so as to offer the practice as an analytical device. The urban walkers represented here have worked through their walking strategies and created their own specific types of urban walking. These customized psychogeographies suit the individual requirements of the practitioners, enabling them to analyse the city in a very specific way. The first two chapters deal with the formulation of psychogeography as a methodology, while the last one looks at the various aspects of setting up a walk for the purposes of research.

In chapter 10, 'Psychogeography and Mythogeography: Currents in Radical Walking,' Phil Smith provides the background to mythogeography, explaining how it emerged and developed over time. He compares mythogeography to historical walking practices, such as those of the SI, and introduces many useful contemporary references. This reflective and critical chapter describes the evolution of a walking practice that has changed over time, providing examples of the walks and collectives involved. The chapter also includes a useful discussion on the depoliticization of psychogeography.

I developed my own form of urban walking critique at the beginning of my PhD. Required to create a methodology that would stand up to academic rigour, I used the psychogeographical practices of the SI to underpin my own approach, which I call 'schizocartography' and explore in chapter 11, 'Developing Schizocartography: Formulating a Theoretical Methodology for a Walking Practice.' Incorporating psychogeography alongside a Marxist-oriented and poststructuralist analysis of space, I use Félix Guattari's theory on critiquing the institution of psychiatry and his work in Brazil to develop schizocartography as a spatial tool. Schizocartography is a process that, while analysing the space under review, looks for the plurivocality presented there, offering counterevents that might be occurring behind the veil of the everyday and that challenge the dominant representation of that space.

Victoria Henshaw specialized in sensory walking and developed it as a methodology that provides qualitative research on the city. Her 'Route Planning a Sensory Walk: Sniffing Out the Issues,' chapter 12, discusses the implications of organizing sensory walks in regard to selecting sites, route selection and research data. Henshaw introduces the 'smellwalks' she carried out in Doncaster and with the Smell and the City Project, explaining the suitability of particular cities for research and the practical considerations for leading the walks themselves. The more formal science-based writing style of Henshaw's chapter (and Bonnett's chapter 4) complement the more 'relaxed' style of the creative-writing aesthetic of the psychogeographical accounts in the volume.

The contributions in part V, 'Outsider Psychogeography,' do not sit within the usual arts-based humanities walking practices previously discussed. Here the authors use the interdisciplinarity of psychogeography within their own academic fields in creative and constructive ways in order to introduce it to a discipline that might otherwise not consider it a standard practice. These chapters look at how psychogeography can be used within the social sciences as a way of helping individuals via a direct engagement with urban space. The chapters also open discussion on the value of psychogeography in its acknowledgement as an affective methodology.

Andrea Capstick, a lecturer in dementia studies, looks at remembering and amnesia in dementia patients and their 'wandering' narratives around a sense of place, such as getting physically lost and the act of forgetting, in chapter 13, 'Rewalking the City: People with Dementia Remember.' The author takes a spatio-temporal look at walking, place and the past, connecting 'signposts' that take the form of real events and places to the patients' narratives as a way of validating and understanding them better. This chapter brings social science, walking-based literature, philosophy, social history and psychogeography together. The chapter includes qualitative research in the form of walking interviews and the author's own research in verifying the validity of the participants' memory of place.

Alexander John Bridger discusses the issues around using psychogeography within a predominantly behavioural or cognitive (and sometimes reductionist) discipline, such as psychology, in chapter 14, 'Psychogeography, Antipsychologies and the Question of Social Change.' The author provides his own examples of walks and drift methodology to elucidate people's experiences in relation to their environments so as to examine the concept of détournement and to open discussion on mobile-methods research. Bridger attempts to introduce psychogeography within his own discipline as a way of helping others to understand their spatial environments and therefore help them realize their lived experiences more fully. He introduces references from his own field and those of urban walking and spatial critique so as to champion psychogeography in a discipline where it might be disregarded due to being considered 'unscientific.'

In order to keep this introduction as relevant as possible in terms of a history of contemporary psychogeography in the United Kingdom, I have had to be concise, which unfortunately means that there are many 'urban walkers' I have not included. For instance, I did not discuss the 'travel writer' Robert Macfarlane or Richard Mabey, whose 1973 book *The Unofficial Countryside* takes a naturalist view of the urban fringes. Due to the vastness of the subject area that psychogeography potentially encompasses, I have had to impose certain limits. Other contemporary psychogeographers and urban walkers (whether they would describe themselves thus, I am unsure) I have not discussed are Alex Cochrane, Tristan Gooley, David Southwell, Paul Conneally, Peter Watts, Graham Hooper and Hamish Fulton. I have not included individuals who practice psychogeography among a variety of other practices, nor have I discussed walking as a form of ethnography or how, on occasion, psychogeography has been used in town-planning projects.

In 2002 Sinclair said of psychogeography that the 'next step is to bury it completely! Let it go and let it re-emerge. I think it needs 15 years to gain some new energy, as I think this energy is rapidly running out' (cited in Pilkington and Baker 2002, 7). Because we are now fast approaching the end of Sinclair's fifteen-year embargo, perhaps this is a salient moment to begin to discuss psychogeography again in a critical way and to take a serious look at the work being carried out in the field. I hope this text contributes to this discussion. Sinclair further comments on this problem when discussing the work Home did with the LPA:

> Stewart Home says that the LPA deliberately mystified and irrationalised their psychogeographical ideas in order to prevent them from being academicised in the future. But they inevitably will be because Stewart himself is a sort of rogue academic, so it's self-contradictory in some ways. By doing it, it becomes part of this machinery in talks and interviews. (cited in Pilkington and Baker 2002, 3)

Nevertheless, Sinclair is in praise of walking despite his concerns with the term *psychogeography*. One thing that many walkers are preoccupied with, from activists to the Ramblers, is not just the marginalization of our public spaces but also the marginalization of the very act of walking itself. As Sinclair says in an interview in the Ramblers' own publication, 'We're at the bottom of the food chain and the day will come when we'll have the equivalent of bike lanes: a narrow suicide strip chucked in among the traffic. We'll have to have ghost walkers, like the white ghost bikes you see to commemorate dead cyclists' (2012, 98). So, it seems, psychogeographers perhaps do have more in common than can be expressed in their differences.

In *The Art of Wandering: The Writer as Walker* (2012) Coverley includes a chapter on 'The Return of the Walker.' Situating the preceding thirty years within a literary tradition that is also reflected in the creative arts, he finishes his closing chapter with Papadimitriou, whose rise in popularity followed Coverley's previous book. *Walking Inside Out* presents the work of some of the contemporary literary psychogeographers alongside those working in academia, thus bridging the gap that would mean that usually these texts are presented to different audiences but also demonstrating the inherent value to academia of the creative psychogeographical account. On 1 May 2014, the BBC online news magazine published an article by Finlo Rohrer, 'The Slow Death of Purposeless Walking,' which is posed rather more as a question than a statement and alludes to the number of recently published books in the field. While his article is not about psychogeography per se, it provides walking advice to the novice, some of which supports and some of which counters psychogeographical practices in the broadest sense. But, despite this, the article is an encouragement to walk, and one of the tips that is common to 'purposeless walking' and psychogeography is to 'walk mindfully' (Rohrer 2014). This mindfulness is apparent in the chapters of this book, as well as in 'Conclusion: The New Psychogeography,' which deals specifically with the direction that the current revival of psychogeography is taking in the United Kingdom and internationally.

The beauty of the inexact art that is psychogeography, appearing in the innumerable forms that it has historically taken and continues to display, attests to the durability and relevance of it today. It can be crafted, manipulated and even reappropriated to suit your particular needs. It can be carried out fundamentally, creatively, or ironically. And it can be picked up and put down like a handy implement that helps you metaphorically whittle away the parts of urban space of which you disapprove, rather like the SI did with their maps. Psychogeography is continually being reworked, reflected upon and reimagined. It has the ability to absorb the urban space it occupies, situating itself sociopolitically and creatively employing innumerable ways to express itself.

NOTES

1. Hay has done much work on looking at the influence of the SI on Sinclair's own work, so I refer you to his thesis 'Form, Place, and Memory: Materialist Readings of Iain Sinclair's London Writing,' University of Manchester, 2012, for his analysis.

2. Stewart Home (from the London Psychogeographical Association, as it was in the 1990s) is known for his critique of the academization of psychogeography and, indeed, anything countercultural.

3. At the University of Leeds, Rebecca Solnit's *Wanderlust: A History of Walking* (2002) was filed under 'Sports Science.'

4. What was left of the county Middlesex (after the forming of the county council system in the 1800s) was incorporated into Greater London and other counties before World War II. However, it is still considered a geographic area, so it remains in that sense.

5. The short-lived online academic resource *Journal of Psychogeography and Urban Research*, circa 2001–2002 and edited by Ian McKay, attested to the variety of origins of psychogeographical writing.

6. Because of his appearance in the broadsheets—often in the form of interviews— but also because of his extensive work in the field, Sinclair is often set up as the 'union rep' of psychogeography and is expected to defend it in the press against its detractors. His vast knowledge means that he has experienced and thought about many of the problems that more recent psychogeographers might still be working through.

7. International urban walking groups of recent times include the New York Psychogeographical Association, Associazione Psicogeografica di Bologna, Toronto Psychogeography Society and the International Psychogeographic Society (Ontario).

BIBLIOGRAPHY

Ackroyd, Peter. 2000. *London: The Biography*. London: Chatto and Windus.
————. 2011. *London Under*. London: Chatto and Windus.
Andreotti, Libero, and Xavier Costa, eds. 1996. *Theory of the Dérive and Other Situationist Writings on the City*. Barcelona: Museu d'Art Contemporani de Barcelona.
Baker, Phil. 2003. 'Secret City: Psychogeography and the End of London.' In *London: From Punk to Blair*, edited by Joe and Andrew Gibson Kerr, 323–33. London: Reaktion Books.
Ballard, J. G. 1975. *High Rise*. London: Jonathan Cape.
Bonnett, Alastair. 2009. 'The Dilemmas of Radical Nostalgia in British Psychogeography.' *Theory, Culture and Society* 26 (1): 45–70.
Bonnett, Alastair, and Catherine Alexander. 2012. 'Mobile Nostalgias: Connecting Visions of the Urban Past, Present and Future amongst Ex-Residents.' *Transactions of the Institute of British Geographers* 38: 391–402.
Coverley, Merlin. 2006. *Psychogeography*. Harpenden: Pocket Essentials.
————. 2012. *The Art of Wandering: The Writer as Walker*. Harpenden: Oldcastle Books.
Cred, C. 2007. 'Counter.Cartographies: Notes towards a Future Atlas.' *Parallax* 13 (1): 119–31.
Dave, Paul. 2011. 'Robinson in Ruins: New Materialism and the Archaeological Imagination.' *Radical Philosophy* 169 (September/October): 19–35.
Debord, Guy. 1996. 'Theory of the Dérive.' In *Theory of the Dérive and Other Situationist Writings on the City*, edited by Libero Andreotti and Xavier Costa, 22–27. Barcelona: Museu d'Art Contemporani de Barcelona.
de Certeau, Michel. 2006. 'Walking in the City.' In *The Practice of Everyday Life*, translated by Steven Rendall, 91–110. Berkeley: University of California Press.
Dunthorne, Joe, and Bradley Garrett, eds. 2013. *Mount London: Ascents in the Vertical City*. London: Penned in the Margins.
Edensor, Tim. 2005. *Industrial Ruins: Space, Aesthetics and Materiality*. Oxford: Berg.
Ford, Laura Oldfield. 2011. *Savage Messiah*. London: Verso.
Garrett, Bradley L. 2013. *Explore Everything: Place-Hacking the City*. London: Verso.
Gros, Frédéric. 2014. *A Philosophy of Walking*. Translated by John Howe. London: Verso.
Harvey, David. 2006. 'Space as a Keyword.' In *Spaces of Global Capitalism*, 117–48. London: Verso.
Hatherley, Owen. 2012. 'How Patrick Keiller Is Mapping the 21st-Century Landscape.' *The Guardian*, 30 March. Accessed 20 August 2014. http://www.theguardian.com/artanddesign/2012/mar/30/patrick-keiller-robinson-tate-exhibition.
Hay, Duncan. 2008. 'Transforming Psychogeography: From Paris to London.' Walled City. 18 October. Accessed 26 October 2014. http://walled-city.net/transforming-psychogeography-from-paris-to-london.
Highmore, Ben. 2005. *Cityscapes: Cultural Readings in the Material and Symbolic City*. Basingstoke: Palgrave Macmillan.
Hine, Dougald. 2011. 'Dériving Scarcity.' Dougald Hine. 10 February. Accessed 21 August 2014. http://dougald.co.uk/writing/dougald_derivingscarcity_feb11.pdf.
Home, Stewart. 1997. *Mind Invaders: A Reader in Psychic Warfare, Cultural Sabotage and Semiotic Terrorism*. London: Serpent's Tail.
Keiller, Patrick, dir. 1994. *London*. United States: Facets Video. DVD.
————, dir. 1997. *Robinson in Space*. United States: Facets Video. DVD.
————, dir. 2011. *Robinson in Ruins*. London: BFI Video. DVD.
Khatib, Abdelhafid. 1996. 'Attempt at a Psychogeographical Description of Les Halles.' In *Theory of the Dérive and Other Situationist Writings on the City*, edited by Libero Andreotti and Xavier Costa, 72–76. Barcelona: Museu d'Art Contemporani de Barcelona.
Kotting, Andrew, and Iain Sinclair. 2012. *Swandown*. Directed by Andrew Kotting. London: Swandown Productions. DVD.

Lefebvre, Henri. 1991. *The Production of Space*. Translated by Donald Nicholson-Smith. Oxford: Blackwell.

London Psychogeographical Association. 1997. 'Why Psychogeography?' In *Mind Invaders: A Reader in Psychic Warfare, Cultural Sabotage and Semiotic Terrorism*, edited by Stewart Home, 136–37. London: Serpent's Tail.

Maxwell, Gordon S. 1925. *The Fringe of London: Being Some Ventures and Adventures in Topography*. London: Cecil Palmer.

McDonough, Thomas F. 1994. 'Situationist Space.' *October* 67 (Winter): 58–77.

Nicholson, Geoff. 2013. *Walking in Ruins*. Chelmsford: Harbour Books.

Papadimitriou, Nick. 2012. *Scarp: In Search of London's Outer Limits*. London: Hodder and Stoughton.

Petit, Christopher, and Iain Sinclair, dirs. 2002. *London Orbital*. London: Illuminations Films. DVD.

Pilkington, Mark, and Phil Baker. 2002. 'City Brain.' *Fortean Times*. Accessed 21 August 2014. http://www.forteantimes.com/features/interviews/37/iain_sinclair.html.

Prescott-Steed, David. 2013. *The Psychogeography of Urban Architecture*. Boca Raton, FL: BrownWalker Press.

Rogers, John, dir. 2009. *London Perambulator*. London: Vanity Projects. Film.

———. 2013. *This Other London: Adventures in the Overlooked City*. London: HarperCollins.

Rohrer, Finlo. 2014. 'The Slow Death of Purposeless Walking.' In *BBC News Magazine*. May 1. Accessed 13 August 2014. http://www.bbc.co.uk/news/magazine-27186709.

Rourke, Lee. 2007. 'Psychogeography: Merlin Coverley.' *3:AM Magazine*. 10 March. Accessed 21 August 2014. http://www.3ammagazine.com/3am/psychogeography-merlin-coverley.

Sebald, W. G. 1995. *Die Ringe des Saturn*. Frankfurt: Eichborn.

Self, Will. 2007. *Psychogeography*. London: Bloomsbury.

———. 2009. *Psycho Too*. London: Bloomsbury.

Sinclair, Iain. 2003. *Lights Out for the Territory: 9 Excursions in the Secret History of London*. London: Penguin.

———. 2009. *Hackney, That Rose-Red Empire: A Confidential Report*. London: Hamish Hamilton.

———. 2012. 'My Perfect Day: Iain Sinclair.' *Walk: Magazine of the Ramblers* (Summer): 98.

Smith, Phil. 2014. *On Walking . . . and Stalking Sebald*. Axminster: Triarchy Press.

Solnit, Rebecca. 2002. *Wanderlust: A History of Walking*. London: Verso.

Stein, Howard F. 1987. *Developmental Time, Cultural Space: Studies in Psychogeography*. Norman: University of Oklahoma Press.

Stein, Howard F., and William G. Niederland. 1989. *Maps from the Mind: Readings in Psychogeography*. Norman: University of Oklahoma Press.

Part I

The Walker and the Urban Landscape

The solitary walker situated within the landscape is not a modern phenomenon, even if the term *psychogeography* is. The cover of Terry Eagleton's *The Ideology of the Aesthetic* (1990) shows *Der Wanderer über dem Nebelmeer* (*Wanderer above the Sea of Fog*; 1818) by Caspar David Friederich. It depicts a man in a frock coat standing on a craggy rock with his back toward us, contemplating the buffeting sea below. He carries a walking stick, telling us that he is a walker and has not just pulled up in his Landau where his coachman awaits his return. The wanderer is elevated above the sea on which he looks down and from which he is separated. What this image depicts is the privileged position of this figure in the landscape. Not just because of his elevated position on the rocks but also because he is male, middle-class, Western and white (his red hair is blowing in the wind, the colour punctuating the image). Our protagonist represents both the eighteenth-century colonizer and the stereotype of a classical psychogeographer.

However, in the twenty-first century, psychogeography takes up multiple positions—from the perspective of the background, gender and age of the individual urban walker to his or her relationship with urban space itself. Today the walker feels some sort of direct connection to the space he or she explores, even if that is from a critical position. It is no longer about the tourist's gaze, but rather a reflexive response in which both the walker and the space in which he or she moves about are momentarily changed. This section looks at the different perspectives a walking critic might take and provides three different urban spaces in order to demonstrate the variety of places available for interpretation. Taking the perspectives of two walkers and providing one analysis of the writing of a walker, these chapters draw upon the place of the contemporary psychogeographer in the everyday landscape.

ONE

Longshore Drift

Approaching Liverpool from Another Place

Roy Bayfield

There was a single silver hair resting between the pages of the free *Metro* newspaper I found on the seat of the train to Waterloo (Merseyside) Station, the starting point for the walk. It was quite early, but the Northern Line train had already been back and forth a few times between the Lancashire market town of Ormskirk and the centre of Liverpool, an artery for a half-hour commute. The strand of hair, with its burden of time, could have belonged to anyone. The cover of the *Metro* that day was a wraparound advertisement for Merseyrail asking the question, 'Want to know more about you and me?' (*Metro* 2013). Inside, a short article stated that 'ONE in six of us is so averse to walking that we rarely venture 500m (1,600ft) from the car' (ibid., 9). Signs were starting to manifest.

I changed trains at Sandhills and travelled to Waterloo, not quite reaching the city before heading out to its edge. At the station I had my first sighting of an image of Antony Gormley's *Another Place* sculptures (a.k.a. the Iron Men) on a fading print over the stairs from the platform up to street level. It would be the first of many—sightings of two-dimensional digital ghosts outnumbering the three-dimensional metal figures of the actual installation. As well as the Gormley image (a lone metal figure staring out to sea), there were other images of people sited around the stairs: pictograms depicting various ways to exit the station—climbing stairs, using the lift in a wheelchair, or pushing a pushchair. Outside the station, a map of the area included a sponsor logo based on a Gormley figure rendered into silhouetted pictogram form; I now knew that (wherever else I was) I was in the territory of the Crosby and Waterloo Business Village Partnership[1] and that an Iron Man was their avatar. From prewalk research, I also knew myself to be in Merseyside; the Metropolitan Borough of Sefton, Church Ward; the L22 postcode area; the Parish of St. John; at one end of the (discontinued) Northern Way and the (continuing) Northern Trade Corridor; part of what was once the County Palatine of Lancashire, also part of what was envisioned as a future Liverpool City Region, and in a place remade as Mongolia in Frank Cottrell Boyce's novel *The Unforgotten Coat* (2011) and its simulated Polaroid illustrations (Hunter and Heney 2013).

I met up with my walking companion for the day, artist Robyn Woolston, and we decided to go for a coffee to consolidate our plans. Crosby's South Street has its share of bars and coffee shops, but the Queens Picture House, a former cinema converted into a Wetherspoon pub, looked spacious and anonymous enough for a discussion involving fully unfolded Ordnance Survey maps and notebooks. It was around 10 a.m. Patrons at the time included a family eating cooked breakfasts; two men drinking beer, their loud conversation sweary and demonstrative; and us with coffee, gearing up to be psychogeographers. Like all of the Wetherspoon chain, the pub was large enough to comfortably accommodate such disparate groups. Also included in the corporate theme were old photos and local history information, making it a kind of drinkers' micromuseum, and a vast wall painting of an aircraft, a reference to pioneer aviator Henry Melly, who, just over a century previously, had flown his Bleriot from Waterloo Sands to make the first nonstop flight from Liverpool to Manchester. I suggested to Robyn that this image of flight was a good omen, reflecting the Aeolian theme that had emerged in the planning of the walk.

Liverpool, Merseyside—as the names suggest, this is an urban place, defined by its relationship to water. The coastline is therefore a natural locale for exploration, walking the most intimate way of going about it. Antony Gormley's statues are widely used as an image of Liverpool; *Another Place* has become one of Liverpool's public faces and therefore a logical way into the city. I knew from colleagues at Edge Hill University that there was a geography research station on the same stretch of coast, analysing the effects of wind on the landscape over long periods. These avatars of art and science, separated by a few miles of beachside, seemed to offer the structure for an urban walk, namely:

Beginning: Gormley statues (art);
Middle: whatever may be encountered; and
Destination: Edge Hill University research site (science).

I contacted Dr. Irene Delgado-Fernandez to find out more about the research station. I had an inkling she would be sympathetic as, despite being a *physical* geographer, she had an interest in *psycho*geography, having been involved in a conference on the subject at the University of Guelph. It transpired that the research station had been obliterated by vandals, but work was still being carried out on the dunes. Irene seemed interested, so I elaborated on the idea of a Liverpool-coast dérive, writing a proposal for a walk that would 'Explore human interventions on the Sefton coast, including Antony Gormley's *Another Place* sculptures; the remains of a scientific research site; participants' own experiences brought to, and emerging from, the walk.'

I was attracted to the aesthetic of geomorphological research undertaken by Irene and colleagues, (mis)reading research papers (such as Delgado-Fernandez et al. 2013) as if they were some kind of Ballardian creative writing. I was struck by the term *Aeolian research*[2] and decided to work that in, too, using Aeolus, the god of winds, as a point of reference, e-mailing Irene to suggest that

> some psychogeography practice has taken mythology, occult and esoteric para-science such as leylines and applied it to real landscape, as a way of destabilising expectations . . . so one could, if only temporarily, choose to interpret the term 'Aeolian' as used in, for instance, the name of the journal *Aeolian Studies* as being on some level a literal homage to the god of antiquity. This could logically lead us to keep a weather eye open for mystical correspondences to Aeolus such as the extensive list provided in Aleister Crowley's *777 and Other Qabalistic Writings* (Crowley 1986)—which includes such things as 'mermaids,' 'a man with bowed head and a bag in his hand,' and 'artificial glass.' That is not to say that literal mystical visions are expected—a mermaid, for instance, might be observed in a Starbucks logo or pub sign. (Roy Bayfield, personal communication, 7 July 2013)

Rather to my surprise, Irene seemed to absorb all of this without demur.

Meanwhile, I had met Robyn Woolston, who was making an art installation for the Edge Hill University campus, *Habitus*, which was to involve information signs for a range of geological eras, pointing toward a Las Vegas–style sign welcoming people to our own, human-influenced Anthropocene Era. As Robyn wrote,

> The word 'Anthropocene,' proposed by atmospheric chemist and Nobel laureate Paul Crutzen . . . refers to the period within which we are currently living—a time perhaps unlike any other where physical markers within the geological record are pointing towards permanent global impacts upon the Earth's ecosystem as a result of human activities. (Woolston 2013)

I gathered from her Twitter account that she had an interest in psychogeography and invited her to be part of the walk. In the end Irene could not make it, which left Robyn and me, sitting in a Wetherspoon's with coffee and maps, planning an expedition.

We worked out an approximate route and got ready to leave—but first I went in search of lavatories. The Picture House stairwell, which would once have led to the screens (last shown film: *I Only Arsked*, starring Bernard Bresslaw, a spinoff from the TV sitcom *The Army Game*[3]; supporting feature: *Buchanan Rides Alone*, starring Randolph Scott), was decorated with a large black-and-white image of the Iron Men, edited to appear more crowded together than they are in reality. Clearly the Wetherspoon designers had been unable to resist referencing the local sculptures (and improving on them) as well as riffing on the building's cinema history and the flight connection, the latter also resonating with today's jury-rigged Aeolian mythology.

We set off down South Street toward the Crosby Coastal Park. A red brick building (a disused toilet block) had some historical photographs mounted on its exterior walls. These had faded so that only cyan, the most persistent print pigment, remained. We walked on further. Sand had drifted into the park, part of an ongoing process that seemed to need keeping in check—a man was busy shovelling sand from the path.[4]

We reached the coast. Behind us, the city; before us, across the water, the hills of the Wirral Peninsula and North Wales. And the Gormley sculptures, now visible in original form—a set of one hundred cast-iron figures, modelled on the artist's own body, positioned over a two-mile stretch of beach, all facing out to sea. Depending on the tide, some of the sculptures can be up to their necks in water. *Another Place* was installed in Crosby in 2005 following appearances in Germany, Norway and Belgium dating back to 1997. Intended to be temporary, the installation became permanent in 2007 as a result of campaigns to keep it in Crosby, supported by the artist ('Gormley's Statues Stay Out to Sea' 2007), a story that is well known locally.

The installation has made this stretch of beach a notable landmark and tourist destination. It has been claimed that the installation 'increased tourist revenue and attracted a reported additional 350,000 visitors per year, with a £5 million impact on the local economy' ('Welcome to the North Public Art Programme' 2011). *Another Place* is, for instance, one of a thousand entries in a book titled *The Most Amazing Places to Visit in Britain* (Reader's Digest 2012, 214); it is featured on postcards and appears on the covers of books about Liverpool (e.g., *Real Liverpool* [Griffiths 2008]). The sculptures have become so strongly associated with the Waterloo/Crosby/Blundellsands area that they almost seem to define the place—for instance, the popular *Liverpool Centre of the Universe* graphic used on posters, tea towels, cards and other merchandise, which substitutes the names of stations on the Merseyrail map with those of notable individuals associated with their locations, like depicting Hall Road (the station at the northern end of the installation) as 'Antony Gormley.'

Another Place, then, is a unique and famous landscape feature. Does anyone arrive at it and see it with fresh and innocent eyes? Gormley has 'always insisted on the work as an "open space" for interpretation; each new viewer finding for themselves a new meaning in it, is, he believes, "making it again"' (Caiger-Smith 2010, 91). However, the artist supplies a detailed and compelling interpretation of his own:

> According to Antony Gormley, Another Place harnesses the ebb and flow of the tide to explore man's relationship with nature. He explains: The seaside is a good place to do this. Here time is tested by tide, architecture by the elements and the prevalence of sky seems to question the earth's substance. In this work human life is tested against planetary time. This sculpture exposes to light and time the nakedness of a particular and peculiar body. It is no hero, no ideal, just the industrially reproduced body of a middle-aged man trying to remain standing and trying to breathe, facing a horizon busy with ships moving materials and manufactured things around the planet. ('"Another Place" by Antony Gormley')

Describing the initial intentions, Gormley stated, 'This was no exercise in romantic escapism. The estuary of the Elbe can take up to 500 ships a day and the horizon was often busy with large container ships' ('*Another Place*' 1997). His statements imply that the proximity of industrial shipping and busyness displaces transcendent, romantic readings. However, the 'romantic gaze,' as described by Urry and Larsen in *The Tourist Gaze 3.0*, does seem to be facilitated by the installation to an extent; the scale and location allow for 'solitude, privacy and a personal, semi-spiritual relationship with the object of the gaze,' although not quite the 'deserted beach, the empty hilltop, the uninhabited forest, the uncontaminated mountain stream' (2011, 19). The sculptures are both in nature (literally immersed in sand and water) and in the human environment of trade, transport and travel. As human figures they are also looking at these things—*Another Place* is a sculpture of seeing—staring out at wind farms, drilling platforms and shipping, as well as at sea and sky. On the edge of a city, an endless act of watching, of the movement between the city and other places, and the natural forces that shape and threaten it.

Evidence of the open readings desired by Gormley can be seen in the playful subversions and additions made to the sculptures. On this day they were mostly unadorned, but I have seen photos of them sporting scarves, glasses, Liverpool football tops, Santa hats, hi-vis vests; coated in paint; endlessly co-opted into posed photos. Other accretions have resulted from nonhuman nature; there are men covered in barnacles visible at low tide, and all of them are slowly transforming into rust. Interaction with the beach itself has a particularly profound long-term effect on the sculptures; some have sunk, while in other cases the plinth on which they stand has been partially revealed. Robyn and I speculated on the reasons for this—how and why the sands are changing—wishing Irene, our physical geographer colleague, were there to explain. Our idle thoughts of underground streams would have to suffice.

A sculpture of a man on a plinth is different from a sculpture of a man standing on sand, and different again from a buried man, the natural changes allowing for new readings. There is also an element of inner workings being revealed. Carl Hunter, a filmmaker and musician who lives locally, recalls seeing the totality of the sculptures in a temporary, preinstallation 'installation':

> By day they were stored horizontally, in a car park, lying in metal bunk beds, very eerie, a dorm for metal men. Men with legs and legs with a huge screw attached to their feet. I became fascinated by this and would watch as the men were lifted from their beds, carried to the sand and like a corkscrew twisted into place. (Carl Hunter, personal communication, 16 April 2014)

We walked on, aiming for a UFO-like leisure centre. Signs announced its fifty-five fitness stations, adverts of a 'Summer Bodies' programme framed with jaunty 'Expressions Fitness' branding. As if to point up this celebration of the body, there was a sudden flurry of joggers running along the sandy path. A fading information sign about *Another Place* bearing Gormley's 'planetary time' quote still spoke of the future removal of the work in 2006. Water incursion had created an estuary of decay through the board's landscape image of the sculptures in the seas.

Drifting along the beach, we scanned the ground for signs. There were dead jellyfish on the sand and some uncanny-looking black capsules, the egg cases of dogfish, ray or skate known as 'mermaid's purses.' Poet Jean Sprackland describes these in *Strands*, her account of a year spent walking this coast, 'cast like small, cryptic gifts all along the strandline. The folk name "mermaid's purse" marks these out as enchanted objects' (2012, 23). She also points out that 'enchantment has its darker side—an alternative name is "devil's purse."' The mermaid connection was pleasing, as it ticked an item on the list of Qabalistic correspondences I had brought along (on an official-looking clipboard). Also the research site destination was called Devil's Hole. Synchronicity seemed to be kicking in as we moved beyond the ambit of the authority-sanctioned artzone, as if we were getting back onto some kind of elusive psychogeography ley lines or reaching the moment when the 'surface of the landscape around you is about to give way to the sinkholes of id' (Smith 2014, 32).

The outer edges of the city were beginning to run out. We walked past a long stretch of large villas, art deco and Tudor, the city's suburban tentacles. As if to symbolize a breakdown of *Another Place*'s dominance of the beach, an information sign at its northern end had disappeared, leaving an empty board streaked with patterns of adhesive tape. There was, however, a panoramic display sponsored by (among other entities) DONG Energy, the developers of the wind farm visible from the shore. The board named the Welsh and Cumbrian hills visible from this point, panning from the land-based windmills of Liverpool to the Lake District. Once again, an Iron Man silhouette was used as a logo.

The city seemed to fade away, at least in the sense that there were no more buildings. We ambled on with a golf course on our right and the sea on our left, still within dog-walking distance of the final streets. And still in Merseyside, still in a Liverpool postcode zone.

After a half-mile, we rediscovered the city, albeit in ruined form. At the mouth of the River Alt, there was a beach made of bricks, worn smooth from decades of tide (see figure 1.1). Red and grey housebricks, parts of stone-carved windows, lintels and concrete blocks were piled in a long profusion, rounded and sometimes overgrown with seaweed. It looked as if the sea had reclaimed a street from the shoreline, and in fact a street of houses was demolished here in the 1920s, victim to the move-

Figure 1.1.   Brick Beach near Hightown, Merseyside, United Kingdom

ment of the river. However, the street would have had to have had many large buildings and bricks anachronistically stamped with dates from later decades to have provided all this rubble. In fact, the debris was imported here, a manmade longshore transport: 'The rubble embankment from which the shingle has arisen was tipped from about 1942, initially using Liverpool bomb-damage debris. Tipping continued at intervals until the early 1970s, when spoil from the construction of the second Mersey Tunnel was used' (Smith 2007, 2). The purpose was to construct a 'revetment shore' to preserve the coastline. The bomb debris, then, was a relic of the city's erasure, remnants of buildings destroyed in the war, each with their own unique history. An erasure of parts of the city now prevents erasure of parts of the shoreline.

A half-deflated birthday balloon was slowly blowing up the brick bank, like a creature crawling away from the sea. A man sat on a section of broken wall, head down, a carrier bag between his legs—another magical image to cross off the list (Crowley 1986, 28). This location felt like Doreen Massey's description of space—

> This is space as the sphere of dynamic simultaneity, constantly discon-
> nected by new arrivals, constantly waiting to be determined (and there-
> fore always undetermined) by the construction of new relations. It is
> always being made and always therefore, in a sense, unfinished (except
> that 'finishing' is not on the agenda). If you really were to take a slice
> through time it would be full of holes, of disconnections, of tentative
> half-formed first encounters. (2005, 107)

—in that our experience of the place included shifting, emergent relations with elements of the environment, with passersby, with each other; the focusing of perception involved in our psychogeographic practice invoking a kind of estrangement, as if we were literally passing through 'holes,' walking through 'disconnections.'

In Hightown, Robyn and I concluded our own half-formed encounter and went our separate ways. Robyn had to meet the sign company that was producing the components of her installation (Woolston 2013); I stopped for lunch in a pub, the Hightown Hotel. There were faded images of ships on the wall, again showing the persistence of blue ink.

I walked on, determined to finish the planned 'art to science' journey. The right-of-way footpaths ran inland for a while. A long stretch skirted an armed forces firing range, part of a much larger 'Danger Area' marked on the Ordnance Survey map. Ordnance was actually being fired at that moment, and a sign on a building inside the fence mentioned a 'raised threat level.'

Eventually I reached the Devil's Hole on Formby Sands, a geographical feature known as a 'blowout,' a large raised crater. I clambered to the top, feet sinking into soft sand, reaching the summit, where I could see the large depression of the Hole. The landscape reminded me of the

Planet of the Apes film and, like Charlton Heston, I ran down the slope, sand pushing down beneath my steps in miniature landslides.

I felt that I had outwalked the city to reach a pocket of pure landscape. This place seemed natural, formed from the effects of wind and sand; Aeolian, physical geography territory. This was largely true: 'Blow-outs form when a sand-dune's protective cover of vegetation is damaged; sand is then blown down-wind and an armchair-shaped hollow develops' (Smith and Lockwood 2013). However, the 'damage' was likely manmade: 'Aerial photographs show that the Devil's Hole began to form on a high dune in the early 1940s, perhaps due to a German land-mine explosion in 1940 or 1941' (ibid.).

I met Irene's students, who were coming to the end of several weeks' surveying the sands, part of an innovative project to produce a 3-D model of the coast to help monitor its long-term changes.[5] The plan for this walk had been to connect art and science; here was the science: documentation, quantification, the creation of an objective record. Gormley set out to 'explore man's relationship with nature' ('"Another Place" by Antony Gormley'); this research was in a sense contributing to an exploration of 'nature's' relationship with 'man': coastal dunes as a protection against erosion, dunes migrating inland, economic and recreational human impacts.

Months later I felt drawn back to the area. Somehow it felt as if I had not seen enough.[6] I again took the train to Waterloo Station and walked back to the Iron Men. It was a breezy, sunny day on school holiday, and the beach was busy, the sculptures interspersed with family groups. I contemplated walking to the brick beach again to commune with the ruins, so I started off in that direction. This felt wrong somehow, so I clambered up a dune and sat down to replan. The walk north was familiar and comprised an officially sanctioned leisure path. To the south were the giant cranes, processing plants and warehouses of the docks; beyond them, glass towers gleamed in the sun. I decided to walk into the city.

Skirting the Crosby Marine Lake (a manmade feature dating from the 1940s), I left the leisure area behind and joined the A565 coast road toward Liverpool. I was walking on a generously sized pavement, but this was not a pedestrian zone. On my right was the container terminal of the Port of Liverpool: a miniature city of steel boxes, the 'intermodal freight containers' that comprise the basic units of global trade. On my left, a three-lane main road, busy with oncoming vehicles behind steel fencing punctuated with the cruciform logo of Sefton Council. Seen in the Christian Holy Week, on a day when the UK prime minister was being quoted in news reports as saying that Britons should be 'more confident about our status as a Christian country' ('Stand Up for Our Christianity, David

Cameron Tells UK' 2014), the crosses appeared to me as an exercise in corporate and state religious iconography, a branding iron aimed at the peripheral vision of passing drivers. However, with postwalk Google omniscience, I note that this type of cross (equal-length arms with curved forked ends, a cross moline) is based on a millrind, the iron support of a turning millstone. This cross has mutated from the arms of the Molyneux (mill of the waters) family, who became earls and barons of Sefton. Interestingly, William Molyneux (nicknamed Lord Dashalong) opposed the surveying of the Liverpool-to-Manchester railway, a link between points that had come up on the earlier walk and would later reappear. These powerful sigils,[7] combining Christ and food-production industry, surround the port's gigantic flour mills like protective charms.

My nose and throat felt as if they were filling with dust—perhaps from the Sefton coast sand, the further-travelled Saharan sand rumoured to be blowing across the country, escaped flour, the traffic fumes or some unholy combination of these particulates. For several miles, my route was lined with dirt and debris—bottles, food boxes, scraps of paper and less identifiable items drifted in a sort of semiorganic dust comprising leaves, seeds and sand blackened in the slipstream of the traffic. Bags and strips of plastic hung in the shrubbery, slowly turning ragged in the wind. I thought back to the many pedestrian approaches I had made on a long, episodic walk to Brighton (Bayfield 2011). For some reason the footpaths, towpaths and disused railways via which I had entered towns and cities always seemed to be covered in litter, the lesser-used pedestrian routes acting as a manifestation of an urban subconscious.

I passed several cathedral-sized dock buildings: processing plants, warehouses and silos. Blank walls faced the road behind large, deep spaces like protective dykes partially covered with scraggly weeds. The road was lined with utility planting, a solitary yellow rose breaking long runs of dark-leaved shrubbery. Once, unbelievably, a rabbit hopped into the green darkness.

Walking in the shadow of the dock buildings felt distant from the beach of subjectivity. I was walking past the backs of the dock buildings—their business-end fronts were facing the water, inaccessible behind fences and safety signs. I recalled a similar perimeter walk around Pinewood Studios, the other side of the fence from the huge blank-walled studios where vast mythologies were created: the Bond franchise, Batman films, a Superman—tales of black-haired orphans fighting monumental adversaries. The products here were more physical but, apart from the sudden scent of timber, equally hard to discern from beyond the fence.

After the A565 separated from the docks, I came to a run of car showrooms and warehouse-style retail outlets for beds, carpets and tents. The marketing logic seemed to be that this was a place for the occasional big-ticket purchase, somewhere to visit once every few years. Outside Rimrose Carpets, several rolls of artificial lawn flanked the entrance. Multiple shades of green but also blue, yellow and black. I quite liked the idea of this stuff—perhaps I would return to buy a hyperreal replacement lawn for my suburban home.

I dropped down to the dock road to try to escape the dust. I was now much closer to the wind turbines I had seen from the beach, able to appreciate their huge size. There were hills of recycled metal, perhaps the largest hills between here and the Devil's Hole. On a lamppost at a height that seemed designed for people in cars to see, there was a poster of a Francis Bacon painting of a screaming seated figure; at the foot of the lamppost, a dead pigeon. Despite these dystopian props, I found this locale quite jolly, perhaps because it reminded me of the south coast port town where I grew up. Also, there was something exhilarating about the vast piles of raw materials, the sense of movement, of the ingredients that had sustained my half-century as a baby boom–born consumer. Still, there wasn't time to linger in the sunshine beneath the windmills. I hiked along a street of ruined buildings housing a couple of car spares businesses and regained the A565.

The roadside now featured public art of a sort—industrial scenes cut from metal, set into a long wall and presumably seen in glimpses by passing drivers. Behind this boundary, the real business was happening: tonnes of raw material, bulk liquids, timber, metal and grain, imported, exported, stored and processed—the mass alchemy of capitalism.

There were closed-down pubs, signs of former opening times and brewery insignia still forlornly on display. Trade had left these behind as relics: The first refreshments I saw available for sale were in a Subway and the Heritage Fish Bar, though perhaps I could have gotten a vending-machine coffee in one of the car showrooms.

Hermann Melville wrote that 'for miles you may walk along [the] riverside, passing dock after dock, like a chain of immense fortresses' (*Redburn*, in Griffiths 2008, 149), and that is what I was doing. Some of the gateways were flanked with castle-like towers. There was an air of abandonment to these walls and structures—crumbling brickwork, buddleia growing in the embrasures and litter jamming the arrow slits.

Shortly after I passed the bridge over the Kingsway Tunnel, the landscape changed, a sudden and dramatic Dorothy-wakes-up-in-Oz type of transformation. Everything now was Singapore tidy. The immaculate roadside planting was even, new and litter-free. I had crossed some invisible boundary. I could now see where the gleaming towers I had seen from Waterloo met the ground, and I made for the tallest of them.

A billboard for the Mersey Waters Enterprise Zone showed an aerial view of a long stretch of the docks. There was a red line depicted as surrounding an area of dockland: the invisible border I had crossed. This was development territory, part of a linked set of regeneration schemes planned to unfold over decades, a nexus of heritage, commerce and culture, whose website promises government-backed superfast broadband, the aetheric data equivalent of the physical tonnage of the port.

Now I had arrived at a space designed for pedestrians. Down by the shimmering water, I was no longer the lone walker; professional-looking people were striding purposefully along the walkways. Outside a dark-glassed Malmaison hotel, couples sat with drinks. A series of coloured banners on lampposts invited me to 'Live, Work and Play at Princes Dock, Liverpool Water,' with words and emblems signifying its set of amenities:

Office
Dine
Leisure
Nursery
Shop
Homes
Hotels

This jaunty codification of utilities implied a sort of holistic completeness to the 'offer' of the regenerated dock—aspects of living and working unified into a neat, branded, owned-by-someone, apprehensible and marketized system.

Finally I was among the glass towers I had seen from a distance. Soaring and pristine, these brought to mind the 'brilliant space platforms of the powerful' described by Donna Haraway (1991, 191). 'Vision is better from below,' writes Haraway. 'There is a premium in establishing the capacity to see from the peripheries and the depths' (ibid.). My playful drifts had certainly been in search of vision, of sidestepping dominant narratives of place without seeking specific counternarratives, just an embodied, partial, momentary view of what was there, trying, at least, to drop some layers of privileged subjectivity and thus 'see from the peripheries.'

It had been fun.

I considered the walk finished. The Museum of Liverpool was in sight, offering the prospect of an encounter with an official narrative of place, which could have been a fitting finish. But it was just about to close, so, in true psychogeographer style, I went to the pub. The Lion seemed like a good choice; at the time I simply fell in there because I knew it had good beer, but as well as this, its semiological setting made it a fitting endpoint. Named after a locomotive that once operated on the Liverpool-to-Manchester line (the one that Lord Dashalong had opposed, on a route parallel to that flown by Henry Melly) and that appeared in the title role of *The Titfield Thunderbolt*, the Lion still advertised a 'News Room' in one engraved window,[8] echoing the setting of the Aeolus episode of James Joyce's *Ulysses* (Joyce [1922] 2008, 113–43). It was opposite the Mercury Court building (Mercury, the god of communication, travel and commerce; with a mystical correspondence to 'Millstones where manna for just is ground for future' [Crowley 1986, 20]), built in the closed-down Exchange Station, dead viaducts rumoured still to exist behind the current building. The walk had finished, but the city continued to appear.

This wasn't my town, although I had lived in its orbit for fifteen years. I had traversed parts of the 'most deprived local authority area in England' (Liverpool City Council 2011, 1) that was also one of the world's 'Top 10 Cities' ('Top 10 Cities' 2013). My approach to the city, framed with my personal take on psychogeography—arbitrary quests, counterrational reference points, validation of coincidence, fetishization of the marginal, poeticized parascholarship, nonlinear linkage, subcultural jouissance, consensual lostness—had given me a succession of viewpoints, a moving sightline grounded in a physical, walked experience of places as they were at that moment—'felt through the feet,' as Robyn observed (Woolston, personal communication, 16 April 2014). A particular type of seeing.

So what had I seen that I had not noticed before? Endless movement. Coastlines and rivers shift, bombs fall, towers rise into the sky, cargo moves, metal eyes rust. Zones are established, boundaries set and breached in an ongoing process of interpenetration. Sand, dust and debris blow alongshore on planetary time. Signs and meanings coalesce and evaporate; 'the raging winds rush thro' the hollow wound.'[9] And on the bridge over the Kingsway Tunnel, some graffiti, someone's idea that I now reproduce and share, in whatever kind of conversation this turns out to be:

> Live with purpose
> Walk without one

NOTES

1. This possibly defunct 'village' pointed to a larger, more nebulous environment: the 'public realm.' On a half-finished undated website, it is stated, 'The Partnership brings together stakeholders in Crosby and Waterloo, [*sic*] to develop and deliver schemes to directly benefit the trading environment, the public realm and the community' ('Visit Crosby and Waterloo' n.d.).

2. The term is used, for instance, in the name of the International Society for Aeolian Research and its journal, *Aeolian Research*.

3. Part of a decades-spanning set of linked comedy series based on National Service and its civilian aftermath and characterized in part by imaginary places: 'Nether Hopping,' an army base in Staffordshire; 'Darawa,' a Middle East protectorate; and 'Bosnik,' a European country.

4. There is in fact a substantial ongoing process of managing the dunes—the result of sand 'overtopping' the sea wall, leading residents to complain of 'nuisance sand blow' (Sefton Coast Partnership 2006).

5. A news story on the Edge Hill University website, 'Students to Help Predict Future of Coastline,' explains:

Winds flowing over beach dunes can influence how sand is transported along coastlines and the force of the wind can shape the surface in profound ways. Now, for the first time researchers have mapped in 3D how air flows over a large beach dune. This novel idea has been developed by Irene Delgado-Fernandez, a coastal geomorphologist at Edge Hill University. She says this could help scientists understand how particular wind events can aid in post-storm recovery of sandy coastlines such as major incidents like 'Superstorm Sandy.' 'Wind flow over dunes has been extensively studied,' said Irene. 'But in most cases, that research has been two-dimensional and focused on straight dunes with smooth slopes and no vegetation or other features that might affect how airflow separates at the crest of the dune. Our first ever three-dimensional field study of airflow patterns is able to monitor much more complex wind patterns.' (2013)

6. Perhaps, like the sailors in Homer's *Odyssey*, I had opened Aeolus's bag of winds (by commencing this chapter) and been blown back to my point of origin.

7. A sigil is a magical symbol, encoding desire into visual form.

8. Newspapers would once have been left out for customers to read (see 'Pub Heritage—Historic Pub Interiors' 2015).

9. A quote from Dryden's translation of Virgil's *Aeneid* (2014). Aeolus opens a wound in his mountain to unleash the winds he controls and bring destruction to the Trojans.

BIBLIOGRAPHY

'*Another Place*.' 1997. Antony Gormley. Accessed 17 April 2014. http://www.antonygormley.com/sculpture/item-view/id/230#p0.

'"Another Place" by Antony Gormley.' VisitLiverpool.com. Accessed 17 April 2014. http://www.visitliverpool.com/things-to-do/another-place-by-antony-gormley-p16 0981.

Bayfield, Roy. 2011. 'From the North to the South You Walked All the Way.' Walking Home to 50. Last modified 14 May 2011. http://walkinghometo50.wordpress.com/.

Boyce, Frank Cottrell. 2011. *The Unforgotten Coat*. London: Walker.

Caiger-Smith, Martin. 2010. *Antony Gormley*. London: Tate.

Crowley, Aleister. 1986. *777 and Other Qabalistic Writings of Aleister Crowley Including Gemetria and Sepher Sephiroth*. San Francisco: Weiser.

Delgado-Fernandez, Irene, Derek W. T. Jackson, Andrew G. Cooper, Andrea C. W. Baas, J. H. Meiring Beyers, and Kevin Lynch. 2013. 'Field Characterization of Three-Dimensional Lee-Side Airflow Patterns under Offshore Winds at a Beach-Dune System.' *Journal of Geophysical Research* 118: 1–16.

'Gormley's Statues Stay Out to Sea.' 2007. BBC News. Last modified 7 March 2007. http://news.bbc.co.uk/1/hi/england/merseyside/6428935.stm.

Griffiths, Niall. 2008. *Real Liverpool*. Bridgend: Seren.

Haraway, Donna J. 1991. *Simians, Cyborgs and Women*. New York: Routledge.

Hunter, Carl, and Clare Heney. 2013. *Making Mongolia from Bits of Merseyside*. Ormskirk: Edge Hill University.

Joyce, James. (1922) 2008. *Ulysses*. Oxford: Oxford University Press.

Liverpool City Council. 2011. 'The Index of Multiple Deprivation 2010: A Liverpool Analysis.' Liverpool City Council. http://liverpool.gov.uk/media/129428/Executive-Summary-2010.pdf.

Massey, Doreen. 2005. *For Space*. Los Angeles: Sage.

Metro. 29 August 2013.

'Pub Heritage—Historic Pub Interiors.' 2015. *Campaign for Real Ale*. http://www.heritagepubs.org.uk/pubs/historic-pub-interior-entry.asp?pubid=108.

Reader's Digest. 2012. *The Most Amazing Places to Visit in Britain: The 1000 Most Unusual, Beautiful and Captivating Spots in Britain*. London: Reader's Digest Association.

Sefton Coast Partnership. 2006. 'Background Information for Working Group: Coastal Processes.' Sefton Coast. http://www.seftoncoast.org.uk/pdf/natconsultcoastproc.pdf.

Smith, Phil. 2014. *Enchanted Things*. Axminster: Triarchy Press.

Smith, Philip H. 2007. 'The Hall Road—Hightown Shingle Beach.' Sefton Coast. Accessed 17 April 2014. http://www.seftoncoast.org.uk/pdf/smith_200706.pdf.

Smith, Philip H., and Patricia A. Lockwood. 2013. 'Devil's Hole 2013.' Formby Civic Society. http://www.formbycivicsociety.org.uk/devils_hole.html.

Sprackland, Jean. 2012. *Strands: A Year of Discoveries on the Beach*. London: Jonathan Cape.

'Stand Up for Our Christianity, David Cameron Tells UK.' 2014. BBC News. Last updated 16 April 2014. http://www.bbc.co.uk/news/uk-politics-27053112.

'Students to Help Predict Future of Coastline.' 2013. Edge Hill University. https://www.edgehill.ac.uk/news/2013/08/students-to-help-predict-future-of-coastline/.

'Top 10 Cities.' 2013. Rough Guide. http://www.roughguides.com/best-places/2014/top-10-cities/.

Urry, John, and Jonas Larsen. 2011. *The Tourist Gaze 3.0*. Los Angeles: Sage.

Virgil. 2014. *The Aeneid of Virgil*. Translated by John Dryden. South Australia: University of Adelaide. Last updated 4 March 2014. http://ebooks.adelaide.edu.au/v/virgil/v5a/.

'Visit Crosby and Waterloo.' Crosby and Waterloo Business Village Partnership. www.visitcrosby.pwp.blueyonder.co.uk/.

'Welcome to the North Public Art Programme.' 2011. Arts Council England. 10 June. Accessed 2 March 2015. http://www.artscouncil.org.uk/funding/funded-projects/case-studies/welcome-north-public-art-programme.

Woolston, Robyn. 2013. '"Habitus" (2013) Statement.' Robyn Woolston. Last modified 13 September 2013. http://robynwoolston.tumblr.com/post/61109384299/habitus-2013-statement.

TWO

Walking the Dog

(For Those Who Don't Know How to Do It)

Ian Marchant

I'm a sort-of-travel writer. I've published three sort-of-travel books. Sort-of-travel books are usually shelved with the actual travel books. I get shelved in 'Travel,' and so does Iain Sinclair, the granddaddy of both British psychogeography and sort-of-travel writers, and so do Will Self's psychogeographical writings. I am on the same shelves as the psycho-geographers, but I'm not of their number. Psychogeography is not what I do. My stuff is too full of people or too full of rambling anecdotes about my nocturial adventures. This would be forgivable, maybe, if I were from a city. Or even interested in cities.

Everyone who has tried to define what psychogeography is, however wildly they might disagree about everything else, agrees that it is some-thing that can only be done in cities, on foot and with a pinch of theory. Theory, fair enough, hands up (or Theory Lite, anyway), but I don't do cities.

I live in a little town called Presteigne. My wife and I go shopping in Hereford, our nearest city, twenty-five miles away. The cathedral is worth a visit, and the best place for lunch is All Saints. Our engagement with Hereford is entirely bourgeois. I work two days in a week at Birm-ingham City University in a respectably edgy part of the city, partway between Villa Park and the Hawthorns. It's a two-hour drive due east of Presteigne, and I never get out of the car until I'm in the university car park, and I never go off campus.

Other than Birmingham and Hereford, the main cities I go to are small French provincial ones on holiday with my wife. We visit the cathedral and have lunch in a bistro. When I go to London, I go to meetings, and afterward I bimble around the bookshops and then maybe go to a show or a talk. I have neither the time nor the inclination to go yomping round abandoned multistorey car parks.

I was born and raised in the countryside. Both my parents can trap and skin a rabbit. My childhood home, where my parents still live, is now three houses from the boundary of the South Downs National Park, though it was just fields when I was a lad. I've lived in rural Lancashire and North Devon, but mostly I've lived in Mid Wales and since 2006 in Presteigne, hard up against the border with England, on the eastern edge of the Great Green Desert of Mid Wales. Cities are not my bag.

What's more, if I didn't have a dog, I'd never walk anywhere because I'm a countryman and we get about by car, except when visiting friends from the city insist on 'going for a walk.' But I do have a dog, and so I go on a walk thrice daily. It's a lovely walk. Presteigne (population 2,100) is the fourth-largest town of the four towns in the old county of Radnor-shire. People retire here because it's lovely and crime-free. And flat—tucked in the valley of the Lugg, with the true heights of the Radnor Forest rising away to the west. Flat is good for retired people, and it's good for heavy smokers too. It's a lovely, crime-free, just-flat-enough walk, with Georgian architecture, good-natured cheery people to stop and chat with, lots of funny dogs on the meadow, silence and a chance to think through the woods by the river. But as a site for psychogeographi-cal exploration, it's hopeless.

A few nights ago, as I was out with the dog, I passed a row of white cottages called 'Castle Dyche.' The cottages face slightly to the north of west. The setting sun had tinted the cottages a rosy hue—a sentence you could find in pretty much any piece of British topographical writing from the seventeenth century until the present day. Thing is, though, the set-ting sun really did turn the cottages rose pink, and you couldn't help but notice because it was beautiful. So what the fuck is psychogeography supposed to do with that? The stuff of chocolate boxes?

Sure, we could nip and get some smack from up Lugg View, our 'social housing' estate, but we're not going to, are we? Why would we? What do we learn by learning that the most beautiful place in Britain has a dark side? Everything has a dark side. It would be easy to walk past the site of what was once the town's biggest employer, the aluminium cast-ings factory, razed to the ground last year, causing high unemployment, especially among young people, who move away and take services with them. In the 2001 census, 25 percent of the population of Presteigne was listed as working in manufacture; in 2011, it was 6 percent. School rolls tumble. Now retirees from Birmingham and Manchester move in. Of course. This is everywhere. The countryside is on its knees. Farming doesn't pay; it's a lifestyle choice, made for you by your parents and grandparents. There are few useful buses, and we are miles from a super-market, which forces everybody to run a car.

But I don't walk that way. That isn't my story to tell. Maybe it was once, but it isn't now. Now I am a writer, a broadcaster, a university lecturer, and when I walk the dog, I want a straightforwardly pleasant walk, one on which I'm highly likely to meet friends but unlikely to come across broken glass, which might incur vet's bills. I am as far from Guy Debord or Sinclair and Self or Stewart Home and the magico-Marxists as it is possible to be.

Nick Papadimitriou in *Scarp* describes what he does as 'deep topography' because he has an intimate relationship rather than an alienated one with his landscapes, and I like that. A reinvention of topography sounds called for to me.

Real topography is bought secondhand years after it was published. Topography is a secondhand book dealer's classification. You can't get topography in new bookshops or find it in libraries. It is shelved either as 'Sort-of-Travel' or in 'Local.' Only at resale do these kinds of books become topography, as secondhand shops have whole sections devoted to it. Intimate, often personal guides to or reflections upon a particular landscape or a particular feature of a landscape, topography holds its value in the secondhand market because people collect it. I collect it, too. Everyone does. Everyone has *Branch Lines to East Grinstead* or *Bus Stops of Huntingdonshire* or *Twixt Torridge and Taw* or *20 Walks in the Breckland* or the local equivalent thereof. My mum only has one book—*Surrey in Bygone Days*. My old man has one, too: *World War Two Airfields of Kent and Sussex in Old Photographs*. It is the most derided of popular literary genres, seen as the trivial outpouring of petit bourgeois Little Britain. Psychogeography, if it could be made to work in the country, would surely aim to turn the other way from traditional topography.

But the cottages are tinted a rosy hue by the light of the setting sun, and I like it. The razed factory, the rural poor, is not the only story. White, middle-aged, middle-class people have a story to tell, too. Concentrating on the dark underbelly of country life is a means of urbanizing the countryside. White, middle-aged, middle-class people like me live in the countryside because it is nice.

And so I accept that my approach to this piece cannot be psychogeographical. But I want it to be at least deep topography, if deep topography means an intimate rather than an alienated relationship with landscape. So I will write what I know; I will write a sort-of-travel piece about my daily walk with the dog through my hometown. But I think I can lift one element from the early Debordist psychotravellers: I will alter my consciousness for the walk.

Debord wrote that he came up with the term *psychogeography* when he was high on hashish and lost in a park. Debord and Wolman's first dérive through Paris was undertaken when they were very, very drunk. Contemporary psychogeographical expeditions seem to have lost sight of the psyche and can be in danger of turning into geographical field trips, albeit field trips to liminal spaces. The point is still, it seems to me, that landscape is altered by consciousness, and that by altering our consciousness, we alter the landscape. So it falls to me, a white, middle-class, middle-aged dog walker, excluded from proper psychogeographical circles by virtue of my Arcadian inclinations, to revive this fine tradition.

I have acquired a small amount of skunk weed from a young friend, have rolled it into a joint and am ready to set out.

The dog, Peggy, is seven months old. She is half English springer spaniel and half standard poodle. She is keen to go. I check my pockets to make sure I have poo bags. I spark up my joint.

I open the gate to our yard, out into the back lane, and turn the corner. The east end of St. Andrew's Church is in front of me as I turn left into Broad Street and walk past our neighbour's house. Outside their front door is a trestle table with a cooler box on top which contains fresh eggs for sale, a pound a half-dozen. You put the pound through their letter box and help yourself to the eggs. When we moved in, their house was called Fold Farm and had once been lived in by a farmer called Ted, but he had died a few weeks before we arrived, and now it's been done up by Ted's daughter Sue and her husband, Kev, and renamed 'Ted's Fold Farm,' with a picture of a teddy bear on the new slate sign. Sue's mum, Molly, lives with them. Molly has never lived here before because Ted was not her husband but her lover. Molly and her husband, Fred, lived on a farm outside Presteigne, where Sue grew up. For a long time, until Ted inherited his family's farm, he was Fred's hand. Fred was, by all accounts, a vile human being. My friend Pope, for example, was for many years Fred and Molly's neighbour, and on several occasions Fred approached Pope and asked him for a wank in return for a crate of Guinness. Sue ran away from Presteigne to Oxfordshire as soon as she could, where presumably she met Kev, an unimaginably colourless man who never speaks. In fact, it was not until Ted's death, when he left the farm to Sue, that she learned that she was his daughter and that naughty Molly had been going up into the long grass with the hired help. So Sue brought Kev home to Presteigne to claim her inheritance. Now Molly has dementia, and when she can, she escapes from Sue and Kev's garden and goes toddling off into Broad Street, which, although very quiet, does occasionally have local boy racers testing out their Subaru Imprezas. Molly's life is in periodic danger.

Next, an electricity substation set slightly back from the pavement, with the 'Danger of Death' signs beloved of traditional psychogeography. The verge in front of the substation, perhaps a metre wide by three metres long, is trimmed, reseeded, looked after and clearly loved by a gentleman called Bert. Bert is ninety-three. He always wears a suit and tie and a trilby as he looks after his bit of grass. Bert has the British Empire medal for his service in the Second World War. He was a dispatch rider who came ashore with the Canadians on Sword Beach on the morning of D-Day and who fought through to the end of the war. He was one of the column that liberated Belsen. Peggy has a piss on Bert's verge when he's not there.

We cross Church Close. Church Close has only just been built, and the first residents moved in last summer. The small development of eight 'affordable houses' has been built by Border Oak, who professes to build in sympathy with local urban landscapes. But Church Close is a horrible mash-up of styles, with half-timbered storied upper floors, faux neoclassical columns and carriage lamps fixed to new brick walls. For years, this site had stood empty, and the only possible response to building on Broad Street would have been stark modernism, leaving a mark that we could still claim as our own in three or four hundred years. Instead, the developers faked the various historical vernaculars that they thought they saw on Broad Street, as though fakery were sympathetic.

Beyond Church Close is 'Roseland,' an early nineteenth-century villa that was once the home of watercolourist J. Murray Ince. I know this because there is a blue plaque on the wall, although otherwise I'm afraid I've never heard of J. Murray Ince, nor seen any of his work. Peggy usually shits outside the front door. I do not think that this is a critique of bourgeois aesthetic values because there are quite a few artists and writers (one an internationally known novelist and screenwriter) who still live in the little run of a half-dozen cottages up from Roseland, and if Peggy were trying to make a point, there are better doors she could shit in front of.

Best place of all for a shit would be the door of the little pink cottage that ends the row. This cottage is called 'The Fort.' There is a plaque on the door that reads 'In 1985 this house was dedicated to the memory of HRH The Duke and Duchess of Windsor.' It is called 'The Fort' after Fort Belvedere, where HRH had his residence when he was Prince of Wales. So far, so pleasingly eccentric, but sadly the owner empathizes so thoroughly with dear David and Mrs. Simpson that he, too, is a Mosleyite, a fact he likes to advertise by putting posters for unpleasant political parties in his window.

Another small run of cottages, and then the dog likes to stop and sniff the steps of the Judge's Lodging. The Judge's Lodging was courtroom, prison and the place where the circuit judges stayed when they were in town; now it is a museum and the town's Tourist Information Centre.

The Radnorshire Assizes moved to Presteigne in 1542, and the last trials were held in 1971. The present building, which also served as Radnorshire's County Hall until the creation of the much-loathed Powys in 1974, was first opened in 1829, twenty-four years too late for the biggest case in the history of Radnor Assizes—namely, the execution of Mary Morgan for the killing of her baby.

Mary Morgan was an undercook at Maesllwych Castle outside Glasbury, south of Hay. In 1804, she was sentenced to death for infanticide. In 1804 in Radnorshire, illegitimate birth was no big thing; approximately one-sixth of all births were outside marriage. Mary Morgan seems to have had 'her head turned' by the birth because, as soon as the baby arrived, she decapitated it with a kitchen knife. There is some suggestion that the 'young master' of Maesllwych Castle might have been the father of the child, but Mary would never say who it was. It is easy to imagine that, in 1804, infanticide was something for which lots of young women were hanged, but in fact cases of execution for infanticide were vanishingly rare, and if anybody was found guilty, the sentence was in almost all cases commuted. But in Mary's case it was not, and she thus became the last woman to be hanged in Wales. The judge who passed sentence, Judge Hardinge, was wildly unpopular, and he still is. Mary Morgan's original gravestone was continuously defaced until it was taken into safe keeping by the Radnorshire Museum. There is now a reproduction in the churchyard. It reads:

> To the memory of Mary Morgan who young, beautiful and endowed with a good understanding and disposition but unenlightened by the sacred truths of Christianity became the victim of sin and shame and was condemned to an ignominious death on the 11th April 1805 for the murder of her bastard child. Rous'd to a first sense of guilt and remorse by the eloquent and humane Mr. Justice Hardinge, she underwent the sentence of the law on the following Thursday with unfeigned repentance and a fervent hope of forgiveness through the merits of a redeeming intercessor. This stone is erected not merely to perpetuate the remembrance of a departed penitent, but to remind the living of the frailty of human nature when unsupported by religion.

In 1818, another stone was erected. The story has it that it was paid for by her defence barrister. The original of this one is still in the churchyard, undefaced, and it reads:

> In Memory of Mary Morgan, who suffer'd April 13th 1805, Aged 17 years. He that is without sin among you, Let him first cast a stone at her.

Beyond the Judge's Lodging, the houses get grander. Posh Sally will often emerge from her grand house at this point, not to say hello to me but to chookle the dog. Posh Sally lives in a double-bayed brick-built three-storey late Georgian mansion called 'The Red House,' and a blue plaque on the side will tell you that this once was the home of Rear Admiral Puget, he of the Sound. Posh Sally is very posh, but as posh people go, she has no side about her. She likes me because I'm on the BBC sometimes and once invited me to dinner with my daughters to meet Arlene Phillips off *Strictly*, who was very friendly and talked about ageism on the telly.

Next to the Red House is the Duke's Arms, run by a brother and sister and their respective spouses. There is a poster in the window advertising a duo from Mississippi called Swamp Thing who is due to play tonight. We get a few American bands coming through because our local booker is a highly connected and respected guy called Pete who is tapped into some interesting gig circuits. The Duke's Arms is famed for the poor quality of its ale, but it's the best place for bands, and when there are no bands, two old guys often sit in the window of the lounge playing cribbage. The Duke's Arms was the last stop on the last ever stagecoach run, which was from Aberystwyth to Presteigne sometime in the 1860s. (I would stop in and check the date, but they don't allow dogs.)

This is the top of Broad Street, and Peggy and I are perhaps a quarter-mile from home. In 1642, a Civil War skirmish was fought up and down Broad Street as the Parliamentarians came to break up a rumoured muster of Royalists, and three men were killed, but now the only fighting is the occasional drunken kickoff on Saturday night, especially when Presteigne St. Andrew's plays Knighton Town in the Spar Mid Wales League (division 2).

We stand at a crossroads. In front Green End, to the left Hereford Street, and to the right the High Street. On the Broad Street/Hereford Street corner of the crossroads is the Assembly Rooms, the finest Italianate gothic building in Mid Wales, with a campanile topped by the town clock, which has kept wildly inaccurate time since 1863 and which chimes around about the hour, roughly every hour or so. It is a good clock for the approximate time of the deep countryside. The ground floor of the Assembly Rooms, once the Market Hall, is now given over to the town library. The Assembly Rooms proper are on the first floor. It's a hundred-seater venue given over to bourgeois artistic endeavour, perhaps a small touring theatre company, or a band slightly too big for the Duke's Arms. Once a month, the Assembly Rooms plays host to the Presteigne Film Society, a relentlessly highbrow organization given to showing Iranian art-house cinema. The nearest commercial cinema is in Hereford, and so if you want to see the latest James Bond film or some such, you face a long drive. But if you want to see the latest offerings from surreal South Korean directors, then Presteigne Film Society will suit you fine.

On the Broad Street/High Street corner is Lorna's Sandwich Shop. Until very recently, this was our post office. It called itself the 'First and Last Post Office in Wales.' At the bottom of Broad Street, fifty yards from our front door, is the Lugg Bridge. The River Lugg at this point forms the boundary between England and Wales. There is a stone on the parapet of the bridge that marks the exact moment that Lloegr becomes Cymru. The post office had a very strong claim to its 'first and last' status. On the Broad Street side, it was written in English, and on the High Street side, it was written in Welsh, but Lorna is an unsentimental local businesswoman who, like most Radnor folk, doesn't speak a word of Welsh and so sees no need to translate her sign.

On the Green End/High Street corner is a now-abandoned shop, which was Lorna's until she bought the old post office. It's a ramshackle half-timbered building, like something from an H. P. Lovecraft story, and the flat above the shop is lived in by a large Polish family. Eastern European immigration has come as a shock to the countryside, which has been largely passed over by Afro-Caribbean or Asian immigration. It strikes me as a great thing, and I get a constant kick from hearing Polish, Russian and Bulgarian spoken in the streets. Next door is Gilly's shop, which is a hippy-ish gift-and-card shop. Gilly is a Scottish immigrant, proudly Scottish, angry that she doesn't get a chance to vote 'yes' for independence in the referendum, who hasn't been to Scotland since the death of her father fifteen years ago. The little run of immigrant businesses and homes is continued by Elda's Colombian Coffee House, run by Elda, who is Colombian. Elda married a Presteigneey ne'er-do-well whom she met while he was backpacking in Colombia. He brought her home and married her, and she took over the Presteigne greasy spoon and then divorced him. It's still a greasy spoon, really, but for the last twenty-five years, she has sold the best coffee for miles around. I have my breakfast there most days. Breakfast in Elda's is a chance to chat with my pals, like Professor Roger, the defrocked philosopher; Bungalow Bill, the failed Canadian gold prospector; and Polly, the Burnt Toast Lady, who always has two blackened slices of toast for breakfast and who gives a soundly left-wing commentary on that morning's *Daily Mail*, which Elda takes for the amusement of her customers.

Between Elda's and the Greek-run fish-and-chip shop is an arch, too small to drive a car through, that leads into Albert Square. I used to live in Albert Square in the flat over Gilly's shop, which is accessed from behind Elda's. My neighbour was called Glenys. She is eighty-nine years old and a great-great-grandmother. You don't get her started on immigration. She hates Elda, despises the Poles and has little time for the Greek family who runs the chip shop or the Australian couple who have come to run the news agents next door to the chip shop or even Gilly, really, who as a Scotswoman certainly counts as being from off. Being from off is a bad thing. Pav, the owner of the Greek chip shop, and Glenys exist in a permanent state of warfare. When I walk the dog at night, Pav comes out and has a smoke if the shop is quiet, which it often is. He looks like Steerpike. On the other side of the road from the chip shop is Deli Tinto, which was started by Leon and Joanna to specialize in Spanish foods. Leon is from Gibraltar. When he and Joanna split up a few years back, Leon and his new lady, Anne-Marie, set up a veg-and-fresh-fish shop called the Salty Dog. Now Deli Tinto and the Salty Dog, although both providers of pleasingly middle-class fare, are at daggers drawn. Leon says that he used to work on the fish counter at Harrods, and I see no reason to doubt him. His specialty is fresh trout from the Lugg, though, if you press him, he admits it comes from a fish farm on the edge of town rather than from the river per se.

A few doors down from the Salty Dog is Carini's, the butcher, and another blue plaque on the wall tells us that this is Sutton House, once the headquarters of the Radnorshire Turnpike Trust. Radnorshire was the main arena of operation for the Rebecca rioters, who in the 1840s blackened their faces and dressed as women in order to smash tollgates on the hated turnpikes. Troops were stationed in Knighton, six miles away, to keep order. One night in 1843, the Rebeccas came to Presteigne. They terrorized the keeper of one of the town tollgates into hiding under his bed, but they were put to flight by Martha, the keeper of the other town gate, and local historians suspect that they were not real Rebeccas at all but practical jokers dressed up as men dressed up as women in blackface.

I do this same walk, or part of this same walk, three times a day, every day. Some elements change slowly; the old post office was empty for a year until Lorna took it over, for example. Other elements of the walk change with the seasons, and not just the straightforwardly natural elements, such as trees or meadow flowers or birdsong. Human elements change from season to season as well. In August, we have a classical music festival that uses St. Andrew's as its principal venue, and then the walk involves restraining Peggy from jumping up at pretty lady violinists on their way to rehearsal in the church or men of a certain age in raspberry trousers limbering up for a bit of Hindemith or Webern. In October, the Vintage Sports Car Club stages their annual Presteigne Rally, and the streets are full of elderly sports cars and their owners. But what changes most dynamically from day to day is the people whom you might meet. Nipping up to the shops to buy a pint of milk or some fags can easily take a half-hour; five minutes there, twenty minutes chatting, five minutes back. In communities of this size, you know your neighbours, and they know you, and unless there is some great emergency, it is the done thing to stop and pass the time of day. There is a poet called Charles whom I often meet, usually at night and usually in transit between pubs, who likes to exchange poetry gossip, poetry being a trade prone to gossip. There is a chap I meet called Ken, who has started teaching me Russian, standing on the High Street, one word per meeting, Peggy straining at the lead, openly bored.

This unpredictable element, the human element, means that the High Street is always the slowest part of the walk. If Gilly and Pav are outside their shops, if Glenys happens to be standing at the entrance to Albert Square, if Sally wants to chookle the dog, if Charles the poet wants to discuss the personal habits of J. H. Prynne, if Leon has a joke to tell, or if Ken is describing the evolution of the Cyrillic alphabet, this quarter-mile strip of small shops can take an hour. But once you're past the Radnorshire Arms and Bryn's Garage, the going gets easier.

Opposite Bryn's is the yard of W. J. Taylor and Sons, agricultural engineers. W. J. 'Eddie' Taylor died a few years back. Five times mayor, on the town council for forty years, he bequeathed a meadow to the town, now known as Eddie's Meadow, which links the site of the Norman motte and bailey (now known as the Warden and a public space since the eighteenth century) with the entrance to Went's Meadow, which Peggy and I are approaching. Eddie was a great engineer, a man who could make and mend pretty much anything. In 1565, good John Beddoes, a local wool merchant, bequeathed money to the town to set up a school on condition that every night at 7:20 p.m. a curfew bell should be rung from the church. By the late 1980s, it was getting harder and harder to guarantee that somebody could be found to undertake this task, and so, theoretically at least, the school was in peril of being closed. Mike Oldfield, of Tubular Bells fame, stumped up a bit of cash, and Eddie Taylor set to mechanizing the ringing. Now Eddie's Oldfield-funded hand-built mechanism rings the angelus bell every evening at 7:20 for five minutes. Eddie and Mike Oldfield therefore saved John Beddoes School, but Powys County Council clearly thinks they are cunts, and this year they closed it anyway after 450 years just because they could. Now the curfew bell tolls for nothing, except perhaps in memory of Eddie Taylor, a man who did his best by his town.

We pass Castle Dyche, a row of cottages that are sometimes tinted a rosy hue by the setting sun. I met a woman by these cottages recently who was urging me to get Peggy's hair cut. She told me she had a number for a dog-grooming parlour in Knucklas. She told me to drop by and pick up the number any time. We live, she said, at One Castle Dye-*ch*. That's how she pronounced it, though clearly it's supposed to be *Ditch*. Perhaps if your cottage is tinted a rosy hue by the setting sun, you can't face admitting that your address is Castle Ditch.

Between two houses there is a path that runs into the corner of Went's Meadow, and it is here I let Peggy off the lead and roll myself a fag. Probably today I should roll another joint to stay in tune with Debordist psychogeographical practice, but I only had a bit. Went's Meadow is divided into two parts. This first section is kept as a meadow, except for the bottom right-hand corner, where a small community orchard has been planted. In January, the hippy part of the community troops down here for wassailing. My friend Pope (of wank-for-Guinness fame) has invented a ceremony that he performs, mostly involving reciting doggerel and banging saucepans. It's only about ten years old, but it already starts to feel like a tradition.

This first half of Went's Meadow has grass, flowers, fruit trees and lots of dogs, and after her second shit, Peggy dances away to play with her pals, while I walk along the side of the meadow and through a gate in the hedge into the other half of Went's Meadow, where the grass is kept shorter. Kids play football, and in summer we sometimes hold a festival here called Sheep Music. Peggy likes the skate park in the far corner over by the Knighton Road; I throw her ball in there, and it bounces in a random way, which keeps her amused all day if I let it. The skate park is covered in graffiti, the only graffiti in Presteigne. There is a standing stone, recently erected by the entrance to Went's Meadow. On it there is a plaque that reads 'Went's Meadow. Bought on behalf of the Community by the Community, 2002.' Peggy and I walk down the far side of Went's Meadow, past the allotments and down to the River Lugg. There is a small, pebbly beach here, where kids come to swim in summer. Wild swimming is one of those rare rural activities that contemporary psychogeography looks on with approval. I can't swim, but Peggy has just learned and will cheerfully chase sticks in and out of the river until she is shivering with cold.

We turn for home, which takes us along the Lugg and through the Withybeds Nature Reserve. This is a marshy area, once given over to the commercial production of willow withies but now tamed and traversed by a wooden walkway. Halfway along this boardwalk, there is a bench overlooking the river, and I stop here for a fag while Peggy roots around in the marshy ground. Today, I think about Debord and how, high on hashish and lost in a Paris park, he had come up with the term *psychogeography*. My conviction at the start of the walk, that I'm not a psychogeographer, can only be strengthened by my enjoyment of the lapping of the benign waters of the Lugg, the knocking of a woodpecker in one of the trees and Peggy sitting hopefully at my feet with a stick, looking up at me with puppy eyes. She is black, but she has a grey beard, and I think about how she looks a bit like Gerry Adams. Debord invented psychogeography after eating a lump of hash, while after a joint of skunk, I think my dog looks a bit like Gerry Adams. I decide that I probably don't have what it takes to launch an art movement and decide against writing a manifesto.

Then we walk out of the Withybeds, back onto the path at the bottom of Went's Meadow, which takes you into a lane that leads past the Powys County Council depot and then turns into Church Street, where Peggy goes back on the lead. Then Church Street peters out and turns into the path through St. Andrew's churchyard. I pass the replica of Mary Morgan's first gravestone.

At the gate to the churchyard opposite my house is a lamppost, just like the lamppost in Narnia. Presteigne is Narnia-esque, there is no doubt, but the fictional place it most closely resembles is Hobbiton, with Radnorshire as the Shire. And I have no real desire to leave. Frodo and the rest can hack off with rings to Mordor as much as they like, but I have modeled myself on Fatty Bolger, the hobbit who stayed behind to smoke a little pipeweed and generally keep an eye on things.

And Peggy always pulls for the last few yards because she knows that her breakfast is waiting, while I normally just have a cup of tea.

But today, for some unaccountable reason, I fancy a couple of biscuits as well.

THREE

Incongruous Steps toward a Legal Psychogeography

Luke Bennett

In *Scarp: In Search of London's Outer Limits* (2012), Nick Papadimitriou conjures many dissonant ideas, images and registers. In this chapter, I dissect two of his strange conjunctions and, in doing so, consider through them the prospects for extending contemporary British psychogeography's embrace of the incongruous—the out-of-place, the absurd and the out-of-keeping—beyond psychogeography's usually aesthetically inclined preoccupation with liminality and into the mundane sphere of law's everyday manifestations within the built environment.

THE MANY TURNS AT SUICIDE CORNER

Papadimitriou takes us—early on in his traverse along the escarpment of what is now the lost county of Middlesex—to 'Suicide Corner,' a stretch of the A41 snaking out its path northwest of London. He recounts for us a succession of fatal car crashes and the people, creatures and other matter caught up in each event that occurred there. In doing so he draws forth isolated incidents from the pages of long-forgotten local newspapers and memory, activating these incidental archives in order to show a reverberation of these events within the landscape itself.

At one point in his rumination, Papadimitriou figures an anonymous 'civil engineer working for the transport ministry' who 'through eyeing the scraggy wood just to the north of the farmhouse, sees only camber, curve and how best to extend the planned M1 extension over this high ground from its present terminus' (Papadimitriou 2012, 20).

Papadimitriou captures in this passage how the task-orientated gaze of the engineer sees the topography as a set of logistical challenges, a puzzle to solve as he works through in his mind's eye the most feasible path for his roadway. Papadimitriou's description seeks to show how all other sensory inputs are blocked (or discarded) as irrelevant to this man's purpose. He is standing there for a reason. He is harvesting the landscape for what *he* needs today. This applied gaze foregrounds certain features and backgrounds all else. This spectator is in the engineering-professional equivalent of 'flow' (Csikszentmihalyi 2008—for whom flow is an optimal immersion in the moment, marked by both physiological and psychological change). He is portrayed as at one with his task, the landscape presenting to him as a specific 'taskscape' (Ingold 1993, 157)—the very perception of a landscape being formed by the requirements of the task to be carried out there.

And yet Papadimitriou then, importantly, shows how even that intent focus is vulnerable to undermining by the assault of the disregarded 'background,' as an irresistible reverie—or least a momentary noticing of other things—takes hold:

> Momentarily distracted from his plans by the chirping of some unnamable night bird, he looks eastwards across the brightly lit Edgware Way, towards the high ground at Edgewarebury. Perhaps moved by some spontaneous memory of childhood holidays spent in the New Forest, his imagination lingers in the woods and fields like a slowly drifting plant community and then dissolves into ditches lined with black waterlogged leaves—a residue of previous summers—and the ghosts of dead insects. (Papadimitriou 2012, 20)

In showing the breaking of concentration caused by the bird's proximate existence, Papadimitriou keys into a number of trends (or 'turns') in contemporary sociocultural theory. I explain each in turn using this paragraph as my anchor. In doing so, I am starting to map out how contemporary British psychogeography has an affinity with cultural geography, even though it is currently regarded with considerable suspicion by academics for—as Alistair Bonnett notes—'Psychogeography is on the furthest margins of the discipline of geography and has attracted little scholarly attention' (2013, n.p.).

If we paraphrase Papadimitriou's passage, we can bring the influence of these turns (or at least the general cultural milieu of which they are part) more clearly into view. Thus, the engineer is shown to be embodied—he is standing somewhere, surrounded by sound and breeze, on and amid the layering of life cycles. He is more than the deportment of his task. He is living and breathing, existing in space. He is there and thus not anywhere else. He is embedded in life and place: his *lifeworld*. He is engaged in a moment-by-moment cocreation of his sense of place; in part he makes this place through the mental (and disciplinary) constructs he brings (his gaze), and in part this place makes him through materially resisting certain options or actions, through presenting certain 'givens' (history, morphology, entropy) that he—this individual—cannot resist. He is entrained in a world, a traveller in time as well as space. This place, and ideas, memories and emotions that he or others associate with it, shapes his experience of it and experiences in it.

This reformulation aligns Papadimitriou's passage to both Maurice Merleau-Ponty's (1962) embodied phenomenology and Kathleen Stewart's (2007) influential advocacy of consideration of the preconscious swirl of 'ordinary affects' (emotions, bodily dispositions, habits) that shape the performance of everyday life. Indeed, Stewart's academic study of the everyday is presented in a similar fashion to *Scarp*—fragments of incisive stories and moments, the multiplicity of happenings, shorn of overarching explanation, emphasizing how 'rogue intensities roam the streets of the ordinary' (ibid., 44), causing us to experience, to react, and then afterward to make sense of where the embodied flow of life has swept us. This focus on preconscious (non-discursive) experience of place is also echoed in the proponents of 'non-representational theory' in British cultural geography (see, for example, Thrift 2008).

Stewart also foregrounds the importance of studying mundane 'everyday' life, of foregrounding the regular, the (ordinarily) unremarkable, the mass of tasks that make up the background of daily life, a concern also to the fore with theorists of 'everyday life,' such as Henri Lefebvre, Walter Benjamin and the surrealists (as chronicled by Highmore 2002). Contemporary psychogeography has an affinity with this scrutiny of the mundane in that it aspires to a restless multiplicity, to an epistemological promiscuity, to an open noticing of *everything*, to a renunciation of conventional filters that push certain elements centre stage and cause others to recede from view. All of these aims can be subsumed within the notion of psychogeography having an embrace of incongruity at the heart of its methodology, as it seeks out the complexity, colour, worth and drama of the seemingly ordinary through juxtaposition, playfulness, embodiment, allusion and heterodoxy.

Meanwhile, Papadimitriou's drift from the engineer's thoughts and their merger into 'ditches lined with black waterlogged leaves . . . and the ghosts of dead insects' (Papadimitriou 2012, 20) is reminiscent of Jane Bennett's 'vibrant materialism' theses—particularly her rumination on the shimmering agency of a pile of refuse (Bennett 2010, 4)—in which she advocates giving greater attention to nonhuman actors and their potency within our human encounters with the world. Bennett's thesis in turn finds echo in an 'object-oriented' pivot toward materialism in a variety of academic disciplines stretching from literary scholars (Brown 2001) and cultural theorists (Bogost 2012) to archaeologists (Olsen 2010), geographers (Whatmore 2006) and philosophers (Harman 2009), and links us back to *Scarp*, particularly around those who foreground the coconstitutive role of human/matter entanglement (for example, Miller 2008 and Hodder 2012) and the mundane, event-forming 'force of things' (Stewart 2007, 16)—the cumulative effects of many tiny encounters with things, people and rules that in aggregate make our daily experience and channel our actions.

Finally, as we have already seen, the engineer brings his own 'way of seeing' (Berger 1972) to this place and through his needs (as embodied within his taskscape) constructs an impression of this place, one likely to be quite different from that assemblage of experience, investigation, action and interaction (with other humans, with other creatures, with others' tasks) that would be composed by any other visitor. This is a relational view of the construction of place—and takes its cue from the work of Doreen Massey (2005) and others applying the work of Gilles Deleuze to geography. For such theorists, the sense of place is dynamic and constantly being re-created because it is only ever an unstable aggregate of the myriad orientations of users of that space.

While it is possible—as Papadimitriou's passage shows in its depiction of a highway engineer's gaze—to point to singular conceptual framings (Goffman 1974) by which a place will be engaged and sense made of it, the embodied nature of the viewer and the temporalities of matter and their interaction deny any one way of seeing (or knowing) total dominion—or even total stability—over that sense-making process. Thus, it would be too simplistic to assert that engineers only see landscapes in one (very instrumentalist) way—and Papadimitriou shows us how the place (and the embodiment of the engineer in it) cannot be entirely eliminated.

But there is more work to be done. While the landscape poet can happily leave us with a romantic resurgence of 'nature' overwhelming an instrumentalist man, psychogeography's embrace of incongruity can—and should—be taken further. Psychogeography should equally be able to show how the workaday preoccupations of an instrumentalist science can invade a thought stream of more affective purpose, showing how the 'straight' world reasserts itself, barging itself back to the foreground—in short, how it recolonizes consciousness and gaze. So, for example, Papadimitriou's engineer's reverie—his tumble back to environment-related childhood memories—is fleeting, itself inevitably undermined by the 'day job' returning to his consciousness, the 'real world' bringing him back down to earth and back to the prosaic task in hand, as he turns away from reminiscence and resumes his survey of this countryside and its future road course.

Using incongruence to tease out and vividly depict *all* aspects of the multiplicity of the experience of place could be psychogeography's rich methodological contribution. In striking out in this even more holistic direction, it would be following in the footsteps of Walter Benjamin's urban investigations (as ably overviewed in Gilloch 1996) and in doing so operationalizing Georg Simmel's (1976) theorizing of the psychic self-survival strategies by which the citizen copes with the sensory overload of modern urban life, and to do so by showing *both* sides of the accommodation of mind and being to space, task and meaning making: thus chronicling the moment of escape (the engineer's romantic rural reverie) as well as the subsequent moment of (re)capture (the *counter*reverie that brings the task at hand, and all of its prosaic strictures, back to the fore).

We will consider why and where psychogeography could gainfully employ an analysis of this counterreverie shortly, but first I must explain what I mean by psychogeography's embrace of incongruity.

PSYCHOGEOGRAPHY'S EMBRACE OF INCONGRUITY

In giving birth to psychogeography (by name at least) in the 1950s, the Situationist International gave contemporary British psychogeography the two core stated aims of psychogeographical enquiry: *détournement* (finding new uses for the built environment) and the urban drift, or *dérive*. Stevphen Shukaitis and Joanna Figiel depict the dérive as a 'way [of] getting lost, of opening up how one is affected by the world, [that] brings to the fore all the richness (and horror) of the everyday that is typically not paid attention to' (2013, 3).

While neither can be formally described as a research methodology, the aspiration that is embodied in each concept has methodological merit and some precedent as an axiom of both social research and creative enquiry. Psychogeographers are not the only explorers (or researchers) who want to 'weird' the world. Thus, in his explication of theories of everyday life, Highmore (2002) points to anthropologist James Clifford's 1981 essay, 'On Ethnographic Surrealism,' which explored the 1920s and early 1930s links between the avant-garde and the emergence of French ethnology. Clifford saw modern ethnology as driven by a need to (in the oft-quoted phrase) 'mak[e] the familiar strange]' (1988, 121; a particularly important dictum for research conducted within the researcher's own cultural reality). But his invocation was more dramatic than those words portray; in embracing the destabilizing principles of surrealism, Clifford then advocated an ethnographic surrealist practice that 'attacks the familiar, provoking the eruption of otherness—the unexpected' (ibid., 146). He situated 'surrealist ethnography' as revelling in difference and semantic indeterminacy (in healthy contrast to the taxonomic—naming and ordering—impulse of a 'scientific' ethnology). Clifford's ensuing methodological prescription co-opted the surrealist practice of collage, assemblage forming in which the 'cuts and sutures of the research process are left visible; there is no smoothing over or blending of the work's raw data into homogenous representation' (ibid., 147).

Contemporary British psychogeography aspires to multiply the readings of any place (thus invoking but widening Lefebvre's exhortation [1996, 159] to do so specifically in relation to cities) and by this commitment to opening up the potentiality of place to avoid the closure (the narrowing down) inherent in instrumentalist meaning making. Papadimitriou shows this urge in our second example from *Scarp*—his strange (essentially incongruent) juxtaposition of a few glimpsed moments at the end of an unidentified old lady's life alongside the recitation of the Mogden Formula, by which water companies calculate sewerage charges.

Here Papadimitriou willfully brings together two entirely separate parts of the modern world and melds them simply in order to delight in their incongruence. There is a playful surrealist stratagem at work here— but also something unusual in psychogeography. The Mogden Formula is presented without explanation—there is no reason for Papadimitriou to mention this formula other than he finds it fascinating, occult even—in the sense that these things do not normally reach the foreground, but rather remain hidden (i.e., 'occluded'); they are normally the infrastructural background of life, important but unacknowledged. Papadimitriou forces us to gaze at the Mogden Formula's complex provisioning, to confront its alien symbols and phrases. *Why* he does so is unclear—taken at face value, it is because (as he says at an earlier point in *Scarp*) 'the thought that anything, any event, should be overlooked horrifies me' (Papadimitriou 2012, 77).

The Mogden Formula passage sits in an appendix to the main (vaguely autobiographical) body of *Scarp*. It is presented as a (presumably) fictitious found text that purports to be the 1974 fragments of 'Perry Kurland's Journal.' The appendix is both the high point of Papdimitriou's embrace of contemporary psychogeography's incongruent intent and the point at which the integrity of his literary text—its *manifest point*—becomes most unstable. The irruption of the Mogden Formula is only held within a vague semblance of narrative progression by the baseline riff provided by the juxtaposed glimpses of the final events of the old lady's life. There is something humanist in this, perhaps an implication that we must always strive to find and foreground the real, modest and anonymous lives that play out alongside such systemic abstractions as waste water management. But whatever Papadimitriou's intent is here, we are certainly left with an embrace of incongruent multiplicity—a simultaneous, parallel reading of multiple, seemingly unrelated fragments of the place under scrutiny, juxtaposing them surrealist collage-like, to see what conjunctions occur. And—for once—it is a juxtaposition that does not quite lapse into a romantic reverie. While the juxtaposition is humanist (perhaps) in overall effect, the reader is left with a glimpse of the strange complexity of the technical bureaucracy by which the most universal of human emissions are 'managed,' and perhaps also a sense of Papadimitriou's fascination with this infrastructural hydrological cycle (a fascination that Papadimitriou happily admits to and performs in John Rogers's documentary film about his life and wanderings: *The London Perambulator* [2009]).

In foregrounding the Mogden Formula, Papadimitriou gives us a glimpse of what a truly rebellious (and also academically valiant) psychogeography could be, a depictive writing that shows the irruption of technical realms into affective life, reversing the psychogeographer's usual discovery of a quirky anecdote, a warm breeze, or a fragment of history to energize a mundane place. Through such bleeding back of technical, bureaucratic and regulatory fragments into psychogeography's 'literary' account forming (as a counter to the predominance of romantic reverie), those accounts would vividly reveal how the everyday world is made both of natural and (affective) human vibrancy *and* of matter, obstruction, systemic regularity, instrumentality and control.

Such a 'counterreverie' turn would seem to take psychogeography back toward the original political reconnaissance envisaged by Guy Debord and the Situationalist International to find in reconnaissance both the ways in which the built environment is experienced creatively by the individual and the strictures and structures by which the regularity and governability of the urban realm is routinely manifested. Thus Papadimitriou's incongruous insertion of the Mogden Formula into the 'human interest' storyline of the prosaic last days of an old woman reveals the 'everywhereness' of technocratic control through its glimpse of a small fragment of the mundane regulatory architecture by which the built environment is (normally) silently constituted and managed.

Back in 1955 Debord advocated that 'Psychogeography could set for itself the study of the precise laws and specific effects of the geographical environment, consciously organized or not, on the emotions and behavior of individuals' (Debord 1955, n.p.). Arguably, Debord set too passive a role for individual place making in that formulation, and the laws that he was envisaging out there to be found betray a greater faith in scientific method than would be found in cultural geography today, bearing in mind where the 'turns' outlined earlier have swept us. But, looked at afresh (and accepting that Debord did little in the way of developing psychogeography beyond a handful of slogans), there is scope—swimming with the academic tide set by the present sociocultural 'turns'—to start searching again for the built environment's effects upon the emotions and behaviour of individuals and of the presence of specific laws and their related effects within the geographical environment.

INTRODUCING LEGAL GEOGRAPHY

And here's where a *legal psychogeography* appears, the prospect of a hybrid fusing of aspects of environmental psychology, institutional ethnography (Smith 2005), all of the sociocultural 'turns' (material, affective, relational, everyday), and legal geography to attain—through psychogeography's embrace of incongruence—insight into the cocreation of place, society and law through localized practices and experiences.

Legal geography is itself an awkward hybrid, seeking as it does to explicate the coconstitutive relationship of the spatial, the legal and the social: how people and law make (aspects of) the world and, in turn, how the world (the physical environment) both shapes the manifestations of law within concrete spatial situations and frames social behaviour. This coconstitutive relationship has its most elaborate statement in David Delaney's (2011) *The Spatial, The Legal and the Pragmatics of World Making: Nomospheric Investigations.* Delaney reworks the standard legal geography trinity to show how places (and by extension objects) are formed from a coconstitutive interaction of material, legal and action-centred processes (practices), none of which is dominant or directive of the others. Thus things, people, practices and the places in which they are found are cocreations. The law does not alone create the world, nor does it have unfettered ability even to shape people, things and places. In many situations law's writ is a strong shaping force, but even in the most controlling society, law's generality must yield to aspects of the specificity of individuals, their actions and their environments—all as imbrications of unique situations and places formed by them.

Legal geographers therefore look to study law's manifestations in (and the curbing of its power by) the social and material world. Thus, to a legal geographer, a road is a product of the application of a law—the Highways Act—to a specific locality. It is a conjunction of the abstract (the generic law) and the site-specific application (particularity). Thus— with Papadimitriou's highway's engineer back in mind—a new road scheme is achieved via a localization of the law through a summoning, humans with money and authority bringing particular matter (tarmac, subbase, paint, rubber) and tasks to a place in order to address a defined individual or social need (the necessity or recognition of which may itself be contested).

With law defined in this modest way (modest in the sense that the limit of its writ—its ability to achieve things in the world—is contingent on both the 'macro' factors of politics and economics and the specificities of place, power, practices and material qualities of any particular road), we can achieve something novel with Guy Debord's definition of psychogeography's project. In Debord's 1955 'mission statement,' we oddly find a concern with understanding the controlling or (at least) conditioning effect of the built environment upon individuals but without an explicit acknowledgement of the force and function of 'legal' laws by which the built environment is constituted. Yet *these* laws are sedimented quietly throughout the built environment. They tell us how wide our roads must be; they demand the auditory signalling and tactile paving of crossing points; they determine the control of traffic flows and of human proximity to them; they mandate the very fabric from which streets, buildings, vehicles and their respective furnishings can be made. These are precisely the shaping forces upon the built environment and its inhabitants—the laws at large in the urban realm—that Debord should have set out to trace through to their material effects and sociopolitical origins.

As Susan S. Silbey and Ayn Cavicchi (2005) show, all of the everyday items that we encounter and that shape our lives within the built environment have—at least in part—origins in legal requirements. Thus law's laws are something that we can search for, and using psychogeographical methods to do so can help us to avoid lapsing in the extremity of 'everything is law or nothing is law.' Thus psychogeography could have a role to play in showing how law is translated (Latour 2005) into seemingly incongruent flows of matter, affect, practices and the resulting assemblages of ideas, materials and actions that form buildings, roads and the urban landscape and—in particular—provide ways to reveal the as-lived effects that those flows have upon individuals, moment by moment.

There is something heady in the prospect of chasing these flows. The day that John Paul Sartre realized that phenomenology—the study of how consciousness constructs objects and understandings—could be gainfully applied to *anything*, he found himself elated by the possibilities opened up to him, declaring, '[N]othing appeared to me more important that the promotion of street lamps to the dignity of a philosophical object. . . . [T]ruth drags through the streets, in the factories and, apart from ancient Greece, philosophers are eunuchs who never open their doors to it' (quoted in Kearney 1994, 3). But beyond the initial, liberating thought that *anything* is fair game for analysis comes the question of how—actually—to depict the mundane, to open it up, via some form of enchantment, to the status of a researchable thing.

While not exclusively, much of legal geography's concern is with the everyday, with the minor site of law's encoding in the built environment: it shares something of Sartre's embrace of the untapped depths of the mundane and previously ignored and has made good progress in explicating the regulatory architecture of everyday space and matter. Thus legal geographers have investigated the local spatio-normative ordering of shopping malls, trees, flower tubs, toilets, pavements, cemeteries, zoos, waste bins and car parking spaces (see, for example, the range set out in the legal geography bibliography in Braverman et al. 2013), and such studies show how such seemingly mundane spaces are in fact rich with constitutive meaning, conflict and symbolism. Under their analytical glare, nothing can be taken for granted as unremarkable—everywhere has a story to tell, and (in keeping with the emancipatory aspirations of the critical legal and critical geographic background of many of these scholars) there is a concern for the everyday experience of the everyday people caught up in law's spatial effects. And yet legal geography has struggled to find ways to write off the localized, affective and flux-like manifestations of the law and its moment-by-moment influence on the minds and orientations of those subject to it. Here—surely—is where psychogeography has something to offer.

Psychogeography's special contribution is its concern to understand the material–human corelationship, particularly as manifested in the emotional (i.e., affective) lives of individuals through their encounters with power and ordering as expressed in the arrangement of the built environment. Maybe it's too neat to suggest that that equates exactly to what legal geography currently lacks, but it certainly offers up a proposition worth exploring, particularly as some UK-based legal geographers are now starting to explore the affective dimension of law's existence within the built environment, as shown, for example, in the programme for the University of Westminster's 2013 symposium on 'Law and the Senses' (Baldissone et al. 2013) and in Andreas Philippopoulos-Mihalopoulos's call for legal geographers to explore the 'aesthetisation of the legal in its urban apparitions. While intimately connected to the biopolitical, this theoretical exploration [would] divert . . . slightly from the emplaced body, and focus . . . more on the sensual adumbration of the legal-urban in its excretal, carnal, aural and other interconnection with the individual' (2007, 5). In this we get a glimpse of a prospective legal *psycho*geography, an interpretive approach that would concern itself with enquiring into the role of sensation as a mediator between law and space—in short, how affect helps make the city, its strictures and its regularities and how they in turn make both the city and its individual citizens sentient. Indeed, this mapping of environment–psyche law–effects is precisely what Debord set as the mission for psychogeography in his 1955 axiomatic formulation.

METHODOLOGICAL AFFINITIES

Thus prospects for a legal psychogeography are good, for there are more methodological similarities between law and psychogeography than we might expect, as both are drawn toward fragments and the incongruous.

Papadimitriou's writing displays a fondness for found, mundane artifacts and texts—'lists dropped on pavements; letters found in attics of condemned houses; personal papers discarded in skips' (2012, 254)—and the promise that these might provide keys to countless otherwise lost stories. There is a parallel here to the meticulous concern of crime scene investigation, or indeed any attempt by law to understand an event that has occurred at a place, by searching for material traces and then piecing them together. Both Papadimitriou and lawyers show a concern with the close, *forensic* examination of fragments in order to explicate the codes, stories and events that lie beyond them. As Highmore notes, the detective and the surrealist have more in common than might ordinarily be acknowledged:

> Surrealism is about an effort, an energy, to find the marvelous in the everyday, to recognise the everyday as a dynamic montage of elements, to make it strange so that its strangeness can be recognized. The classic Surrealist can be seen as Sherlock Holmes-like: faced with the deadly boredom of the everyday, the Surrealist takes to the street, working to find and create the marvelousness of the everyday. (Highmore 2002, 56)

Highmore's invocation of Sherlock Holmes gives us a direct bridge between a precursor of psychogeography (surrealism) and law's forensic examination of the minutiae of the built environment. In the framing of a road traffic accident (or of an incident: a mugging, sexual assault or Saturday night drunken brawl), an otherwise unremarkable portion of the street becomes suddenly noticed, foregrounded and subjected to forensic scrutiny, combed inch by inch for evidence (meaning) by which the incident can become known, categorized and dealt with by the law and its technicians. Upon arrival at the (suddenly constituted) 'crime scene,' everything—no matter how ordinarily unimportant—may be key. Suddenly every discarded cigarette butt, sweet wrappers, any irregularity in the lie of the pavers, tyre scuffs upon tarmac, bodily excretions and the pooling and ponding of rain water on local surfaces all come under scrutiny.

Thus the psychogeographer and the detective each pore over both the dusty archive and the dross—the fragments found in event spaces—and construct a narrative by stitching their disparate findings together in accordance with codes of assembly. The only difference between them being one of purpose rather than method, in that while the detective seeks to 'close' a case through his forensic attention to these fragments, a psychogeographer seeks to open up the space and its things to an amplification—via an incongruent multiplication of meanings. And yet even this distinction is unstable, for the initial stages of a detective's investigation require him to adopt an 'open mind'—almost creative—posture, as a crime scene manager explains:

> When I arrive at the scene, it's my thinking time. . . . What am I seeing? What am I hearing? . . . Which lights are on? Which are off? Has the toilet been flushed? Is the seat up or down? You may not know the relevance, but take in the details—a ring of dust, an open drawer . . . maybe 70% of what you retrieve is not relevant. That doesn't stop you from finishing with a fingertip search, looking for that last piece of detail. You retrieve and work out the relevance later. (Taylor 2012, 25)

Both then comprise a creative rummage based around the application of genres to the swirl of matter, events and energies in the world. Yes, law aspires to a conclusive ordering of the world—but given that it is based on the formation and contesting of versions of events, it actually lives and breathes incongruent multiplicity—it is part of the partisan process, albeit that court judgements ultimately (in the sense of eventually bringing an end to that multiplicity) require a judge to select which version of events or interpretation of legal principles he or she prefers. Still, in all areas but the final scene, law's practice is to *directly* multiply meanings in partisan fashion within disputes and to do so *indirectly* by summoning anxious images of contingencies, as future risks to be ironed out within partial contract negotiations, in each case within the scope of given frameworks. As played out day to day in offices, courtrooms and elsewhere across the built environment, the law more than matches psychogeography in its dwelling on darkness, excess, ghosts and incongruent multiplicity.

Yet—somehow—law manages to assert a myth of its own self-image, of applied reason stripped of fancy, self-contained and truth-focused. Legal geography takes issue with this faith in law's closure. As demonstrated earlier, legal geography rests on an assumption that the law is not self-contained in this way—that it is in fact a cocreation of matter, meaning and pragmatic action. Legal geography, then, has a natural affinity with the anticlosure sentiment of contemporary psychogeography, and a psychogeographically inclined reckoning of law's incongruous traces, flows, eruptions, artifacts, loose ends, mess and symbolism is long overdue.

CONCLUSION

The affective relationship between the arrangement of things in space and the experience of place remains a central trope of psychogeographical account writing. Research in this mode can present rich reflexive description of the story-stacking processes by which instances of place are encountered and the terms (and sense) of that encounter negotiated between the creative agency of humans and the resistances and affordances of matter and of normative systems like law (following here Ewick and Silbey 1998, Smith 2005 and Stewart 2007). Psychogeography's embrace of incongruence can make toward the opening up (explication and potential transformation) of other sense-making strategies at large in the built environment. But just as law's closure is a myth, so is psychogeography's aspiration to the propagation of boundless incongruent multiplicity, for it tends too often to multiply meaning only in the direction of an obsessive pleasure–pain poetic excitation. Psychogeography needs to challenge itself, to explicate *all* matter–text–affect intersections, not just those that lead to whimsy or romantic reverie. Co-opting psychogeographically inclined place accounting into studies of law's manifestations in the built environment, an area that psychogeography—despite all of its talk of multiplying the readings of the city and a politically inspired urban reconnaissance—has conspicuously avoided treading, would be a fruitful next step for both legal geography and psychogeography.

BIBLIOGRAPHY

Baldissone, Riccardo, Anne Bottomley, Nathan Moore, Bela Chatterjee, Nayeli Urquiza Haas, Eric Heinze, Daphne Bidstrup Hjorth, Marta Iljadica, Danilo Mandic, Amber Marks, Ariane Monnier, Caterina Nirta, Tanyel Oktar, Andrea Pavoni, Andreas Philippopoulos-Mihalopoulos, Nicola Pozzani, James Parker, Kanika Sharma, Mayur Suresh, Jessica Worden, and Daichi Yoshikawa. 2013. 'Law and the Senses.' Presented at the Westminster Law School, London, 18–19 April. Accessed 3 April 2014. http://nonliquetlaw.files.wordpress.com/2013/04/law-and-the-senses_booklet.pdf.

Bennett, Jane. 2010. *Vibrant Matter: A Political Ecology of Things*. London: Duke University Press.

Berger, John. 1972. *Ways of Seeing*. London: British Broadcasting Corporation and Penguin Books.

Bogost, Ian. 2012. *Alien Phenomenology, or What It's Like to Be a Thing*. London: University of Minnesota Press.

Bonnett, Alistair. 2013. 'Psychogeography.' Oxford Bibliographies. Accessed 31 March 2014. http://www.oxfordbibliographies.com/view/document/obo-9780199874002/obo-9780199874002-0020.xml.

Braverman, Irus, Nicholas Blomley, David Delaney, and Alexandre Kedar. 2013. *The Expanding Spaces of Law: A Timely Legal Geography*. Buffalo Legal Studies Research Paper Series, Paper No. 2013-032. New York: SUNY Buffalo Law School.

Brown, Bill. 2001. 'Thing Theory.' *Critical Inquiry* 28 (1): 1–22.

Clifford, James. 1981. 'On Ethnographic Surrealism.' *Comparative Studies in Society and History* 23 (4): 539–64.

———. 1988. *The Predicament of Culture: Twentieth Century Ethnography, Literature, and Art*. London: Harvard University Press.

Csikszentmihalyi, Mihaly. 2008. *Flow: The Psychology of Optimal Experience*. London: Harper Perennial.

Debord, Guy-Ernest. 1955. 'Introduction to a Critique of Urban Geography.' *Les Levres Nues* 6. http://library.nothingness.org/articles/SI/en/display/2.

Delaney, David. 2011. *The Spatial, the Legal and the Pragmatics of World Making: Nomospheric Investigations*. Abingdon: Routledge.

Ewick, Patricia, and Susan S. Silbey. 1998. *The Common Place of Law: Stories from Everyday Life*. London: University of Chicago Press.

Gilloch, Graeme. 1996. *Myth and Metropolis: Walter Benjamin and the City*. Cambridge: Polity Press.

Goffman, Irving. 1974. *Frame Analysis: An Essay on the Organization of Experience*. New York: Harper and Row.

Harman, Graham. 2009. *Towards Speculative Realism*. Winchester: Zero Books.

Highmore, Ben. 2002. *Everyday Life and Cultural Theory*. London: Routledge.

Hodder, Ian. 2012. *Entanglement: An Archaeology of the Relationships between Humans and Things*. Chichester: Wiley-Blackwell.

Ingold, Tim. 1993. 'The Temporality of the Landscape.' *World Archaeology* 25 (2): 152–74.

Kearney, Richard. 1994. *Modern Movements in European Philosophy*. Manchester: Manchester University Press.

Latour, Bruno. 2005. *Reassembling the Social: An introduction to Actor Network Theory*. Oxford: Oxford University Press.

Lefebvre, Henri. 1996. *The Production of Space*. Translated by Donald Nicholson-Smith. Oxford: Blackwell.

Massey, Doreen. 2005. *For Space*. London: Sage.

Merleau-Ponty, Maurice. 1962. *The Phenomenology of Perception*. London: Routledge, Kegan and Paul.

Miller, Daniel. 2008. *The Comfort of Things*. Cambridge: Polity.

Olsen, Bjørnar. 2010. *In Defense of Things: Archaeology and the Ontology of Objects*. Plymouth: AltaMira Press.

Papadimitriou, Nick. 2012. *Scarp: In Search of London's Outer Limits*. London: Sceptre.

Philippopoulos-Mihalopoulos, Andreas. 2007. 'Introduction: In the Lawscape.' In *Law and the City*, edited by Andreas Philippopoulos-Mihalopoulos, 1–20. London: Glass-House.

Rogers, John, dir. 2009. *The London Perambulator*. London: Vanity Projects. Film.

Shukaitis, Stevphen, and Joanna Figiel. 2013. 'Metropolitan Strategies, Psychogeographic Investigations.' *Cultural Studies* < = > *Critical Methodologies* 13 (6): 536–43. http://csc.sagepub.com/content/13/6/536.

Silbey, Susan S., and Ayn Cavicchi. 2005. 'The Common Place of Law: Transforming Matters of Concern into the Objects of Everyday Life.' In *Making Things Public: Atmospheres of Democracy*, edited by Bruno Latour and Peter Weibel, 556–65. Boston: MIT Press.

Simmel, Georg. 1976. 'The Metropolis and Mental Life.' In *The Sociology of Georg Simmel*, edited by Kurt H. Wolff, 409–26. New York: Free Press.

Smith, Dorothy E. 2005. *Institutional Ethnography: A Sociology for People*. Oxford: AltaMira Press.

Stewart, Kathleen. 2007. *Ordinary Affects*. London: Duke University Press.

Taylor, Craig. 2012. 'The Real CSI: What Happens at a Crime Scene?' *Guardian Weekend*, 28 April, 25–26.

Thrift, Nigel. 2008. *Non-Representational Theory: Space, Politics and Affect*. Abingdon: Routledge.

Whatmore, Sarah. 2006. 'Materialist Returns: Practicing Cultural Geography in and for a More-Than-Human World.' *Cultural Geographies* 13 (4): 600–609.

Part II

Memory, Historicity, Time

Our relationship with the city is intrinsically tied up with our knowledge and memory of it. If a particular city is somewhere we know—from today or from our past—we are unable to separate our psychological responses to it from the materiality of the place itself. This, in fact, is psychogeography, and it is what makes us all psychogeographers (to a degree). A sense of place connects us to a geographic region in a specific way that becomes apparent when we start to explore the emotions attached to particular urban pockets that spark something in us. It might be a memory from our adolescence, such as an independent record shop in our hometown where we purchased our first piece of vinyl, or a more recent memory of moving to a new town or city and the differing aesthetics of that place compared to our last home.

These memories are not separate from ourselves; they inform and form us. The experiences of the everyday that are played out in space—walking to the train station, going to the supermarket, taking the dog for a walk—make up a significant part of our days. These practices are imprinted on our psyches over time, forming our relationships with space, and at the same time they are laid down in our memories of that place, creating our attachments to it. What is particularly pertinent to our memories of place is that they are subjective and partial—they cannot be anything other. It is this that lends itself to the multifarious and often contradictory accounts of specific spaces.

In this section, contributions range from qualitative research on memory and place to personal accounts that interweave fact and fiction. They express the variety of styles of writing on place but also the effects of time and memory in the way that they become part of our own histories.

FOUR

Walking through Memory

Critical Nostalgia and the City

Alastair Bonnett

This chapter explores how nostalgia for the city shapes the way we use it and think about its future. I examine how fond memories and a sense of loss among ex-residents shape their movement within and relationship to the city.[1] Building on recent reappraisals of the role of nostalgia in psychogeography, I point out overlaps and connections between avant-garde psychogeography and the supposedly conservative and backward-looking sensibilities of ex-urban residents.

PSYCHOGEOGRAPHY AND URBAN NOSTALGIA

Psychogeography was born with a sense of loss for the city. The name *Situationist International* (SI) obscures the fact that this was a movement born and bred in one particular place, postwar Paris, and that the relationship many Situationists had with Paris was framed and informed by the confluence of revolutionary and nostalgic sentiment. In part this connection was secured by the perception that 'their' Paris—the street-based, intimate and organic Paris of the bohemian and working-class community—was under assault by the forces of banalization and modernization (Sadler 1998; Chevalier 1994). Twenty-four percent of the surface area of the city was demolished and rebuilt between 1954 and 1974 (Pinder 2000). This figure may appear modest—Paris was not obliterated in the way many less prominent cities were in the last century—but it represents the uprooting of much of the inner-city working-class population.

Between the same two dates, their numbers in the Ville de Paris fell by 44 percent (Sadler 1998). Massive road-building programs, housing developments on the city limits, the eradication of such ancient markets as the Halle aux Vins and Les Halle all signalled to the Situationists the dawn of a homogenized, passionless and historically brainwashed city.

The Situationists interpreted these changes through Guy Debord's notion that, within a society of the spectacle, history was 'outlawed,' to be replaced by 'frozen time.' Debord established this link in *Society of the Spectacle* through a comparative urban example:

> The 'new towns' of the technological pseudo-peasantry clearly inscribe on the landscape their rupture with the historical time on which they are built; their motto could be: 'On this spot nothing will ever happen, and *nothing ever has.*' It is obviously because history, which must be liberated in the cities, has not yet been liberated, that the forces of *historical absence* begin to compose their own exclusive landscape. (Debord 1983, 177)

In Raoul Vaneigem's terms, 'The new towns will efface every trace of the battles that traditional towns fought against the people they wanted to oppress' (1961, 36). What is being articulated here is a nostalgia for the authentic attachments and political memories contained in buildings and streets that have witnessed past conflicts. It is not, ostensibly at least, a mourning for the loss of the picturesque or quaint but for popular memory. The SI and their direct forerunners, the Lettrist International (LI), were conservationists in a strictly political cause: 'beauty, *when it is not a promise of happiness,* must be destroyed' (Lettrist International 1985, 178).

The Situationists' favourite illustration of the extinction of popular memory through urban renewal programs was the suppression of the street. Construed as the social and imaginative centre of working-class community, the street was presented as endangered by modern urbanism—more specifically, modern urbanism as devised by Situationist bête noire, Le Corbusier. In 1954, the LI noted, 'In these days where everything, across all areas of life, is becoming more and more repressive, there is one man in particular who is repulsive and clearly more of a cop than most. . . . Le Corbusier's ambition is the suppression of the street . . . [and] an end to opportunities for insurrection' (1985, 34–35). The SI's attachment to the Paris of intimate streets and their search for more authentic and passionate relationships to place were reflected in their footloose (and foot-based) geographical praxis. The old market at Les Halles was pyschogeographically mapped out following two drifts by Abdelhafid Khatib in 1958. The same area was lovingly observed by Debord a year later in his film *Sur le Passage de Quelques Personnes a Travers une Assez Courte Unite de Temps* (1959).[2] The prospect of the demolition and displacement of Les Halles, Khatib noted, 'will be a new blow to popular Paris, which has for a century now been constantly dismissed, as we know, to the suburbs. A solution aimed at creating a new society demands that this space at the centre of Paris be preserved for the manifestations of a liberated collective life' (1958, 17). Debord's own drunken, slightly boorish drifts (1989), as well as the collaborative cut-up maps (in which zones of intensity are snipped out, separated and connected by arrows) he made with Asger Jorn (*Guide Pyschogéographique de Paris* of 1956 and *The Naked City* of 1957), can be read as typical avant-garde transgressions. Yet they are propelled by a deep sadness and a desire for a passionate connection to the city. Although 'French Situationism' is today stereotyped as rationalist and aloof in comparison with the sensuous and open approaches found in 'Scandanavian Situationism' (see Ohrt 2014), both repeatedly declared the value of intense, emotional connections to places and landscapes. In retrospect, it is apparent that this intensity was a product, at least in part, of the anger and melancholy of loss. Tom McDonough suggests that Debord's maps 'stand as the last articulations of a city which is irretrievable, a Paris now lost to us' (1996, 65). For Simon Sadler, Debord's cut-up maps may be seen as 'guides to areas of central Paris threatened by development, retaining those parts that were still worth visiting and disposing of all those bits that they felt had been spoiled by capitalism and bureaucracy' (1998, 61). In *The Situationist City*, Sadler goes on to discuss the 'drift' as a form of heritage survey. The drifters, he explains, gravitated toward old working-class streets and spaces, 'recording them for posterity, fastidiously avoiding the fluid traffic of the boulevards in favour of the still pools and backwaters of the city' (1998, 56).

Although they liked to boast that they regarded 'les souvenirs audessous de tout' (Situationist International 1958), nostalgia played a creative and productive role in shaping the Situationists' hostile attitude toward late modernity and the 'society of the spectacle.' This was nostalgia that acted not as a retreat from time but as a challenge to 'frozen time,' not a desire for all things gone but for landscape as an arena of popular identity and memory. But, as we shall now see, the avant-garde do not have a monopoly on critical urban nostalgia. In exploring how memory shapes the routes and routines of ex-residents, we also encounter a hostile engagement with the destruction of the popular past within the modernizing city.

THE CRITICAL URBAN PAST: RESEARCHING EX-RESIDENTS

My interest in the city among those who have left it but live nearby reflects this group's intriguing status as doubly dislocated (by time and space), yet geographically proximate. They are a provocative comparator with the Situationist psychogeographers: the one a famous example of avant-garde radicalism, the other a byword for conservatism. According to the cultural stereotypes of our era, the two groups should have nothing in common. And yet they do: for, as we shall see, they both employ and deploy images of the past to offer a critical perspective on the banalizing and inauthentic nature of urban modernization, and they both privilege passion and popular memory over mere aesthetics and walking, and intimate scales of urban attachment over modernist grand plans. Another similarity suggests itself: a number of important Situationists ended up as escapees from the city, going to live in rural locations that they imagined, as René Riesel puts it, as places where one can 'relearn practices that in many respects make up the genuine riches of humanity' (cited by Léauthier 2001, 13).

The image of ex-residents of the city as 'escapees' offers one of the most influential stereotypes of counterurbanization (for example, Osbaldiston 2010; Salt 2004) . Yet the twenty-six interviews this chapter draws on suggest we should expand our vision of ex-residents toward a more complex picture of continuing engagement.[3] It also allows us to begin mapping individuals' memories of the city upon their contemporary use of the city. Our interviews were carried out with long-term ex-residents of Tyneside (an urban area comprised of the four metropolitan boroughs of Newcastle upon Tyne, North Tyneside, South Tyneside and Gateshead) now living along the Tyne Valley to a distance of twenty-two miles (the principal towns in the study are Prudhoe, Corbridge and Hexham). 'Long-term ex-residents' were defined as those who lived in Tyneside for more than ten years and left Tyneside more than ten years ago.

Our interview technique directed interviewees to talk about their early memories and then their contemporary use of the city. Each interview began with the request, 'Tell me about your earliest memory of Tyneside,' eliciting a variety of rich accounts and pictures of the city. The start of the interview schedule contained a number of simple temporal and spatial questions. Informants (each of whom is identified in the following account by a pseudonym and by age) were asked to tell us the span of years when they first lived in Tyneside and the whereabouts of their first home or place of work. We would then, gradually, move on to how interviewees used the city today. While they were speaking, respondents were asked to draw mental maps of Tyneside. They were encouraged to pick out points of interest and focus on personal routes and uses, including areas of attraction and places they would avoid. Thus we encouraged them to talk about and map both routes taken on an everyday basis and buildings or streets that their most important or significant memories were tied to. They were asked to undertake this exercise in relationship to their past (often evoking their early youth) and the present, the latter map being overlaid on the former (different-coloured pens were provided for these different periods). The two techniques—of interview and mental mapping—acted together, each supporting the other. As respondents drew, they would remember, and as they remembered, they drew.

Although the resultant maps are not assessed in this chapter, they proved invaluable in encouraging interviewees to begin to talk about their memories of place and pathways in the city. The physical and spatial act of drawing appeared to open up ideas and recollections of place.

A little context on the city these people have left is useful here. Over the past fifty years, Newcastle has been through several periods of widespread demolition and rebuild, although the retail centre remains largely Georgian. However, around this small core, there has been intensive redevelopment in the east and west central parts of the city. Three notable developments have been the demolition of the Georgian Eldon Square in the 1960s (a new shopping centre opened on the site in 1977), the opening of A167 (M) in 1975 (a motorway that cuts through the middle of the city) and the expansion and construction of two city centre university campuses and subsequent large and extensive student accommodation blocks. Conservationism had a relatively low profile until the early 1980s. Since then, a number of conservation-led policies and initiatives have emerged, although they have mostly focused on the retail core. From the 1970s in the United Kingdom, the rediscovery of the street and the importance of memory and continuity in the creation of 'liveable' cities began to reshape attitudes toward urban planning. What Hebbert describes as an 'end-of-the-century postmodernism' (2005, 583) sought to 'repair' and respond to the 'grief and anger' at the loss of the street (ibid., 586). Yet although today in Newcastle, as elsewhere, the rhetoric of conservationism is entrenched within the planning and consultation process, the city remains a site of near-continuous large-scale redevelopment, and what remains of the old urban fabric continues to be eroded through either 'facadization' or demolition.

THE CITY THAT IS LOST

One of the most popular arenas of nostalgia for respondents was the lively bustle of family-run and otherwise unique shops that they recalled existing before Newcastle's redevelopment in the 1960s and 1970s. But such recollections were rarely straightforward: '[It] would be marvellous if you could get Grey Street as it was, and the old Fenwick window, and the Grainger Market—those are the things you really need—and the old-fashioned pubs. . . . We've lost the plot. And why can't they soften Newcastle? It's very hard' (Pat, aged fifty-five). What Pat offers is a vision of the future based on the persuasive power of a vision of the past. It is not a passive reverie but an intervention into debates about the future of the city. Pat's critical agenda turned on the idea that the contemporary city suffers from a lack of heterogeneity and distinctiveness, and that these problems could be solved by looking to the past for inspiration. This was a theme raised by twenty-two of our twenty-six interviewees. In part, it reflects their present relationship to the city as out-of-town shoppers looking for interesting consumer experiences. However, the idea that '[t]here are no individual shops anymore' (Sylvia, aged sixty-four) also provided the route through which a wider set of issues was articulated — issues that concern the decay of individuality, heritage and uniqueness — and the rise of more uniform and corporate identities and urban landscapes. The commentary from Susan that follows provides an intriguing statement regarding this interplay:

> It's a shame we haven't got that individuality anymore — and that is one thing that is happening to a lot of big cities — it doesn't matter where we go in England. Wherever we go to visit, it is the same as the last place. I can go to any town and know there will be a Topshop or Next or any store. . . . What I *want* to find is somewhere that has *independent little shops,* and they are the kind of places I look for. You can still get them in Newcastle; you just have to know where to look. [Go] off the main street, and you will find them. Some of them are still hanging on by the skin of their teeth. It's just a shame you can't do something to help them. Concessions or something — to stop them disappearing — because they will disappear, and where we used to live, we had three corner shops, we had a co-op at the top of our street, and it was one of them where you had the tin boxes with the glass lid and the biscuits in and the end one always had the broken biscuits in, and they used to slice your meat individually, and everything was rationed, and they've all gone, and [now] you've got Tesco's. (Susan, aged sixty)

The 'individuality' that Susan finds in the past and sees disappearing in modern England is represented as something that can be fought for and brought back. Susan makes concrete suggestions as to how this might be done. But the issue is clearly a concern that goes beyond 'concessions' for local shops. Toward the end, Susan's commentary slips, without even a pause for breath, from this policy suggestion to an intimate and almost dreamlike set of memories and associations. The images and connections that Susan creates indicate how place-based nostalgias operate and can swing between a variety of forms and scales, from the abstract and general to the personal and detailed. It is the latter that appears to animate many of the most intense feelings of loss. Time and again respondents would commence their accounts with broad depictions and argument but then, often suddenly, begin to narrate a very personal and 'small-scale' recollection. These narrations were not merely illustrative or subsidiary to the general argument but opened onto a new type and tone of recollection. This mixture — and to-ing and fro-ing — between the intimate and the general provided a central mechanism through which different nostalgic forms were brought into conversation and collision. In the following recollection we see this collision, and slippage, in more dramatic form. We hear respondent Thomas (aged sixty-eight) move seamlessly from nostalgic recall of the destruction of the old to nostalgic recall of his own part in the construction of the modernized city:

> We have lost a lot of the quaint old things in the city centre, whether it's the tripe shops or the old-fashioned seafood shops [and] . . . all the old-fashioned secondhand bookshops. . . . [S]o many of those old, quaint historical things have gone. . . . [T]he small historic facilities have gone. So as a student I mixed concrete to build the Civic Centre across the [Great North] road. And I worked four years, Easter, summer and Christmas I worked, mixing concrete. And I am very proud, and I can say that concrete there is what I mixed, and that was part of the huge redevelopment of the city, the building of the motorway bypass and modernization, but [it caused] a loss of the historic element of Newcastle.

Thomas's fond memories of his time mixing concrete for the new city are personal ones; yet they deploy a mixture of emotions and attachments. His account refers to the old and 'quaint' shops and streets that have disappeared but also to a different past, the now widely reviled days of modernist, car-centred redevelopment. These memories collide but also provoke and shape each other. Thomas is reminded by his own narration of the 'quaint' of a very different story he wants to tell. He concludes that tale by circling back to where he began. Neither of these pasts is being offered as a fixed golden age. They interrupt each other, creating a dialogue of memories and attachments that is both 'simple' and 'reflexive,' sentimental and personal, but also restless and forward-looking.

This combination was also apparent in respect to the theme of community that emerged (alongside the nature of shops and shopping in the city) as another key locus of nostalgia for respondents. For our interviewees, the loss of community was not a matter of an abstract social or moral decline but a material consequence, occurring in specific, named locations, of urban redevelopment schemes driven through by the local council (and other government agencies) or by one of the two city universities (Newcastle University and Northumbria University). Speaking of the large-scale demolition of the terraced houses that used to run along and down to the Scotswood Road in the west end of the city, Mike (aged seventy-eight) depicts it as the literal and metaphorical 'breaking-up' of community: 'The soul had gone out of the place definitely, just like the roof had. [verbatim pause] You know everybody went to different places—some went to Killingworth, some went to Newbiggin Hall, some went to Kenton—and it broke the whole community.'

The most politically engaged respondents often allied their sense of loss with a sense of anger at the consequences and causes of this loss. Our respondents were convinced that urban planners, politicians and universities were at the root of the problem. However, this antagonism, along with the idea that destructive redevelopment is inevitable, was eased by the hope that the local authorities are becoming more sensitive to the value of the past.

NOSTALGIC PATHS AND LOVE FOR THE CITY

Nostalgia shaped respondents' use of the city through their use of routes and places that they turned to and returned to because of a sense of attachment to the old city. As we also see, this attachment was not an instrumental form; rather, it offers an enactment of a loving relationship to the city.

Our respondents were not interested in returning to live on Tyneside (indeed, they were uniformly pleased to have left it). However, proximity allows them to maintain an active relationship with the city. It also means they can be continually reminded of the reasons why they left. Pat (aged fifty-five) describes his urban routine as follows: 'I park in "The Gate," and I walk down, and I go to Fenwick, and I still go and have a look at Fenwick window . . . and I go past the monument, and I still go and have a look at these shops, and then I go and have a look at Eldon Gardens — which wasn't there in my day — and that now is my favourite part.'

Pat's journey combines the old and the new: parking in the 'The Gate,'[4] Pat then walks toward familiar sites before ending up in a new shopping centre. This choreography of past and present was found repeatedly among respondents. Connerton (1989) has demonstrated that the social process of remembering is bound up with a bodily practice of commemoration, often in the form of ritualized performances. In this way, buildings, squares, statues and street names all 'facilitate commemorative performance by reproducing and producing social relations' (Connerton 1989, 8). Repeatedly during our interviews, it was the same specific features of the urban landscapes (Fenwick, the Quayside, the Grainger Market) that participants brought up and wanted to talk about at length. These acted as what Meusburger, Heffernan and Wunder call 'mnemonic devices; as the storage vessels of cultural identity and information . . . as triggers for sensations, emotions, and sensibilities' (2011, 8) and as 'spatial anchors for historical traditions' (Foote and Árvay 2000, 305). Indeed, for some respondents going into Newcastle was akin to going back in time: '[B]ut funny enough, when I go into Newcastle, I don't see it through the eyes of what it is now. I see it as it was. . . . I can see the old Fenwick and the old Binns, and I can see Carricks, and if we go past that way and Mawson, Swan and Morgan, I see it like that. I never really let the changes affect how I see the place' (Sylvia, aged sixty-four). Sylvia's wishful relationship to the city is an extreme example of a more general tendency among respondents to go back to familiar haunts and retrace their steps around the centre of the city (though none of them claimed to do so in the parts of the city where they used to live). For some respondents, these sites and routes also held another pleasure, of meeting up with friends. Here we encounter the practice of mobile nostalgia: memory and attachment structure ex-residents' use of the city and their desire to return. Commenting on where and when he met up with old friends, Mike (aged seventy-eight) noted, 'You do tend to end up in the older section of the town.' However, the sentiment that one has 'got to go back' (Pat, aged fifty-five) represented far more than an instrumental desire to meet friends or go shopping. Indeed, as it was pointed out to us several times, if this was all ex-residents were interested in, they would go to the large 'out-of-town' shopping centres (and get the benefit of free parking). For Pat, 'I couldn't do without Newcastle. I've always, always got to go back.' Like other respondents, Janet (aged forty-five) recounted how she comes into the city to walk about, even at night: 'I will walk around at night. I don't feel threatened, but I think that's maybe because I've always done it.' However, the sympathetic attitude of respondents to the civic trend toward urban conservation appears to encourage their interest in going back and walking around:

> [No]w when I go, I always feel proud of Newcastle because I think now there is more flowers everywhere—they have tried to make it look better—and I don't know if it's because I'm older, but you really notice that. I love loads of it. Like, I love the station buildings and the Centurion the pub, and I love Grey Street. And I suppose it is the buildings that you don't see if you go to the Metro.[5] . . . I just love all the old architecture, and I really appreciate it now. I don't so much like shopping; I love just walking down the streets. It is such an event just to go. (Janet, aged forty-five)

Janet's testament was prefaced by the observation that 'even though I was young, I remember everything was dirty.' The clean city of today is fascinating to her, in part because of the contrast with the 'dirty' place of her youth. The sense of excitement at seeing a familiar place transformed, by being either cleaned and preserved or comprehensively redeveloped in a way that enhances the city, is something that our group of ex-residents found themselves continually drawn to. This sentiment may be judged as uncritical, but, in fact, it emerges from the 'lived' alienation of our subjects from their city: In conservationism they see a kind of reclaiming of popular space. But this relationship also touches on another theme found in Situationist psychogeography: the need for a passionate, loving relationship with place.

Respondents told us they would stand and marvel at how the 'gloomy Quayside' has changed and at the relatively thriving Georgian streets of the city centre. This kind of 'gawping' is stereotypically associated with tourists. But for our ex-residents, it emerged from a sense of identification, belonging and love. Indeed, the thrill is so powerful that they return time and again to these sites. Mike's (aged seventy-eight) deep attachment to the city extends to documenting its many faces:

> I suppose I just like going around and getting the atmosphere of the place. I can walk for miles in Newcastle around, erm . . . you know, the usual Grey Street, of course, but around by Central Station. And of course the Centre for Life has changed around that area a lot as well, and then there is the Pink Triangle, which is the gay area of Newcastle—which I don't know anything about—and then the museum, of course. I love the big museum.

There is rhapsodic quality to Mike's depiction. And although there is unintended comedy to his hastily parenthetic remark about the Pink Triangle (something 'which I don't know anything about'), it is acknowledged and included as part of a city that he loves.

This section has shown that the desire to return to the city for ex-residents clearly does have a number of practical causes: shopping, meeting friends and entertainment being the most often mentioned. But the most frequent explanations given for 'going back' relate to ideas of memory, sentiment and attachment. If any term stood out in respondents' accounts of their relationships with the city, it was 'love.' In Thomas's (aged sixty-eight) terms, 'The City of Newcastle which I love and value, and here are the people which I love and value.' For Pat (aged fifty-five), the enduring attraction to the city is noted with 'I've got the most wonderful, wonderful memories of a city that to me is just magical.' These ex-residents cared—and continue to care—about 'their' city to a degree that speaks of a critical but passionate relationship.

CONCLUSION

Whoever sees the banks of the Seine sees our grief:

> [N]othing is found there now save the bustling columns of an anthill of motorized slaves. (Debord 1991, 44–45)

It is no surprise that nostalgia was an object of contempt for the Situationists. Debord and Wolman's gnomic declaration that 'life can never be too disorienting' (1981, 13) is merely an extreme expression of the totemic status accorded to deracination found across Marxist revolutionary movements in Europe and North America. It is, perhaps, only since the collapse of left radicalism as a significant phenomenon in Western political life, along with the end of Soviet communism, that it has become possible to see the nostalgic content of radical politics as a chronic dilemma rather than a form of ethical and political failure. The Situationists and the avant-garde world they inhabited, with its certainties and self-confidence, are gone. But the paradoxes of their nostalgic radicalism remain. These are being worked though in a variety of different ways. An openness to the power of the past is a characteristic of the neo-psycho-geographical groups that developed magico-Marxism in the 1990s (see Home 1997) as well as literary psychogeography (best exemplified in the work of Iain Sinclair) and the 'urban explorers' of the late 2000s and 2010s. Yet the same period is also seeing more far-reaching reassessments of nostalgia, reappraisals that both question and connect conservatism and ultraradicalism. Nostalgia is being interrogated as an inherent and productive aspect of the modern imagination (Boym 2001; Bonnett 2010). The a priori categorization of nostalgia as irremediably passive, conservative, or uncreative may still be commonplace, but it is starting to look like a dated and simplistic view of the world. With these developments comes the possibility of bringing previously disconnected communities of psychogeographical knowledge into dialogue, or at least into a comparative analysis. As this chapter has shown, when we do, some interesting parallels emerge, but different routes and mobilizations of critical urban nostalgia also become visible. Both the SI and the ex-residents I have introduced were in flight from the homogenized, deracinated city ushered in during the wake of large-scale modernist redevelopment. Yet neither are merely escapees, for both groups' attachment to the past of the city is a condition of their engagement with its future. The critical interests and nostalgic paths identified among our interviewees were not articulated as part of an insurgent, revolutionary narrative—far from it— yet in their intimate, street-based engagement with the city they love, they offer a set of challenges and practices that suggest a different and unfamiliar (at least within the literature on psychogeography) kind of psychogeographical paradigm. It is a paradigm based not on avant-garde discordancy and extremism but on everyday experience and ordinary needs. Perhaps for these very reasons it is an enduring commitment. The evident care and love toward the city we find among this group also suggest that the 'nests of kindness' spoken of by Nigel Thrift (2005, 143–45; Thrift 2004) as central to a renewed urban culture should include those who no longer live there.

NOTES

1. This chapter draws on research carried out with Catherine Alexander and published as A. Bonnett and C. Alexander, 2013, 'Mobile Nostalgias: Connecting Visions of the Urban Past, Present and Future amongst Ex-Residents,' *Transactions of the Institute of British Geographers* 38 (3): 391–402. This work was based on research funded by an ESRC research grant (RES-000-22-3833) titled 'Urban Memory, Nostalgia and Use of the City amongst Ex-Residents of Tyneside.' This chapter also draws on material published as A. Bonnett, 2006, 'The Nostalgias of Situationist Subversion,' *Theory Culture and Society* 235: 23–48.

2. 'On the passage of a few people through a rather brief moment of time.'

3. Further details on the project can be found at the project website, http://tynesidememories.mfbiz.com.

4. Opened on 28 November 2002, 'The Gate' is a new city centre retail and leisure complex that gets its name from the street on which it is sited, Newgate Street. It is part of the historic Grainger Town area of Newcastle.

5. The MetroCentre (often simply referred to locally as 'the Metro') is a large out-of-town shopping centre located in Gateshead on a former industrial site close to the River Tyne. It opened in 1986 with more than 340 shops occupying 168,900 square metres.

BIBLIOGRAPHY

Bonnett, Alastair. 2010. *Left in the Past: Radicalism and the Politics of Nostalgia*. New York: Continuum.

Boym, Svetlana. 2001. *The Future of Nostalgia*. New York: Basic Books.

Chevalier, Louis. 1994. *The Assassination of Paris*. Chicago: University of Chicago Press.

Connerton, Paul. 1989. *How Societies Remember*. Cambridge: Cambridge University Press.

Debord, Guy. 1959. *Sur le Passage de Quelques Personnes a Travers une Assez Courte Unité de Temps*. Paris: Dansk-Fransk Experimenatalfilmskompagni. Film, 20 mins.

———. 1983. *Society of the Spectacle*. Detroit: Black and Red.

———. 1989. 'Two Accounts of the Derive.' In *On the Passage of a Few People through a Rather Brief Moment of Time: The Situationist International 1957–1972*, edited by E. Sussman, 135–39. Cambridge, MA: MIT Press. First published 1956.

———. 1991. *Panegyric*. London: Verso.

Debord, Guy, and Asger Jorn. 1956. *Guide Psychogéographique de Paris*. Copenhagen: Permild and Rosengreen.

———. 1957. *The Naked City: Illustration de Hypothèse des Plagues Tournantes en Psychogéographique*. Copenhagen: Permild and Rosengren.

Debord, Guy, and Gil Wolman. 1981. 'Methods of Detournement.' In *Situationist International Anthology*, edited by Ken Knabb, 8–14. Berkeley, CA: Bureau of Public Secrets.

Foote, K. Tóth, and A. Árvay. 2000. 'Hungary after 1989: Inscribing a New Past on Place.' *Geographical Review* 90: 301–34.

Hebbert, Michael. 2005. 'The Street as a Locus of Collective Memory.' *Environment and Planning D Society and Space* 23: 581–96.

Home, Stewart, ed. 1997. *Mind Invaders: A Reader in Psychic Warfare, Cultural Sabotage and Semiotic Terrorism*. London: Serpent's Tail.

Khatib, Abdelhafid. 1958. 'Essai de Description Psychogéographique des Halles.' *Internationale Situationniste* 2: 13–18.

Léauthier, Alain. 2001. 'Les Progrès de la Soumission Vont à une Vitesse Effroyable.' *Libération*, 3 February.

Lettrist International. 1985. *Potlatch 1954–1957*. Paris: Editions Gérard Lebovici. First published 1955.

McDonough, Tom. 1996. 'The Derive and Situationist Paris.' In *Situacionistas: Arte, Politica, Urbanismo (Situationists: Art, Politics, Urbanism)*, edited by Libero Andreotti and Xavier Costa, 54–65. Barcelona: Museu d'Art Contemporani de Barcelona.

Meusburger, Peter, Michael Heffernan, and Edgar Wunder, eds. 2011. *Cultural Memories: The Geographical Point of View*. New York: Springer.

Ohrt, Roberto. 2014. 'Fin des Modifications: Common and Contested Ground between Asger Jorn and Guy Debord.' In *Asger Jorn: Restless Rebel*, edited by Dorthe Aagesen and Helle Brøns, 176–201. Copenhagen: Statens Museum for Kunst.

Osbaldiston, Nick. 2010. 'Elementary Forms of Place in Seachange.' *Journal of Sociology* 46 (3): 239–56.

Pinder, David. 2000. '"Old Paris Is No More": Geographies of Spectacle and Anti-Spectacle.' *Antipode* 32: 357–86.

Sadler, Simon. 1998. *The Situationist City*. Cambridge, MA: MIT Press.

Salt, Bernard. 2004. *The Big Shift*. Victoria, BC: Hardie Grant.

Situationist International. 1958. 'Les Souvenirs Au-Dessous de Tout.' *Internationale Situationniste* 2: 3–4.

Thrift, Nigel. 2004. 'Summoning Life.' In *Envisioning Human Geographies*, edited by Paul Cloke, Philip Crang, and Mark Goodwin, 81–103. London: Arnold.

———. 2005. 'But Malice Aforethought: Cities and the Natural History of Hatred.' *Transactions of the Institute of British Geographers* 30: 133–50.

Vaneigem, Raoul. 1961. 'Commentaires Contre l'Urbanisme.' *Internationale Situationniste* 6: 33–37.

FIVE

Selective Amnesia and Spectral Recollection in the Bloodlands

Phil Wood

> Urban walking is a way of contacting the ghosts and levels of a city, the
> past and the future. . . . The solitary walker soon gathers with him a
> commonality of other walkers behind, all whispering and talking in his
> ear, and trying to seduce him to turn right into this mystery or turn left
> into that building, go up that church tower. You're aware of them, and
> I don't think you can do that any other way than by walking.
>
> —Iain Sinclair (quoted in Pinder 2001)

Why I should spend my time walking around places that most people
would choose to avoid has never been entirely clear to me. My parents
suggest the experience of falling unnoticed into a subterranean coal cellar
as a toddler and spending several hours there has burned itself into my
subconscious. My childhood playgrounds were old colliery spoil heaps,
slowly slipping back into nature, and I can recall the uncanny thrill of my
first illicit entry to an abandoned building—the recently closed mine near
my home at Lepton Edge in the British town of Huddersfield. Doubtless
there is also the eerie experience of seeing the film *Stalker* (Tarkovsky
1979) at an impressionable age. Regardless, I can endorse Iain Sinclair's
view that the act of walking, or purposeful drift, is the route to revelation.

Yet it also seems (in my case, at least) to be the places of past or recent
tumult, where the silt has been stirred and agitated, that the greatest
spectral potential lies. Thus, in Britain, it is no surprise I should be drawn
to the remnants of the Industrial Revolution and its long tail (Edensor
2005; Hill 2013). But for decades I have been drawn also to the east of
Europe—particularly the regions dubbed 'the Bloodlands' (Snyder

2012)—where past and present still coexist in a more dynamic and occasionally dangerous relationship. And, while industrial ruination proliferates (Pusca 2010; Schönle 2006), there are other sources of tumult, too. In Britain most boundaries are defined by the sea, and ethnic identities have remained fairly stable for centuries, whereas a twentieth-century resident of Lviv in western Ukraine, for example, might feasibly have been a subject of five different national jurisdictions without once having moved house (Snyder 2003). They would also have witnessed mass deportations of neighbours and other atrocious acts, many of which remain psychologically and politically unresolved, leaving behind unexorcised ghosts.

This is an account of my unaccompanied walks, imaginings and hauntings through the cities of Odessa and Lviv in Ukraine. I have chosen them specifically because each has experienced trauma, absence and loss and is in some sense a 'wounded city' (Till 2012), and yet each has amnesia and has been quite selective in what it has remembered and forgotten or even removed from the record, making for a disjointed and only partial therapy. The German language has evolved the concept of *Vergangenheitsbewältigung*[1] to express these complex processes, but, to my knowledge, there is no equivalent in Ukraine. There ought to be. Writing this piece during the period of the Ukrainian crisis in 2014 was a reminder, if I needed it, that an unresolved past can suddenly and violently blow up in our faces.

Each city is following its own course in search of a post-Soviet identity, but I have encountered and written about them through my own peculiar lens, influenced by walking writers like Sinclair, W. G. Sebald and Nick Papadimitriou. I have drawn encouragement in particular from Sebald's statement that he was 'patiently engraving and linking together apparently disparate things in the manner of a still life. . . . I have kept asking myself since then what the invisible connections that determine our lives are, and how the threads run' (2005, 200–201). For Sebald, the places we wander through are not fixed in time and space but are restlessly in motion, like a series of tableaux that are connected but constantly changing their position in relation to each other and to us (Wylie 2007, 176).

Walter Benjamin was the first to teach me that 'progress' is a dubious notion and that life and history rarely unfold in an orderly fashion 'through a homogeneous, empty time' (1968, 261). Jacques Derrida (2006) has taken me further to a deeper understanding of the spectral, beyond conventional notions of the merely 'spooky.' He coined the term *hauntology* to suggest that the present can only exist with respect to the past. But he was agitated, too, by the fall of communism in 1989 and the subsequent fatuous assumption in the West that this represented the 'end of history.' He asserted that wilful forgetfulness or negligence of recent traumas would return to haunt the new regimes, providing the impetus for future turbulence. As I write this, the media is reporting a column of Russian tanks entering Ukrainian sovereign territory.

Like many of my walks, the drift through Odessa turned out to be something other than I'd expected it to be. My shabby Soviet-era hotel, Yunost, at the wrong end of Frantsuzkyi Bulvar, seemed to be isolated in an unpromising part of town, close to the sea and surrounded by large areas of scrubby woodland. I paid it no heed, but as I was rummaging for a few hryvna for the tram fare into the centre, I started to realize it wasn't as empty as it had first seemed. As my eyes acclimated, I could pick out a shape here and there—walls, buildings, statues—or the remains of them. By the time the tram swept by, curiosity had already taken me, and I was off, probing for a weak point in the perimeter fence. I didn't have to look far before discovering a decrepit gateway through which I could slip.

Before long I found an empty building, then another, and finally a whole cluster—all abandoned and in a shocking state of disintegration. There was no great architectural merit or antiquity to any of them, and it seemed their demise must have been quite recent, as there were none of the telltale signs of long-term decay, such as shrubbery or saplings, poking through roof tiles. They had, however, quite obviously been robbed of any valuable metals they had once harboured.

I picked my way around, trying to rebuild some sense into the apparent chaos (see figure 5.1). It seemed like it had been a diverse and integral community, with homes, offices, shops, what looked like a former cinema and even a library. They had probably been built between the 1950s and the 1980s, but their level of decay suggested they should be much older than this, and that meant just one thing to me: they were of a woefully shoddy Soviet construction, whereby seemingly adamantine concrete could be reduced to flakes and dust within only a generation's wear and tear.

Clearly, though, this was no mere functionalist suburb. It had been designed as a place for pleasure—even, hard as it might seem, a place in which to delight. There was a bandstand and the remnants of benches encircling it. And scattered around were several fountains from which water would once have sprinkled with no purpose other than to relax or enrapture people now long since dead. *Et in Arcadia ego.*

My mind was starting to drift, and I was hearing voices, sensing ghosts, even smelling the medication.

'Can I do you now, sir?'

He was ready. He'd been ready for five years at least, so Vitali slipped off his gown, handed it to the attendant and slid effortlessly into the bath of warm, dark, viscous gloop. People had been coming to Odessa for treatment with Kuyalnik estuary mud almost since the city was founded by Catherine the Great and the time when Pushkin made it his home. Vitali comforted himself with the thought that, at last, he was living the good life. Heaven knows it hadn't been easy—far from it. But now, as the

Figure 5.1. Ruined library in Arkadiya, Odessa

whole of the mighty Arkadiya Sanatorium seemed to throb with the sole and collective purpose of making him, Vitali Olexandrovich Semerenko, once again 'vital,' it felt worth it. It had been such a relief when his employers, the Maxim Gorky Mine in Donetsk, had agreed to subsidize his three weeks at the fabled Arkadiya resort in Odessa's Boulevard of the Proletariat. Mining was a young man's game.

The mud was already working, and he relaxed as the pain faded from his knees. He began to dream—backward from 1987 to a time decades earlier. Even now, forty years later, he still had twinges of fear that somehow he was under suspicion. It was more painful than the arthritis.

'Who was this guy, Vitali, and who were the others?' I thought, as I picked my way gingerly through the rubble. Their world might have been trashed and ridiculed, but they were real people who had made and used these places—and I sensed them still.

Vitali felt woozy and pleasurably delirious. He recalled in his mind's eye a smile. That smile—the only smile that mattered. The one his twin brother, Ihor, had given him in July 1944 when they parted for the last time. The rampaging Red Army was on the outskirts of Lviv, and the Wehrmacht, along with its Galicia Division of Ukrainian volunteers, was in headlong retreat. Ihor hadn't been with them long—he was only a teenager—but long enough to mean that, if the Soviets got him, he'd be dead meat. He was always the physical one among them, while Vitali doubted the Galicia would have taken him—even if he'd offered.

For years after, he heard nothing from Ihor and feared he'd ended his days in some squalid ditch in the Carpathian Mountains or somewhere. Only in the last few years—thanks to Glasnost, he guessed—did he get a bundle of letters that Ihor had been sending to the old family home in Volynska Street in Lviv—intercepted by the police. It turned out he'd survived the Carpathians and made his way to safety in Austria by the end of the war. Those who remained of the Galicia Division surrendered to the British and were put in a camp in Spittal an der Drau and then moved on to Rimini in Italy. They all thought they'd be repatriated to the Soviet Union and certain death, and many were. But Ihor had talked his way into the group of 8,570 who were transported through Venice to Britain. They put him in a prisoner-of-war camp at Hallmuir Farm near Lockerbie until 1947. He even claimed in one letter to have built a Ukrainian chapel[2] while he was there. The National Coal Board eventually came along with the offer of a job, and he ended up in Yorkshire at Lepton Edge Colliery in Huddersfield. That's where he caught the eye of Edith, his English wife.

I pushed on through Arkadiya's tangle of undergrowth and encountered building fragments of a much older vintage, from the time of Pushkin and the tsarist elite who once basked here. But whatever hauntedness they might have had was outweighed on that day by Soviet-era ghosts.

Vitali chuckled and wondered how he, the weedy one, with his head always in a science book and not interested in politics, should have ended up being arrested by the NKVD[3] and exiled to Kustanay in Kazakhstan, all for being the brother of a suspected traitor. And he was still here—which was more than could be said for old Ihor, though he had died happy, according to that last letter from Edith.

'Ahhhh.' The mud was good. Vitali decided to take another half-hour before getting spruced up for the show. Odessa's top Jewish comedian Mikhail Zhvanetsky was giving a rare performance. 'He's his own man, old Mikhailo,' smiled Vitali. 'Tells it as he sees it, even if *they* don't approve. He's seen off Brezhnev and all those bastards. He's like me: a survivor.'

Vitali had tickets for the sanatorium's theatre that night, where generations of *shansoniers*[4] had crooned and recuperating Stakhanovites[5] had been tickled back to health by Zhvanetsky and other saucy Odessan comedians.

As I crunched my way across its shattered floor, it echoed cavernously, and the Black Sea breezes whistled through the skeletal rafters.

The zinc bathtub in which Vitali had luxuriated was long gone. I'd spotted where it had been torn from its moorings in 1999 by Gennady and Iryna, a homeless couple who sold it to a scrap merchant for the price of a few wraps of scag.

I was rudely jolted from my reverie. Scanning the wreckage of a housing block across from the theatre, I did a double take. Was it? No, surely not. But yes, it really was a washing line full of someone's drying smalls. With a shudder it dawned on me that, along with its Soviet ghosts, Arkadiya now had a new clientele—part of Odessa's small army of homeless and destitute people. I left quickly, not wishing to impose myself as a gawping intruder in their world.

Nevertheless, I couldn't remove the image from my mind, nor the thought that, every time I passed an exposed cellar opening or airshaft, there might be someone within, eking out a living. Odessa is remarkable in having built itself from Pontic limestone it quarried from tunnels beneath its very feet. These catacombs stretch for miles and have long offered a bolt hole for people who have been drawn to Odessa and then fallen on hard times.

Just over the wall from here, however, I could sense there was another intruder in waiting that would impose itself soon enough. *Biznesmen* had not been slow to recognize the availability of prime real estate with sea views and dubious tenure. A new Arkadiya was rising. Brasher and even more charmless than its predecessors, a rash of new seafront development was now erupting to tempt the cash-rich winners of the all-or-nothing game that has been Ukraine's twenty-two years of independence.

Mikhail Mikhaylovich Zhvanetsky still lives to this day and has become a wry commentator on what has become of his city. In his ballad 'Lost Generation,' he sings, 'People are disappearing in our country. We've already got used to it. But how come we lost the whole generation? All of a sudden. They disappeared. And we keep on pretending that nothing has happened.'

Both Odessa and Lviv are cities where whole generations have indeed disappeared. At best, consigned to the condescension of posterity. At worst, to total oblivion. Zhvanetsky was a remnant of an Odessan Jewish community that, in 1941, had numbered 233,000, representing more than a third of the total population. Within two years, there were virtually none (King 2011).

Jews had always flocked to Odessa because it was a port and a place of possibility, not so encumbered by the oppressive atmosphere of the surrounding Pale of Settlement, where both ingrained anti-Semitism and the stuffiness of rural rabbis held sway. Even so, the Odessans, too, would occasionally indulge in violent pogroms in which the Jews were blamed for everything from the plague to the price of bread. But even as they were doing this, the cityscape, music, sense of humour and very language of Odessa were uniquely influenced by the Jews, as exemplified by the loveable mobster Benya Krik from Isaac Babel's *Odessa Tales*. Odessa was dubbed the 'City of Rogues and Schnorrers'[6] (Tanny 2011).

What tends to be forgotten is that the Nazis played little or no part in this mass disappearance. In 1941 Odessa was overrun by the Romanian army, which was tagging onto the coattails of Hitler and Mussolini in the hope of acquiring territory. An unknown number of Jews fled with the retreating Red Army and were eventually scattered across Soviet Central Asia, but many stayed.

Continuing my walk, I was a little startled to be suddenly disgorged from the jagged, oppressive confusion of the resort district into the city proper and the open, orderly spaces of Shevchenko Park. It may have felt like a benign haven, but at 5:35 p.m. on 22 October 1941, things had been otherwise. It was then known as Alexandrovsky Park and had been the scene of a massive explosion, and as the dust settled, locals realized that the former NKVD building had been shattered. In recent days it had been commandeered as the headquarters of the occupying Romanian army and was destroyed by a time bomb left by retreating Soviet forces. It was deeply shocking and personally embarrassing to General Constantin Trestioreanu, whose troops had supposedly swept it for booby traps, and in his rage, he needed a scapegoat. Thus ensued one of the most savage and visceral episodes of the whole war, as Odessa's remaining Jews were hounded down and murdered in their tens of thousands. Sad to say, the exercise was made much easier by the fact that they were often denounced (and subsequently looted) by their Gentile neighbours.

This aspect of Odessa's history is little acknowledged today in Romania or in Odessa. Its sole Holocaust memorial stands on a busy street. According to Charles King, 'The fountain doesn't work, the pavement is cracked and broken, and the trees want watering. An inscription inaccurately reminds visitors of the crimes committed by "the Nazis," not by Romanians or local Odessans. The small park in which it sits is littered with plastic bottles and overflowing trash bins' (2011, 239). And closer inspection revealed that the memorial was not actually to the Jews at all but to the Ukrainians who risked their lives trying to save them. A little like the postwar Germany as described by Sebald (2004), which collectively failed to talk about its own trauma and complicity, there is much that Odessa has yet to address.

My walk came to an end in this city that has lost so much, not least its memory. It is now wallowing as deeply in nostalgia as Vitali in his mud bath. Bizarrely, though, if we are to draw any conclusions from the brash neoclassical oligarch pleasure domes starting to rise from the ruins of Arkadiya, it is not a nostalgia for the Odessa of Pushkin, Babel or Trotsky but for a fantasy of ancient Greece—which never even existed in the first place.

I left the coast and travelled to western Ukraine. Vitali followed me, or, rather, I followed him.

> We lived in Volynska Street before the War, Ihor and me. We were the
> only Ukrainians in the street or in much of the Pidzamche district. Dad
> worked as a tile-maker in the Bracia Mund ceramics factory in Sykstus-
> ka Street. Pidzamche was mainly Jewish people and of course a lot of
> Poles—Lviv being part of Poland then. Mum and Dad liked it that way.
> They said we ought to get on with other kinds of people, and anyway
> Mum didn't want to be under the prying eyes of her mother-in-law
> back in the village. You know, I've always had this nagging feeling that
> we even had some Jewish blood ourselves, through Dad's side of the
> family, but no-one ever talked about it.

My walk in Lviv took me on a long curving arc from the original Old
Town Square, north across the rail tracks, through Pidzamche, and back
around the west side of town through Krakivski district, finishing at the
Kropyvnytskogo Square. It was a journey through a city that is now
largely monoethnic and monolingual and with one dominant Orthodox
religion. Yet Lviv is a city with at least six other names (L'viv, Lwów,
Lemberg, Leopolis, Lemberik, Ilov), reflecting a turbulent history of settlement and conquest. Until 1918, it had been an outpost of the Austro-
Hungarian Empire and was then drawn into newly independent Poland;
throughout this time, it was populated mainly by Poles and Jews, with
smatterings of Germans, Armenians, Serbians and Ukrainians, although
the latter were much more in evidence in the surrounding countryside.

This uniformity reflects a terrible decade of liquidation and forced
deportation from which virtually no section of Lviv's citizenry was im-
mune. The Nazis, of course, were responsible for the extinction of Jewish
Lviv, but on either side of this, the Soviet Union perpetrated murder and
deportation of many ethnic Poles and Ukrainians. But what is also overlooked is that in a substratum of the titanic struggle between Germany
and the Soviet Union was fought a particularly vicious local war between
Poles and Ukrainians. Ultimately, the Poles who survived the bloodbath
were scooped up and deposited in the late 1940s in the new parts of
Poland that had been wrested from a defeated Germany, such as
Wrocław, while any Ukrainians formerly living within the borders of the
new socialist Poland were thrown out, and many came to live in the
vacated houses of Lviv. But you'd be forgiven for not knowing any of
this, as there really are few public or officially sponsored acknowledge-
ments that Lviv ever was anything but a bastion of Ukrainian national
purity (Givental 2011). But if you get your eye in and look a little deeper,
there are 'ghost signs,' for example, from shops that once advertised their
wares in German, Hebrew, Yiddish, or Polish.[7] The contemporary poets
and authors of Lviv have recognized the significance of these palimp-
sests, even if the authorities have not. For instance, Yuri Andrukhovych
writes, 'I love those inscriptions that come to the surface from out of

every possible hole, every crack in the foundations, from under thresh-
olds, from the subconscious of the city' (2002, 14).

Meanwhile, Andrij Pavlyshyn has written of his youthful realization
that there was more to his hometown than met the eye:

> I grew up in this beautiful place where one could always find lots of
> strange things. Old bits and pieces in the attic written in an unknown
> language: walls where the plaster peeled off and names made up of
> foreign words appeared. . . . I dream even now, sometimes, that I am in
> a city, in which the walls stayed, only people were not there. It is only a
> dream, only an impression because the streets of today's Lviv are filled
> with crowds of people. . . . But why was the city from my dreams
> deserted? (2001, 145)

As I walked around Pidzamche, I was struck by the jumble of styles
and usage, with a fine *Sezession* villa wedged between a rustic cottage
and small holding on one side and a gerry-built Soviet-era workshop on
the other. Here, away from the commercial bustle of the centre, I felt the
walk slipping into a different atmosphere. Unmolested, I ghosted up alleyways, alongside rail tracks, into backyards, through vegetable patches.
It was quiet, almost deserted, but somehow I didn't feel alone. Down
Volynska Street, I was drawn toward an open door of a shabby but beau-
tifully adorned fin de siècle apartment block. I had no idea who originally commissioned this house or who might have lived here. It could have
been a group of reasonably well-off Polish families between the wars, or,
as Pidzamche was designated the ghetto under German occupation, it
was probably bursting with desperate Jewish families for a while. The
fact is they were all gone now. I would have liked to have asked the
current residents what they thought of this—or indeed to what extent
they knew or cared about their own district's recent history.

A neglected but still-charming vestibule was tiled in an art nouveau
style, advertising the manufacturers as 'Bracia Mund Lwów' (see figure
5.2). It seemed to lead me onward into a triangular hallway with a stairwell stretching upward and a shaft of light bathing the floor. It was
nothing more than one might encounter in a million other such places in
the former Habsburg lands or *mitteleuropa*, but it held me at that point in
a trance. Did I hear the rattle of feet on the stairwell and perhaps voices?
Were they the voices of excited weekenders intent on an afternoon in the
park or even the teenage Vitali and Ihor heading for a kick-about in the
street? Or were they the shrieks of the terrified being hounded out by
their persecutors?

Furthermore, if I were sensing these spectral presences, were they also
sensing me? Haunting is an experience rarely far from the surface in the
Bloodlands because so many wrongs remain unrighted and so many
questions remain unasked and still less answered. But maybe these
ghosts weren't even from the past at all but from a future yet to be played

Figure 5.2.   Vestibule in Volynska Street, Lviv

out in this portentous city. I am with Derrida in not seeing haunting as
only a one-way street. Maybe it was not Vitali haunting me at all but me
haunting him.

As Derrida stresses, the spectral is not simply the invisible or the
spiritual. Being 'neither soul nor body, and both one and the other' (2006,

6–7), it exhibits a 'supernatural and paradoxical phenomenality' (ibid.), in between visibility and invisibility and between observer and observed. The spectre is visible, it appears, but 'there is something disappeared, departed in the apparition itself as reapparition of the departed' (ibid.). Equally, the spectre is invisible, but it watches, it is the unseen seeing, and 'we feel ourselves observed, sometimes under surveillance by it even before any apparition' (ibid., 101). Places, people, are always already haunted insofar as 'they (specters) are everywhere where there is watching' (ibid., 175).

Going further, Derrida says of spectres, 'They pass through walls, these revenants, day and night, they trick consciousness and skip generations' (2006, 30). This reminds me of the character John Osborne, who appeared in Papadimitriou's book *Scarp* (2012, 196). Although a documented character from English history, Papadimitriou embellishes him into one of the most disturbing time- and shape-shifters of contemporary imagination. Being the victim of terrible injustice, Osborne becomes a vengeful spirit empowered, or maybe enslaved, to return through history often to commit gruesome and unsolvable murders. He can be like the therianthrope of classical mythology who took on the forms of various beasts, but the most intriguing aspect of Osborne is his propensity to transmogrify into inanimate objects for decades or more, such as a manhole cover in Finchley.

I wandered on through the busy market, which had once been the main Jewish cemetery. For all the pain Lviv has experienced, I felt no spirits here who meant me, or anyone else, ill. It wasn't until the end of my walk that I encountered malignancy, and this was not from a lost or restless source but one cast in bronze on a marble plinth. Having climbed the St. George's hill out of the Krakovski District, I approached the grand Church of Saints Olha and Elizabeth and behind it Kropyvnytskogo Square. I assumed the vast bombastic statue of a man in the square to be a Soviet leftover, but no. It was clearly bright, shiny and very new. Only erected in 2007, it was the memorial to Stepan Bandera, founder and racist ideologue of the Ukrainian Insurgent Army (UPA),[8] a guerrilla force that was set up to resist the Red Army but also fought the Germans, participated in anti-Jewish pogroms and, most notoriously, led an ethnic cleansing and almost medieval butchering of the Polish population of western Ukraine.

These war years had been messy, treacherous times, and for most Ukrainians, the question had not been 'Which side are the good guys?' but 'Can I trust anyone?' Ihor Semerenko opted for the Galicia Division, but many others joined the UPA. It's not surprising that contemporary Ukraine should want to look into its recent past for patriots it can honour, particularly when taking its first stumbling steps as a nation-state and still under the beady eye of its big neighbour, Russia. Nor is it shocking that in those brutal times such men would have had blood on their hands. But what did shock me at the end of my spectral walk in Lviv, and still brings a shudder now, is that a city that claims to embrace the values of liberal cosmopolitan Europe should (in the twenty-first century) erect such an ugly, gloating edifice to a genocidal psychopath and dictator manqué as a symbol of how it wants to be seen in the world.

This spurred the realization of another recurrent theme of these walks: selective memory and amnesia in relation to traumatic experience. To some people (for example, Archbishop Desmond Tutu, Vaclav Havel or Adam Michnik), remembering what was done to you but also what you did to others is a confessional responsibility and the only way to reconciliation and peace (Eyal 2004). But in most of the former communist lands, memory has been purloined for less therapeutic means. And where leaders do not take responsibility and information is not freely available, the human mind has an ability to fill the void with nonsense. For example, a survey in 2000 asked the general public in Lviv what percentage of the city's total population they thought was made up of Jewish people. They settled on a figure of 18.7 percent, when in fact the true figure was 0.2 percent (Susak 2009)!

Vitali moved back to Lviv in 1991 and died contentedly five years later. Most days you could find him drinking coffee and holding court at *Pid Synoyu Plyashkoyu* (Under the Blue Bottle Coffee House) on Ruska Street. He often reflected upon his life: 'All the time I was exiled in those Kazakh boondocks, and every day down that Donetsk mine, I dreamed of one thing: Lviv coffee. Nowhere else in the god-forsaken USSR could you get a decent cup of coffee. The Habsburg influence you see—*Kaffee und Kuchen*.'

The former gulag inmate Yuri Vynnychuk has shown in his series of books, *The Mysteries of Lviv Coffee*, that the city goes gooey with nostalgia over its former colonial masters (Blacker 2012), and there are even suggestions to raise a statue to the old Austrian emperor Franz Joseph. Meanwhile, local entrepreneurs make a killing from a string of novelty restaurants, where punters can variously act out sick fantasies of being heroic Stepan Bandera or anti-Semitic stereotypes (Narvselius 2012). From the evidence of my experiences, Lviv might be better served visiting Vienna, not for the coffee but to enrol in a course of psychoanalysis. I would certainly adopt Etkind's reading of psychoanalysis that both Lviv and Odessa suffer dangerously unstable levels of melancholia: 'In Freud's logic, if the loss is not recognised, it is repressed; when repressed, it turns into new and strange forms; henceforth, it threatens to return as the uncanny. The failure to recognise death as death produces the uncanny. When the dead are not properly buried and mourned, they turn into the undead' (2009, 186).

Alternatively, the citizens of both Lviv and Odessa might try taking a few walks around their own streets to get better acquainted with some of their ghosts and to form their own opinions. Who, after all, am I to reproach anyone on whose truth and which reality to adopt? As psycho-geographic walkers and writers, we would be wise to abide by Sebald's dictum: 'You adulterate the truth as you write. There isn't any pretence that you try to arrive at the literal truth. And the only consolation when you confess to this flaw is that you are seeking to arrive at poetic truth, which can be reached only through fabrication, imagination, stylisation. What I'm striving for is authenticity; none of it is real' (2011, 164).

NOTES

1. 'Coming to terms with the past.' This refers to the periods of Nazism and of the former East Germany.
2. For more information and pictures of the chapel, go to http://skipcottage. blogspot.co.uk/2010/05/lockerbie-secret.html.
3. The People's Commissariat for Internal Affairs (*Narodnyy Komissariat Vnutrennikh Del*), charged with protection of the Soviet Union's internal security between 1917 and 1953.
4. *Shansoniers* were purveyors of a uniquely Odessa-Russian style of melancholic song with roots in the French chanson.
5. In Soviet history and iconography, a *Stakhanovite* is a patriotically diligent worker who follows the example of Aleksei Grigorievich Stakhanov, a supremely productive coal miner.
6. *Schnorrer* is a Yiddish term meaning 'sponger' but distinguished from an ordinary beggar by dint of his boundless chutzpah.
7. There is a fine collection of old shop signs at http://shadowsofaforgottenworld. blogspot.co.uk/2012/06/lvivs-ghost-signs.html.
8. The Ukrainian Insurgent Army (*Ukrayins'ka Povstans'ka Armiya*, UPA) was a Ukrainian nationalist paramilitary and later partisan army that engaged in a series of guerrilla conflicts during World War II against Nazi Germany, the Soviet Union, Czechoslovakia and both underground and communist Poland. The group was the military wing of the Organization of Ukrainian Nationalists; the Bandera faction (the OUN-B) formed in 1942.

BIBLIOGRAPHY

Andrukhovych, Yuri. 2002. 'Tu i tylko tu.' In *Ostatnie Terytorium: Eseje o Ukrainie*, edited by Yuri Andrukhovych, 13–20. Wołowiec: Czarne.
Benjamin, Walter. 1968. 'Theses on the Philosophy of History.' In *Illuminations*, by Walter Benjamin, translated by Harry Zohn, 253–64. New York: Schocken Books.
Blacker, Uilleam. 2012. 'Popular Literature, the City and the Memory of Vanished Others in Poland and Ukraine: The Cases of Marek Krajewski and Iurii Vynnychuk.' *Slavonica* 18 (1): 37–50.
Derrida, Jacques. 2006. *Specters of Marx: The State of the Debt, the Work of Mourning and the New International*. Abingdon: Routledge.
Edensor, Tim. 2005. 'The Ghosts of Industrial Ruins: Ordering and Disordering Memory in Excessive Space.' *Environment and Planning D: Society and Space* 23 (6): 829–49.
Etkind, Alexander. 2009. 'Post-Soviet Hauntology: Cultural Memory of the Soviet Terror.' *Constellations* 16 (1): 182–200.
Eyal, Gil. 2004. 'Identity and Trauma: Two Forms of the Will to Memory.' *History and Memory* 16 (1): 5–36.
Givental, E. 2011. 'A Tale of Two Cities: Re-Establishing Cultural Identities in Eastern Europe.' *Yearbook of the Association of Pacific Coast Geographers* 73 (1): 52–68.

Hill, Lisa. 2013. 'Archaeologies and Geographies of the Post-Industrial Past: Land-scape, Memory and the Spectral.' *Cultural Geographies* 20 (3): 379–96.

King, Charles. 2011. *Odessa: Genius and Death in a City of Dreams*. New York: W. W. Norton.

Narvselius, Eleonora. 2012. 'Collective Memories and "Blank Spots" of the Ukrainian Past as Addressed by the Lviv Intellectuals.' In *Painful Pasts and Useful Memories: Remembering and Forgetting in Europe*, edited by Barbara Törnquist-Plewa and Nik-las Bernsand, 51–72. CFE Conference Papers Series 5. Lund: University of Lund.

Papadimitriou, Nick. 2012. *Scarp*. London: Hachette UK.

Pavlyshyn, Andrij. 2001. Nie ma tego miasta. Zesz'o pod ziemi̞e. Przesz'os´c´ w tra-dycji wspo´ 'czesnego Lwowa i Gdan´ ska. Dyskusja ['The city no longer exists. It went underground.' Past in the tradition of contemporary Lwo´w and Gdan´sk. Discussion]. In *Tematy polsko-ukrain´skie. Historia, Literatura, Edukacja (Polish-Ukrai-nian Topics: History, Literature, Education)*, edited by R. Traba, 145–47. Olsztyn: Wspo´ lnota Kulturowa Borussia.

Pinder, David. 2001. 'Ghostly Footsteps: Voices, Memories and Walks in the City.' *Cultural Geographies* 8 (1): 1–19.

Pusca, Anca. 2010. 'Industrial and Human Ruins of Post-Communist Europe.' *Space and Culture* 13 (3): 239–55.

Schönle, Andreas. 2006. 'Ruins and History: Observations on Russian Approaches to Destruction and Decay.' *Slavic Review*: 649–69.

Sebald, W. G. 2004. *On the Natural History of Destruction*. New York: Random House.

———. 2005. *Campo Santo*. New York: Random House.

———. 2011. *The Emergence of Memory: Conversations with W. G. Sebald*. New York: Seven Stories Press.

Snyder, Timothy. 2003. *The Reconstruction of Nations*. New Haven, CT: Yale University Press.

———. 2012. *Bloodlands: Europe between Hitler and Stalin*. New York: Basic Books.

Susak, Anna. 2009. 'Jewish Heritage in the Historical Memory of East-European City Dwellers: The Case of Lviv in Comparative Context.' Master's thesis, Department of Sociology and Social Anthropology, Central European University.

Tanny, Jarrod. 2011. *City of Rogues and Schnorrers: Russia's Jews and the Myth of Old Odessa*. Bloomington: Indiana University Press.

Tarkovsky, Andrei. 1979. *Stalker*. Film.

Till, Karen. 2012. 'Wounded Cities: Memory-Work and a Place-Based Ethics of Care.' *Political Geography* 31 (1): 3–14.

Wylie, John. 2007. 'The Spectral Geographies of W. G. Sebald.' *Cultural Geographies* 14 (2): 171–88.

SIX

The Art of Wandering

Arthur Machen's London Science

Merlin Coverley

In summer 2013, I was among a small group of fellow writers and enthu-
siasts who gathered in Caerleon in South Wales to celebrate the 150th
anniversary of the birth of Arthur Machen. Here, in Machen's birthplace,
surrounded by the enchanted landscape that inspired him so greatly, we
discussed his experiences of both Wales and his adopted city, London,
and sought to account for the enduring impact of his work. In recent
years Machen has enjoyed something of a comeback; his many works, for
so long out of print, have gradually been reissued, and his unique voice
has found a new audience. And, as his inclusion in a book such as this
would suggest, this renewed interest has resulted to a large degree from
his having been adopted, retrospectively, into the psychogeographical
tradition, that community of writers and thinkers that enables a diversity
of figures to come together, finding common ground where perhaps none
might have been sought previously.[1] It is Machen's role within this tradition and his continued relevance to contemporary debates surrounding
psychogeography that is the subject of this chapter.

As should be apparent to readers of this volume, however, the subject
or practice or tradition of psychogeography—even here there is little una-
nimity—is itself by no means a fixed concept, but rather a fluctuating
series of ideas and positions whose borders are uncertain and whose
meaning is unclear. With characteristic playfulness, Guy Debord describes the adjective *psychogeographical* as 'charmingly vague' (Debord
2007b, 8), and before I attempt to place Machen within this context, it

might be helpful to outline briefly what I understand by the term and its application.

Psychogeography is generally considered to describe the point at which psychology and geography collide, in an attempt to calibrate precisely the psychological impact of place. How such an impact should be documented, however, and to what purpose, remains much less clear: Are we dealing here with a principally literary or documentary enterprise, or rather a practice or intervention? Is the purpose of psychogeography primarily political or aesthetic? Should the 'rules' governing such an activity remain those articulated by Debord and his circle in a particular time and place—Paris in the 1950s—or is it legitimate to apply psychogeographical ideas within a much broader historical and geographical context? In answering these questions, it seems to me that psychogeography can best be understood through the series of oppositions such questions provoke: centre and suburb, urban and rural, literature and practice, the political and the aesthetic. It is the oscillation between these opposing poles that gives psychogeography its dynamic, as well as a framework within which psychogeographical ideas can be discussed.

Amid such flux, however, two clear strands of psychogeographic thought can be identified: On the one hand, we can trace the emergence of the flâneur on the streets of Paris in the work of Baudelaire and Benjamin before passing through the activities of the surrealists to Debord and the Situationists. On the other, we have the current of esoteric thought that originates with Alfred Watkins and his theory of ley lines, resurfaces in the work of John Michell and the earth mysteries school of the 1970s, and can be seen today within the accumulation of occult paranoia that surrounds the work of Iain Sinclair. Phil Baker has summarized these two opposing streams of psychogeographical thought, labelling them 'Situationist and Earth Mystery' (2012, 282), and, following his schema, it would appear that it is to the latter camp that Machen's work naturally gravitates; yet, as we shall see, Machen's work tends to resist such easy categorization. Before discussing Machen's work in detail, however, we must first continue our retrospective descent through psychogeographic tradition still further by turning to one of Machen's predecessors, the man whose work has been identified as marking the origin of urban psychogeography—'retrospectively, and from a Situationist-influenced perspective' (Baker 2012, 281)—Thomas De Quincey.

THE NORTHWEST PASSAGE

> Some of these rambles led me to great distances: for an opium-eater is too happy to observe the motion of time. And sometimes in my attempts to steer homewards, upon nautical principles, by fixing my eye on the pole-star, and seeking ambitiously for a north-west passage,

instead of circumnavigating all the capes and headlands I had doubled in my outward voyage, I came suddenly upon such knotty problems of alleys, such enigmatical entries, and such sphynx's riddles of streets without thoroughfares, as must, I conceive, baffle the audacity of porters, and confound the intellects of hackney-coachmen. I could almost have believed, at times, that I must be the first discoverer of some of these *terrae incognitae*, and doubted, whether they had yet been laid down in the modern charts of London.

—De Quincey (2003, 53–54)

If De Quincey has been identified as a precursor to—indeed, the progenitor of—psychogeography in its Situationist form, then his *Confessions of an English Opium Eater*, first published in *London Magazine* in 1821, is the urtext, the founding work in the psychogeographical canon. De Quincey's search for a 'northwest passage' amid the streets of nineteenth-century London is the commanding metaphor that continues to illuminate our own attempts to make sense of the city some two centuries later.

The search for the Northwest Passage, a navigable sea channel that was believed to link the North Atlantic and the Pacific Oceans, is a tale of hardship, despair and delusion spanning more than four centuries. Ever since Columbus first encountered the American landmass in 1492, there have been those convinced of a way to pass through or around the American continent in a shortcut to the dreamed-of riches of the Orient. European seaman thus embarked on numerous attempts to steer a passage through, the failures of early Spanish and French attempts gradually leading to ever more northerly voyages through the ice fields of the Arctic. The voyages of the Elizabethan adventurer Martin Frobisher between 1576 and 1578 and his discovery of what he believed, wrongly, to be gold were to be followed by those of John Davis, Henry Hudson and Luke Foxe. All were unsuccessful. Mutiny, scurvy, death and disappearance were invariably the result. The idea of the passage waned, and by the late eighteenth century its existence had been largely dismissed; yet speculation continued, and by the time De Quincey was attempting his own navigation of London's uncharted topography, the British Navy was continuing to map the Arctic coastline. Once all the Arctic waterways had finally been mapped, several possible routes were revealed, although it wasn't until the turn of the twentieth century that Roald Amundsen finally completed the first sea transit of the passage.

For De Quincey, however, the Northwest Passage was symbolic of a journey both through and out of the city, an act of faith as much as a voyage of discovery, through which the secrets of the city could be exposed and a path out of the labyrinth revealed. His genius lies in his recognition of the nautical metaphor of the passage, in which the city is imagined as a 'psychogeographic sea pushing and pulling the sensitive soul along its eddies and currents' (Sadler 1999, 88).[2] With its sense of shifting currents and inherent disorientation, De Quincey's metaphor is perfectly suited to the mysterious and seemingly impenetrable maze of alleyways and courtyards that characterized the city of his youthful wanderings. Yet inasmuch as De Quincey's search for the 'terrae incognitae'[3] of the city—its unknown and unexplored locations—is an act of physical exploration, so, too, is it an act of mental discovery, a means of imposing his imagination upon the city and recording the results, and it is this that has ensured that his metaphor remains a motif for today's breed of urban explorer.

It is from precisely this passage that Guy Debord was to quote De Quincey in 'Psychogeographical Venice,' in which he writes, 'We must recognize in Thomas de Quincey . . . an undeniable precursor to psychogeographical derives. . . . Perhaps there exists a more irrational tendency, a tendency to expect the discovery of a kind of psychogeographical Great Passage, beyond which we will attain mastery of a new game: the adventures of our lives themselves' (1957).[4] It is easy to see how De Quincey's drifts, albeit under the influence of the opium dream, would fascinate the Situationists—his attempts to find a channel through and out of the city, overcoming any impediment to his passage, mirroring the action of the dérive and their own attempts to navigate a path through Paris in a similar fashion almost 150 years later. Elsewhere, Debord states, 'We need to discover and open up the "North-west passage" toward a new revolution that cannot tolerate masses of followers, a revolution that must surge over the central terrain which has until now been sheltered from revolutionary upheavals: the conquest of everyday life' (Debord 2007a, 148). And while Debord's revolutionary rhetoric may read a little incongruously alongside De Quincey's more dreamlike prose, the impact of De Quincey's vision on the history of psychogeographical thought is undeniable.

If De Quincey's search for the Northwest Passage propels him through the nightmarish streets of central London while Debord was to navigate those of postwar Paris, so, too, has Iain Sinclair described his own search for the 'Arctic Grail,' applying De Quincey's metaphor to a contemporary setting. Describing his attempts to replicate De Quincey's bid to escape from the gravitational pull of the centre, Sinclair writes, 'The ritual can still be experienced in Bishopsgate, the City, Clerkenwell, Holborn. You progress like a stream of water, running up against barriers and blockages, detouring, doubling back. You're flung out onto the street, you duck and dive' (Sinclair 2013b, 56–57). While elsewhere he describes the search for the Northwest Passage as 'like the thread in the maze, like Ariadne's thread—which could lead you out of London if you contact it. . . . This is an alternate form of psychogeography: we walk in a particular way and its [sic] going to lead us out of the density and clutter and noise of London. I've attempted that for many, many years. Without success' (Barfield 2008).

As Sinclair's remarks make clear, the search for the Northwest Passage is not to be conducted within the centre of the city but at its perimeter. If one is to successfully navigate a path through the city, one must head for the suburbs and, it would appear, one part of suburban London in particular: Stoke Newington. Just as psychogeographical tradition can be retraced to an original figure and, as we have seen, an original text, so, too, can it be followed to an original location, a site where these myriad histories, people and texts intertwine. All cities possess such a location, and in London such a place is Stoke Newington, once home to Defoe, later the setting for Poe's schooldays and finally the focal point for Arthur Machen's own search for the Northwest Passage. Machen, a devotee of both De Quincey and Poe, spent a lifetime searching for an escape from the centre, for the elusive path that would take him to the perimeter of the city and beyond, and it was in the North, in Stoke Newington, that he was to find it.

N

By 1936, when *N* was first published, Arthur Machen was seventy-three years old, and the books that had established his reputation, such as it now was, were long behind him: *The Great God Pan* (1894), *The Three Impostors* (1895), *The Hill of Dreams* (1907). This final period of Machen's long career has since elicited little critical attention, and yet *N* is perhaps his strangest and most revealing story. The title is intriguing, for while its meaning is impossible to establish with any degree of certainty, it may well refer simply to the area in which it is set, Stoke Newington being represented by the single letter *N*, the postal district for North London at this time.[5] In this sense, then, the story is almost but not quite the perfect backdrop to Machen's search for the Northwest Passage, instead revealing a route to the northeast, but in any event a more romantically inclined title, to my mind, than its contemporary equivalent—N16.

The subject of the story is one that dominates much of Machen's fiction, the interpenetration between the commonplace world of our everyday experience and the imaginative, transcendent landscape that for Machen lay just beneath the surface, its marvels apparent only to those with the vision to apprehend it. The term Machen uses here to describe this process of interpenetration, as one world bleeds into another and the boundary between reality and illusion momentarily gives way, is *perichoresis*, a concept more usually found in Christian theology, where it describes the interrelational nature of the Trinity—but, in Machen's hands, it becomes a term employed to encapsulate his own peculiar worldview. An alternative description of this twofold vision, however, that also contrasts the world that is with the world as it might be, albeit one born of wholly different circumstances, can be found in the anonymous slogan that was to briefly adorn Paris in 1968: 'Sous les paves, la plage!' or 'Beneath the pavement—the beach!'[6] An unlikely echo of Machen's position, certainly, yet one that also shares a sense of the imaginative potential repressed by contemporary life, a potential that could break through to radically transform our perception of reality.

N begins in classic Machenesque fashion: Three gentlemen sit together in comfortable armchairs in front of an open fireplace, sipping punch and discussing Machen's favourite topic, London. The conversation sways gently from the Strand to Kings Cross and Bloomsbury before moving 'farther afield, into stranger, less-known territories' (Machen 2010, 6). Soon the conversation moves to Stoke Newington, and one member of the party recalls the name of Canon's Park, which, it has been asserted, is a paradisiacal wilderness of streams, temples and abundant foliage quite unlike anything else in London. Shortly afterward, another member of the same party, Arnold, comes across an old volume of London recollections entitled *A London Walk: Meditations in the Streets of the Metropolis*, written by the Reverend Thomas Hampole and dated 1853. Here, in a style curiously reminiscent of Machen himself, we are introduced to the world of beauty that lies behind our own:

> Some have declared that it lies within our own choice to gaze continually upon a world of equal or even greater wonder and beauty. It is said by these that the experiments of the alchemists of the Dark Ages are, in fact, related, not to the transmutation of metals, but to the transmutation of the entire universe. . . . This method, or art, or science, or whatever we choose to call it (supposing it to exist, or to have ever existed), is simply concerned to restore the delights of the Primal paradise; to enable men, if they will, to inhabit a world of joy and splendour. It is perhaps possible that there is such an experiment, and that there are some who have made it. (Machen 2010, 14)

Hampole's book reveals the disturbing tale of a man who finds an enchanted domain in this same corner of Stoke Newington, the sight of which is so unearthly that the rapture it initially inspires soon gives way to revulsion and terror. By now convinced that Hampole's story must confirm the existence of Canon's Park, Arnold sets out on a journey of discovery to the 'wild no-man's land of the north' (Machen 2010, 11) to confirm his suspicions. His first impressions of Stoke Newington, however, merely reveal an unattractive suburban scene in which all traces of the past have been eroded by the inexorable tide of red-brick expansion, and amid this anonymous landscape, he can find no trace of Canon's Park and its wondrous vistas. Finally, however, having retreated to the pub, Arnold's perseverance is rewarded, and the story is revealed: Canon's Park used to be the site of an asylum. It was an escapee from this institution who had been the subject of Hampole's narrative and who claimed to have witnessed the splendours of Canon's Park. It would appear that to those of a saner disposition, however, no such vision is to be disclosed. Arnold returns to his companions, puzzled by his experience and unsure what to make of those who claim to have glimpsed a vision of an enchanted reality withheld from the mass of common humanity. 'I believe that there is a perichoresis, an interpenetration,' he concludes. 'It is possible, indeed, that we three are now sitting among desolate rocks, by bitter streams' (Machen 2010, 33).

Machen's tale, like so much of his writing about London, is concerned with borders and borderlands, the point at which the underlying fiction of the city breaks through to the surface, disrupting our experience of reality, and also the point at which the city reaches its suburban perimeter and becomes something quite different, a liminal zone in which the rules governing the centre no longer apply. Here the city becomes something unformed or incomplete, a landscape whose seeming anonymity, in which all traces of the past appear to have been erased or displaced, may in fact conceal its true nature as a repository of unexpected mystery and delight. In this sense, Machen's work (particularly *N*) marks an extension, or rather an anticipation, of the use to which the Situationists were to put De Quincey's metaphor of the Northwest Passage, revealing a perception of the city as not merely a place to be explored or traversed but to be passed through and, ultimately, to be overcome. Machen was to realize in his endless journeys through the suburban streets, on foot and alone, that if the fabric of the city was to be transformed, what was required was a transmutation of perception, an act of imaginative reconstruction in which the commonplace topography of everyday experience could be made strange, defamiliarized, by seeking out that single image or experience that might radically alter one's perception of the landscape. It is here, then, that the true meaning of *N*, and, indeed, the legacy of Machen's work, can be found. The search for the lost domain of Canon's Park was to successfully anticipate the trajectory that the Situationists and their successors were to follow, outward toward the overlooked margins of the city in search of that elusive point of access through which an imaginative leap might allow one to transcend the city altogether.

ARTHUR MACHEN'S LONDON SCIENCE

In *Far Off Things* (1922), Machen recalls his first visit to London in June 1880, describing the sense of awe he was to experience on first glimpsing the Strand: 'No man has ever seen London,' he writes, 'but at that moment I was very near to the vision—the *theoria*—of London' (71). This sense of awe was to remain with him throughout his life, and his search for the *theoria*, or essence, of his adopted city was to become something of an obsession.

Machen's early years in London, which he was later to recollect in his three volumes of autobiography, were a period of unremitting hardship as he struggled both to make his way as a writer and to come to terms with the immensity of his new surroundings. These years were marked by an acute sense of loneliness, and it was initially as a means of combating his isolation that Machen would endlessly walk the streets, his traversal of the centre that had first captured his imagination soon giving way to an exploration of London's outer suburbs. By the 1890s, however, the decade during which he was finally to establish his name as a writer, these seemingly aimless rambles had begun to assume a more systematic role, as he attempted not merely to come to terms with this alien city but also somehow to grasp it in its entirety. By losing himself, wilfully, amid the endless suburbs, Machen hoped to face down his fears while also mastering the unknown geography of the city. Soon he was attempting to transform these unknown names on the map of London into real, living locations, all the while aware, of course, of the impossibility of ever completing such an undertaking. And it is this element of his work that makes Machen so appealing a figure to today's generation of urban wanderers.

Iain Sinclair has described Machen's ability 'to get lost creatively, how to navigate through a web of coincidences and confusions, and how to live and thrive in a plural city where all of these things happen at once' (2013a, 14). But in Machen's eyes, this role as pioneering explorer, mapping London's ever-expanding outer limits, was itself merely one aspect of a greater work that had less to do with charting London's topography than with transforming it, for just as the alchemists were to describe their great work of transmuting base metal into gold, so was Machen's own project an attempt to transform the matter of London from the mundane and unremarkable into something magical and wondrous. It was from this impulse that the Ars Magna of London was born:

> I will listen to no objections or criticisms as to the Ars Magna of London, of which I claim to be the inventor, the professor and the whole school. Here I am artist and judge at once, and possess the whole matter of the art within myself. For, let it be quite clearly understood, the Great Art of London has nothing to do with any map or guide-book or antiquarian knowledge, admirable as these are. . . . But the Great Art is a matter of quite another sphere; and as to maps, for example, if known they must be forgotten. . . . Of all this the follower of the London Art must purge himself when he sets out on his adventures. For the essence of this art is that it must be an adventure into the unknown, and perhaps it may be found that this, at last, is the matter of all the arts. (Machen 1923, 62)

At first glance, it can appear difficult to distinguish Machen's approach from that of the flâneur operating on the other side of the channel at just the time Machen is describing. Machen was certainly familiar with this figure, and some critics have interpreted his work in exactly this light; yet there are also clear differences between Machen's project and those of his Parisian counterparts.[7] While the flâneur is the man of the crowd, the invisible spectator who observes his fellow city-dwellers from within their ranks, Machen's exploration of the city was conducted alone and was directed precisely toward those quarters of the city where the flâneur would be unlikely to stray. Furthermore, Machen's journeys were less a saunter through the centre than a race for the perimeter, an attempt not so much to observe the city as to escape it altogether. There is something fevered, even desperate, in Machen's recollections of his endless suburban walking that has little in common with the more sedate movements of the dandified stroller. In fact, Machen's insistence that his Great Art must be conducted without guidebooks and maps, the initiate purged of all historical knowledge, is reminiscent less of the flâneur than of the early surrealist attempts at a kind of perambulatory automatism as well as the later aimless drift of the Situationist dérive.

Machen's final autobiographical volume, *The London Adventure, or the Art of Wandering*, was published in 1924, and it is here that Machen is most explicit, in as far as Machen is ever explicit about anything, in outlining the crucial role that the exploration of the urban environment was to play in his life and work. It is in *The London Adventure* that Machen acknowledges most clearly his debt to the city that had provided him with not only the inspiration for his seemingly inexhaustible supply of anecdotes but also the stage on which his search for the miraculous was to be played out:

> But as to this plan of mine, that was to turn into a book to be called *The London Adventure*. It originated in old rambles about London, rambles that began in 1890 when I lived in Soho street and began to stroll about Soho and to see that here was something very curious and impressive. . . . Such were the beginnings and first elements of my London science, unless I were to take account of earlier wanderings in the 'eighties, when I roamed out north and west and saw the red brick villas and streets of shops gaining on the quiet fields and old lanes overhung with trees that then made a veritable countryside within ten minutes of Acton. But in writing this book of mine I was to dip rather into the later years; into the 1895–99 period when I first found out the wonders that lie to the eastward of the Gray's Inn Road, when Islington and Barnsbury and Canonbury were discovered, when Pentonville ceased to be a mere geographical expression. (Machen 1924, 30–34)

Here, then, Machen's 'great art' becomes his 'London science,' and, whether art or science, this was a discipline he was to refine over the course of his lifetime in attempting to overcome the fear that London, in all its immensity, was to instil in him.[8] London was, of course, then as now, vast and unknowable, but Machen sought to combat the disorientating sense of awe that it provoked in him by the simple expedient of

walking its streets. Walking, in all its simplicity, is the activity that links
Machen's experience of the city with our own, the activity that through
its very resistance to prescribed routes becomes an expression of both
personal freedom and radical disregard for the conventions of the day.

Iain Sinclair has described walking as the 'last radical act' (Kobek
2014, 31), and by studiously avoiding the familiar and the well known in
favour of the neglected and the overlooked, Machen was to resist the
perambulatory conventions of the nineteenth-century city in precisely the
way that Sinclair and today's urban explorers resist the prescribed and
promoted topographies of the twenty-first. Machen's act of resistance
was a highly personal one, entirely free from political allegiance and
quite unconcerned with intellectual or literary fashion; however, his attempts to navigate a Northwest Passage out of the city and to access the
imaginative landscape behind the everyday resonate clearly in the works
of multiple later writers, from Breton and Aragon to Debord, Sinclair and
Self. And yet, as a consequence of his resistance to, or rather his disinter-
est in, any particular school or philosophy, his work, while establishing a
certain trajectory and a highly idiosyncratic sense of the city, finally falls
short of establishing an exact model or template for those who were to
succeed him. In the end, Machen's worldview was uniquely his own, and
while we may try to follow in his footsteps, no single set of practices or
principles will enable us to replicate his vision. While practices can be
learned or followed, Machen's own sense of his surroundings was gov-
erned ultimately not by technique but by temperament, and though we
may strive to lose ourselves as he once did, Machen, as it turns out, was
lost all along:

> I was deep in all these matters, as I said, in that June of 1896; and after
> one very heavy and terrific night at this dismal old game of invention, I
> went out for my customary stroll in the Gray's Inn—Bloomsbury quar-
> ter . . . when I suddenly became aware that I had utterly lost the sense
> of direction. I was disorientated, though I was in a part of London most
> familiar to me; north and south, east and west had no more any mean-
> ing. . . . I got home somehow by complicated and dubious calculations,
> and in a somewhat confused and alarmed frame of mind. And odd as it
> may seem, this perplexity has never wholly left me. (1924, 140–41)

NOTES

1. Will Self (2014) writes, 'There's a sense, I think, that psychogeography—which
isn't so much a field as the traversing of one—gathers into its practice the productions
of writers and thinkers who might otherwise be regarded as having little in common.'

2. Further evidence in support of this nautical link is provided by McKenzie Wark,
who describes the origins of the word *dérive*:

> Its Latin root 'derivare' means to draw off a stream, to divert a flow. Its
> English descendents include the word 'derive' and also 'river.' Its whole

field of meaning is aquatic, conjuring up flows, channels, eddies, currents, and also drifting, sailing or tacking against the wind. It suggests a space and time of liquid movement, sometimes predictable but sometimes turbulent. (2011, 22)

3. Geoff Nicholson writes:

> De Quincey's fantasy of an unknown London is an attractive one, since London is, in every sense I can think of, exceptionally well-trodden territory: a place of walkers, with a two-thousand-year-old history of pedestrianism. . . . No part of London is genuinely unknown. However obscure or hidden the place and its history, somebody has already discovered it, walked it, staked a claim to it. (2010, 41)

4. These comments, written by Debord in 1957, were originally intended as a preface for a book by Ralph Rumney. However, Rumney was excluded from the Situationist International a short time later, having failed to write the book as promised.

5. 'Its mystery is not confined to the meaning of its title,' writes Christopher Palmer, 'which may or may not refer merely to that area of London in which the scene is set, i.e. Stoke Newington (in those days elaborate postal codes were blessedly unknown and unwanted)' (1988, 16).

6. McKenzie Wark has identified Debord's sometime collaborator, René Viénet, as the likely author of this slogan (2011, 149–50).

7. In his introduction to *The Three Impostors* (1895), David Trotter discusses Machen's relationship to the flâneur:

> Machen's familiarity with home-grown varieties of the phenomenon is evident from a later story, 'A Fragment of Life,' whose hero, a suburban newly-wed, recalls with mixed feelings the fecklessness of his bachelor existence, the 'innumerable evenings on which he had rejected his landlady's plain fried chop, and had gone out to *flâner* among Italian restaurants in Upper Street, Islington.' (1995, xxii)

8. Describing Machen, Philip Van Doren Stern has written, 'He seems never to have fitted into the life of the huge metropolis. He explored London endlessly and came to know it well, but it evidently terrified him' (1949, ix).

BIBLIOGRAPHY

Baker, Phil. 2012. 'Secret City: Psychogeography and the End of London.' In *London from Punk to Blair*, edited by Joe Kerr and Andrew Gibson, 277–91. London: Reaktion.

Barfield, Steven, ed. 2008. 'Psychogeography: Will Self and Iain Sinclair in Conversation with Kevin Jackson.' Transcribed by Karian Schuitema. *Literary London: Interdisciplinary Studies in the Representation of London* 6 (1). http://www.literarylondon. org/london-journal/march2008/sinclair-self.html.

Debord, Guy. 1957. 'Psychogeographical Venice.' Not Bored! http://www.notbored. org/psychogeographical-venice.html.

———. 2007a. 'The Counter-Situationist Campaign in Various Countries.' In *Situationist International Anthology*, edited and translated by Ken Knabb, 145–49. Berkeley, CA: Bureau of Public Secrets.

———. 2007b. 'Introduction to a Critique of Urban Geography.' In *Situationist International Anthology*, edited and translated by Ken Knabb, 8–11. Berkeley, CA: Bureau of Public Secrets.

De Quincey, Thomas. 2003. *The Confessions of an English Opium Eater and Other Writings*. Edited by Barry Milligan. London: Penguin.

Kobek, Jarett. 2014. *Walking Is a Radical Act: An Interview with Iain Sinclair*. 24 March. http://solarluxuriance.com/walking.html.

Machen, Arthur. 1894. *The Great God Pan*. London: John Lane.

———. 1895. *The Three Impostors*. London: John Lane.

———. 1907. *The Hill of Dreams*. London: Grant Richards.

———. 1922. *Far Off Things*. London: Martin Secker.

———. 1923. *Things Near and Far*. London: Martin Secker.

———. 1924. *The London Adventure, or the Art of Wandering*. London: Martin Secker.

———. 2010. *N*. Leyburn: Tartarus Press. First published 1936.

Nicholson, Geoff. 2010. *The Lost Art of Walking: The History, Science, Philosophy, Literature, Theory and Practice of Pedestrianism*. Chelmsford: Harbour Books.

Palmer, Christopher. 1988. Introduction to *The Collected Arthur Machen*, edited by Christopher Palmer, 1–21. London: Duckworth.

Sadler, Simon. 1999. *The Situationist City*. Cambridge, MA: MIT Press.

Self, Will. 2014. 'The Frisson.' Review of *The View from the Train: Cities and Other Landscapes*, by Patrick Keiller. *London Review of Books*, 23 January. http://www.lrb.co.uk/2014/01/20/will-self/the-frisson.

Sinclair, Iain. 2013a. *Our Unknown Everywhere: Arthur Machen as Presence*. Newport: Three Impostors.

———. 2013b. *Swimming to Heaven: The Lost Rivers of London*. London: Swedenborg Society.

Trotter, David. 1995. Introduction to *The Three Impostors*, by Arthur Machen, xvii–xxxi. London: Everyman's Library.

Van Doren Stern, Philip. 1949. Introduction to *Tales of Horror and the Supernatural*, by Arthur Machen, v–xv. London: Richards Press.

Wark, McKenzie. 2011. *The Beach beneath the Street: The Everyday Life and Glorious Times of the Situationist International*. London: Verso.

SEVEN

Wooden Stones

Gareth E. Rees

It's the sea air, as I stand by the ruined pier, that brings me the first whiff of Mike's memory. The instant the salt hits my nostrils, I'm transported to that morning when he was found, laid gently on the rocks beneath the castle at low tide, by a dog walker. It didn't happen here in Hastings, though. You'd have to travel nine hundred miles up the British coast to St. Andrew's in Fife and nineteen years back in time to see me beside the castle, staring in horror at what lay below. Mike was still wearing his tweed jacket, jeans and leather-soled shoes. But his glasses were gone. It looked as if he was curled up asleep.

He was buried in a cemetery on the outskirts of Edinburgh among myriad rows of glittering marble on the brow of a vast manicured lawn high above the city. Months later I left Scotland for a job writing radio adverts in Cardiff. A few years after that, I migrated to London, where I lived for fifteen years, morphing into a middle-aged man with a wife and kids. I've been back to Edinburgh several times but never to that ceme-tery. I never thought about why. Not until I came to live by the sea once again.

Not until I discovered the wooden stones.

THE PROMENADE

Hastings Pier is a charred skeleton, burned by arsonists in 2010, now on the brink of regeneration. A faded campaign banner flapping from the rusted Victorian gantry bears the word *Save*. Outside the entrance, hoardings tell the story of a renovation that hasn't yet begun, while men in yellow hats scratch their heads at the shredded decking.

There is a lot of writing on this part of the promenade. Vested interests clamour for their say. Danger signs warn, 'Falling Debris'; 'Beach Levels May Change'; 'For Your Safety Keep Off Groynes and Other Structures.' The rails are dotted with advertisement posters for '1066 Country,' weather-worn to the point of dementia. All but a few flecks remain: the façade of a Tudor house, a knight's helmet, a child's face. There's a fresh poster for a concert in the White Rock Theatre: 'The Upbeat Beatles: Come and Party Like It's 1963.' Dead flowers, empty cans of Stella, and the words *Gone but Not Forgotten* are Sellotaped to a lamppost.

This is not a place to sit and reflect. The narrative insists you *move along, move along*. It's all about the flow. Bollards separate the promenade from the busy road; a lane separates bicycles from pedestrians; railings separate the promenade from the sea. Cars, walkers, cyclists and water are meant to move in their designated channels. I'm forcibly swept down an avenue of joggers, pensioners, teens and tourists toward the old town nestled between two outcrops: West Hill, home to the castle ruins, and East Hill, serviced by a funicular railway lift overlooking the fishing boats, cafés and amusement arcades.

As the danger warnings are left behind and the scent of chips wafts through the petrol fumes, I pass benches, positioned so that the sitter can stare out to sea. Some bear inscriptions. On the first: 'Ruth Wakefield, 1911–1990, a wonderful wife, mother and grandmother.' Then there's a row of them together:

In Loving Memory of Ron Dunk

In Loving Memory of My Husband Tom Higgins

In Loving Memory of Dolly & Jack Chad

In Memory of Olive & Lancelot (Lyn) Bolton-Dunk

The four inscriptions are so alike in tone, style and levels of weathering that I wonder if Ron Dunk is any relation to the Bolton-Dunks, and, if so, why they are separated by Higgins and the Chads. What does this bench arrangement mean? Perhaps there was a grand wedding where Olive Bolton was hitched to Lancelot Dunk in double-barrelled matrimony. A handsome couple. There was dancing and drinking. A scuffle broke out between members of the two families. Long-standing tensions unleashed by Buck's fizz. The Higginses and the Chads stepped in to break it up:

'Leave it, Jack! He's not worth it!'
'My God, look at his face!'
'You've ruined everything!'

Years of estrangement followed, until death reunited them. Or perhaps that's total nonsense. Perhaps the Dunks had nothing whatsoever to do with the Bolton-Dunks. Never even met the Bolton-Dunks. It was simply that the person who planned the position of these memorial benches believed a Dunk at either end would have pleasing symmetry. Perhaps they mischievously wanted to imply a relationship between these people that never was. Or perhaps they thought nothing at all, and I'm reading meaning between the lines of a text that has no author.

Beyond the benches I take the steps from the promenade to the beach, where the broken spine of an outflow pipe gushes freshwater into the sea. There's a long line of hollows in the shingle where someone has walked earlier. I follow it, placing my feet in the pits their feet have left behind. There's something forlorn about the way the trail meanders toward the water's edge, suggesting a distracted mind tugged by emotional currents. For me, these prints are just as poignant as those prehistoric footprints exposed on Norfolk shorelines by storm tides. After all, what's the difference between an 850,000-year-old human footprint and a five-minute-old human footprint? Nothing but sentimentality. In the grand, cosmological scheme of things, we are all fellow ancients together, sharing the blink of an eye.

It's low tide. The shingle gives way to a wide slab of sand, shimmering like meat, peppered with mollusc shells. Looking out toward the horizon, I lose all sense of the town behind me. There's only the universality of sand, sea, rocks, sky. Suddenly this beach is all the beaches of my past. Family visits to Tenby. A trip to Blackpool. Holidays on the Costa Brava. Dover, where Mike and I became best friends at school and talked of there being a giant mutant eel in the harbour waters with a head the size of an armchair. Folkestone Beach, where we went underage drinking on Saturday afternoons. The West Sands of St. Andrew's, where, one afternoon in 1996, Mike and I raced each other across the beach in a parody of *Chariots of Fire*, which was filmed there. In our school days, I had been the sportier one, but at Sheffield University I'd done little other than booze, smoke, read and sleep. By the time I came up to St. Andrew's to study for a master's, Mike was in training for the army. So much for his lefty leanings. Gone were the days when we busked on the street, bellowing out Dylan and Billy Bragg songs. Now they made him do things like haul a backpack full of rocks up a snowy Munro without any sleep while being attacked by ninjas, or so he told me, anyway. He could be full of shit like that. But I couldn't deny the evidence on the beach that day. He accelerated away from me with surprising speed, suddenly faster, stronger, seemingly unstoppable.

Lungs heaving, I crumpled onto the sand and watched him run toward his destiny. That castle, looming.

WEST HILL

There's a castle in Hastings, too, on West Hill overlooking the town. Someone has painted an eye onto a small bulge in the cliff face, giving the outcrop the appearance of a beached leviathan wearily watching human life scuttle beneath.

My house is nestled in the valley behind the hill. On my daily walks, I rise up to the castle through elevated Victorian streets, facades painted pastel yellows, pinks and blues. The town centre drops away as I climb. Below, the Priory Meadow shopping centre clutters the space where a harbour used to be in the Middles Ages, when Hastings was a Cinque Port, before it became filled with silt, wrecking her dreams of power. The windows of many houses on my ascent are adorned with figurines of sailors and fishermen, boats in bottles and conch shells, icons of coastal life curated for the benefit of passersby or to appease aquatic gods I have not yet encountered.

These Victorian terraces finally open onto the crest of West Hill. A lush green park sweeps down toward the slate roofs of the old town, jumbled between the thighs of this hill and East Hill. Beyond is the ocean, where gulls boomerang in the headwind and tankers crawl on the horizon. That threshold where the world ends and outer space begins. A spotlight of sunshine blasts through a gap in the cloud, turning a disc of sea to silver, as if something gigantic is about to rise from the water and break into song.

With this sort of view, it's unsurprising that the hill is striated with benches (see figure 7.1). It's an amphitheatre for a grand oceanic performance where the audience is made up of the dead, for every bench is a memorial, demarking a viewpoint where the viewer is no more. I walk past inscription after inscription:

Pat and Wynne Wells 1920–2008 remembered with love

In Loving Memory of Doris Green, Sadly Missed by Family and Friends

In Loving Memory of Our Mum Olive Martin 1921–2006
Who loved Hastings

In Loving memory of my dear wife Florence Lansell

In Loving memory of Flo and Alf Longman
Down memories [sic] path we will walk with you forever

Vincent James Penny beloved Husband and Father
A quiet sleep and a sweet dream when the long trick's over

Doris Rosalind Robinson 1930–2001 Forever In Our Hearts

In Loving Memory of John Sydney Mellor
1931–2007
He enjoyed the sea

Miss Jean Povey
Born 1926–2003
Who loved to walk this hill

Eileen Butcher
21.3.1939–22.7.2009
Who Loved Hastings

Margaret E. Sands
30 April 1989 Age 63
Much Loved

Freda May Longman 1925–2008
Smile and Remember All We Shared

In Memory of Martha Robertson 1917–1997. She loved it here.
In Memory of Henry Robertson 1948–2003. So did he.

I'm reminded of that Edinburgh cemetery where they laid Mike, except these stones are wooden, and I'm merrily taking photographs of them with an iPhone. It's vampiric, this appropriation of other people's memories for my own ends. But the whole point of these benches is that the grieving immortalize their loved ones in a written form. Words only become meaningful when they are read, so the dead on West Hill are only truly remembered when there is a reader. Whether they like it or not, I am a necessary part of this equation. One day the grievers who commissioned the bench will also die. When that happens, all that will remain are words on a landscape, detached from their authors, with strangers looking upon them, forming their own impressions, indulging their own private remembrances. But all they can ever really know is that someone called Jean, Eileen, Henry, John, or Martha once came here to enjoy the landscape.

Or did they? There's something odd about the benches. Rather than located in positions where someone would stand to appreciate a view of the sea or the old town, they are infrastructural, aligned according to the trajectory of footpaths that cut across the park in diagonals, decreed by municipal planners for the needs of walkers who wish to get from A to B—from the West Hill lift to the Smugglers Adventure caves, from the steps of the old town to the Victorian terraces on the hill's crest. It may be

Figure 7.1.   Memorial bench on West Hill, Hastings

that at no time ever did the deceased sit in the precise location of their memorial bench and look out. Unless he was some kind of misanthrope with a loathing for the picturesque—or perhaps a psychogeographer— it's unlikely that Richard Bexhell's favourite spot on West Hill was in the corner by an allotment fence, facing away from the castle and sea, over-looking a steep littered path and two bollards.

The benches don't signify an actual moment in space-time as experi-enced by the deceased. They're a utility for rest. A public narrative to be read as people walk by on their ways to other places of local interest—the castle, West Hill Café and the historical town. If their true purpose were to signify moments in a life, they would be placed in those invisible loci where dog walkers, lovers and loners leave the path to weave across the grass, gaze out to sea, clamber over rocks and talk—kiss—declare their love—end the relationship—reveal the secret! Memories are made in those moments of transgression. But they are often kept private, taken to the grave, unknown to those family members who write epitaphs like this:

In memory of Susan Lowescroft (1936–2012) she loved this hill

It might be more accurate to place Susan's bench in the long grass near the castle, with an inscription like this:

> In memory of Susan Lowescroft (1936–2012). She got pregnant here in 1953 by John Truman (1932–2008), who wanted nothing to do with it. Then the baby died, and she came here every Sunday to cry.

Of course, this would never happen. Memorial benches are the narratives of survivors. Many proclaim in their inscriptions that remembrance is the 'last gift of love.' Their function is to keep a family's memory of a loved one alive in the landscape they use every day rather than a cemetery on a ring road. This desire to reconnect memory with topography sees epitaphs proliferate in locations where people congregate for leisure: parks, cliff tops, outdoor markets, promenades. It is *words* that forge this connection. A blank bench placed in a beautiful spot could as easily commemorate a loved one. Although the family would know it was their loved one's bench, it must bear an inscription in order to activate that memory. It works in the same way that a diary is both a means of preserving an experience through the act of writing and a means of returning to that experience through the act of reading. For many, it's not enough to enjoy a fleeting moment. It must be recorded for it to exist, for it to *endure*.

There's writing all over West Hill. Not only on the benches but also on the cliff by the castle, where bulbous grey rocks form a viewing platform over the sea front. Every inch of rock is carved with names and initials. Unlike the benches, these inscriptions demark the exact location where someone has sat. They recorded the experience in stone, forging the moment in a physical groove as if marking a piece of vinyl. These rocks are an LP library of educational field trips, marriage proposals, inaugural joints, first kisses and family holidays. I run my fingers over the text:

> *Leah and Shane . . . Sexy . . . Sara . . . Lenka . . . Kristian . . . Peace . . . Elliott . . . Perla . . . Zoe . . . Joy Larkin 1930 . . .*

Many of the markings are indecipherable, worn smooth over decades by the feet and buttocks of thousands of visitors, overlaid with new inscriptions. There is writing upon writing. Memories upon memories. Generation upon generation. These engravings seem a vain attempt at immortality in a world where people keep coming in crashing cycles of birth and death, rubbing each other out, endlessly forgetting.

Down below the dangling legs of tourists, the cliff has been reinforced to stop erosion and landslips. Much of the original castle was lost to the sea. Subsequent sea defences and a widened promenade now keep the waters at bay. But the torment of weather is unrelenting. Angular red walls are built into the cliff to prop it up. Caves are bricked up like defunct church windows. Chunks of rock are fused with mosaics of mortar and stone. West Hill is mutating into a manmade monument, a temple of memory that the town is shoring up with every means possible. As savage storms and rising seas threaten the coast, Hastings is determined to hang onto itself, much in the same way as those who carve their initials onto the rock are determined to fuse with the landscape. There's a terror of it all slipping away. We don't want to live in the moment, only then to forget and be forgotten. We want to endure. We want our loved ones to endure. We look to the landscape as a medium through which we can preserve our identities in a form of afterlife. But this is an impossibility. Long after those who have scrawled names on rocks and wooden benches have died and their children's children die, their inscriptions will remain on this cliff, detached from any human connection. Names that nobody recognizes. Viewpoints with no viewer. Until what remains of the cliff crumbles, taking a jumble of meaningless words into the sea.

THE STADE

Winding steps take me down from West Hill to the church of St. Clement's in the old town, where there is an even greater sense of this shoring-up of memories. Antique shops are piled high with curios. There are skeletons everywhere. Human skeleton with a sheep skull head. Dapper skeleton in a straw boating hat and suit. Dwarf skeleton in a wedding dress. Replica Tyrannosaur skeleton leering from a ledge. On the walls, framed old maps of Sussex, stuffed mammals, World War II memorabilia, vintage soldier's uniforms. Tables are heaped high with grenades, documents and medals. It's as if professional grave robbers have appropriated the town to flog their wares. On a corner opposite the church is a memorial garden, where a plaque commemorates the White Swan Hotel, obliterated by German bombs one Sunday afternoon in 1943, killing sixteen people.

I push through the bustle onto Rock-a-Nore Road with its pubs, chippies, arcades, seafood stalls and ice cream parlours. A Kinks track blasts from inside the Lord Nelson, where fishermen unwind after work. Outside, a skinny old man in a suit stands by an upturned bicycle, smoking a fag, frantically turning the pedal so that the back wheel spins. As I approach for a closer look he steps forward and yells, 'Stop copying my fucking idea!'

Across the road is the Stade, a shingle beach from which the fishing fleet is launched. The premium on space meant that the fishermen built their net huts extremely tall with multiple floors. Many of the early Victorian examples still stand, black lacquered boards stretching to peaked roofs. In the midst of the huts is the fisherman's museum, on the wall of which four plaques are lined in a row:

In Memory of Boy Ashore
Jimmy Read
Killed Tragically
In the Hurricane of
16th November 1987

In Memory of Hastings Fisherman
Darren Fox
Lost at Sea
2nd February 1998
Aged 23

In Memory of Hastings Fisherman
Russell Stewart
Who died tragically
6th November 1998
Aged 25

In memory of
Steve Weatherall
Fisherman
Lost at Sea 21-3-2000
Aged 37

These memorials are positioned where fishermen pass by on their way to work, facing peril to catch cod, plaice and sole. Despite the museum pieces, this is still a working fishing community. In the shadow of the newly constructed Jerwood art gallery, a line of shacks sell the latest catch from beneath white painted signs. 'Fresh Fish,' reads one, with an abandoned sofa outside it. 'We do not sell drugs,' explains another.

I stop for a drink in a new café built on the Stade in 2011, a companion piece to the gallery, constructed from the same shimmering black brick. At the adjacent table, an elderly woman talks with two friends, folded wheelchairs stacked beside them. I catch some of her monologue. It's about a conversation she had with a male friend a long time ago, when she was accused of getting pregnant by a man who was not her husband:

> He sat me down and patted me by the hand. And then he says, 'So you gone and you seeded yourself again, Rose? You only gone and seeded yourself.' I said, 'It's not—not another man. You don't have to worry about me having a man.' And he says, 'Don't telly porky pies.' I says to him, 'Why worry about having a man? Who needs one when I got one sitting in a box in me wardrobe?' Ha ha ha ha ha! One day Harry finds it and says, 'I can't believe you let me sleep in the room with *that thing* in there.'

Her companions assume outraged faces, but I get the impression they've heard this one before. I think about Rose's old friend patting her hand all those years back. It must have seemed to him an insignificant gesture at the time, one of many that occur in any given day. But the passing years have enshrined that moment in Rose's narrative. That old friend may be dead now, but he endures in an anecdote she tells over and over. It's funny to think that none of us knows which of those things we do and say will outlive us in the memory of the living. We're all accidental authors of our own epitaphs.

I leave the café and push past the miniature railway station and aquarium; past the last few shops selling buckets, spades and soft drinks; into the car park. Then it all stops. The town ends abruptly at a sea wall and railings festooned with signs: 'Unstable Cliff / No Access.' Sandstone cliffs stretch into the distance. The walkway drops onto a beach with arches of weathered rock and wet slabs tilted like broken tables. The vinegar stench of seaweed. Yawning mussels and the stripped bones of a fish. A rusting anchor. Fisherman's rope. Plastic bottle. Things returned that have been taken away.

It was surprising how gently the sea delivered Mike to us that morning in May 1996. The waves could be so violent on the Fife coast. The rocks sharp and unyielding. Yet there were barely any signs of damage on his body but for a single small bruise on his head, or so his father told me after he'd been to the morgue. I never went that close. By the time I got to the castle, there were already police on the beach. I'd stayed the night at my girlfriend's house a few minutes down the road, so I took the phone call there. I knew from the first word, just the way that Ben said, 'Gareth . . .' that something terrible had happened.

The moment you hear that someone has died is like a universe collapsing. All your energy is sucked through a hole in your gut until you are turned completely inside out and hoovered into the hole yourself, falling through space. There are no words. There is no air. Sound won't carry. I ran up the road toward the castle, mouth open in a silent scream. It was a numb nothingness that I wanted to hold onto for fear of what would come next, that realization that hit me like a fist. An explosion of pain. Then all the noise rushing back. Talking, crying, police sirens. Questions. *What happened? How did this happen? Is this really happening?* Strangers inside our house, and people milling around outside. Our flat was opposite the castle, overlooking the beach, so even when the police cars had gone, we were left with the ebb and flow of tourists. They took photographs, big smiles and thumbs up, right where we had clambered over the railings the previous night. Giggling children looked for crabs in the rock pools where Mike had lain only hours before. A Labrador splashed in the waves. It was like nothing had happened. And, of course, for them nothing *had* happened. They existed in that world in which I'd lived until that morning. Now I'd crossed to a parallel universe where there was no laughter, no light, no Mike. I watched the tourists from our window, seething with envy.

It all comes back to me at the edge of Hastings, looking at the shore's broken maw, listening to the waves churn. There's a universality to the sea. The smell. The sound. It dissolves your sense of time. It's the sea of your youth. It's the sea of now. It's the sea that will be there after you're gone. It's that same vastness of water, endlessly taking things out, then pushing them back in again. So many life stories have ended on the coast. Death by falling, drowning, suicide. People swept off boat decks and harbour walls, carried away by deadly currents. Really, we should stay well away from it. The East Hill promontory beneath which I stand is rapidly being eaten away by tidal surges. During the storms of 2014, a tower of stone broke from the cliff and exploded into the sea, filmed by screaming onlookers. Moments later, another column slid away with a thunderous roar. It was like the last days of Atlantis. The following morning I came to the edge of the car park to join a crowd of spectators by the 'Danger of Falling Rocks' signs. We looked upon fresh sandstone exposed to the air after millennia and piles of ochre stone on the beach. I wondered if eventually there would be a memorial bench located here:

In loving memory of Gareth E. Rees
He liked to come to this place
and watch the world collapse

The coast has a strange torsion. We're drawn to these perilous outcrops to remember, contemplate, throw ashes, carve our names on rock. But in these places, we also make memories. Here's where families and friends descend at the weekend to eat, drink, smoke, scream on fairground rides, howl at slot machines, dance on the beach. There's an industry built around this process of memory creation. Adverts for holiday resorts and package tours guilt-trip us with sepia film reels of family seaside holidays. They tell us that these are the days our children will remember us by. These are what fill the family photo albums. These are the times we will come to the sea to remember when we're older.

These are the stories we will tell.

EAST HILL

On a crankily humid day, I slip through an alley beside the Dolphin pub and climb the steep steps alongside the Victorian railway lift that takes tourists to the top of East Hill. There are memorial benches toward the summit. The epitaphs are different in tone from those on West Hill, looser and wittier, with hints of an authorial voice—or even the voice of the deceased themselves, humming in the depths of their wooden chambers.

Jim & Trixie Butchers
A Wonderful Hastings couple

Olly '9 Toes' Carey 31.12.82–5.10.05

Michele Campling
I don't know where I'm going from here but I promise it won't be boring

Never a Dull Moment—In Loving Memory of Gary Batcheler

At the very top, by the exit of the funicular lift, there is a single bench beneath a tourist information board that reads:

Mad John?
1945–2009

Who on earth were *you*, Mad John? I sit down by his name. His bench is positioned so that it takes in the whole Hastings vista—the Stade, the promenade, the pier and the curvaceous rump of West Hill rising from the old town. Unlike the infrastructural location of many benches on that rival elevation, this seems the most natural spot where someone would stand to soak it all in. I can imagine John's gaze as if it were my own. I smirk on his behalf at the stuffy formality of those memorial benches on West Hill, some of whom he knew when they were more than just names on wood. There's Mrs. Jenson, who was 'much beloved'—oh yes, *beloved* alright. She was known as the town bike back in the 1950s. Everyone had a go. Then there's Dicky Pierce. Christ only knows why he's up on that hill. The lazy fat sod barely left his bar stool at the Stag. Harry and Jill Michaels, a 'loving couple'—God, you should have heard Harry going on about her behind her back until that day she whopped him with a sauce-pan and everyone laughed at his black eye. Yet there they all are, laughs Mad John. Dead and turned to benches instead of dust, arranged in rows, seething at each other for taking the superior spots. Oh, how they'd love to wrench their little wooden legs from the earth, grow big eyestalks and go clattering across the hill like crabs to find a viewpoint away from those tourists and their big sweaty arses. Ah, for shame, you dead of West Hill. It's here on East Hill where the benches are arrayed according to human nature, wild and random, with the most majestic vistas. East Hill is where the chaos happens.

From John's bench I can see a weather system approach, an opaque twister moving over Bexhill-on-Sea. Rain falls on distant boats. Sensing a squall, restless gulls spiral up from the cliff side like cinders rising from a fire. I envy them sometimes. Birds are the expression of the wind. They travel invisible paths in the sky, gone as soon as they are created, never to be repeated. These animals are free to live in the moment. But we humans are entrenched in the earth. The routes we travel are scars on the topography. Memory trails where we can't help but leave our footprints nor avoid following the footprints of others. Walking is unavoidably an act of writing *and* reading. Even without memorial benches, the landscape is heavy with text.

I cross the rolling green baize of the West Hill, formerly a golf course, past the benches of Bill Gausden (12th February 1933–30th November 2012), Janet Harling (1943–2008) and John Mantle, who 'loved this park.' Ahead of me a path stoops from the hill, then sweeps up along the bitten cliffs and over a freshly farmed crest. Logs are hammered into the path at intervals to prevent it turning into a mud chute. As I descend awkwardly, I pass a man with his young son and dog as they duck under a barrier and follow a gulley to the rocky beach below. I'm sure they know what they are doing, but it seems treacherous. As I rise up the incline and look behind, I see more clearly the effects of erosion. Old stone steps truncated at sheer drops. The remains of a building's foundations on a ledge, crumbled and overgrown. Patches of grass weep over the broken brow, trees in slow motion topple toward the sea, roots dangling in the air. This landscape is dying. Slowly but surely.

The path takes me higher and closer to the precipice. Encroaching clouds bruise the sky. I catch voices in the wind. They sound alarmed. Is it that boy and that man I saw earlier? *Are they in trouble?* I try to look down. I can see a man, tiny at the foot off the cliff, picking his way through the rocks, knee-deep in water, clutching onto the sandstone to steady himself. There's a frenzy of dog barks. Someone shouting. A dark shape in the water. I'm sure I can see the hump of something's back — shiny and black like a giant eel — break the water's surface, momentarily, before the waves fold upon it. Another cry, a child's. It could be a completely innocent scene, or something terrible is happening. I cannot tell. But there is nothing I can do about it. I'm too remote, too alone, too afraid to step beyond the barrier. It's not the height that frightens me; it's the edge. Being on the threshold between existence and obliteration. I fear that moment where I'm in the air suddenly, the cliff edge falling upward, I've surrendered control to gravity and there's nothing I can do. That split second where I am both alive and dead. That moment Mike must have experienced when he slipped off the castle wall. I can't get it out of my head. I've never been able to.

We drank a lot that day. A friend was up visiting, and we wanted to show him a good time, taking him on a crawl of the pubs. It was dark, and there was drizzle in the air by the time we went to the castle, as we'd done so many times before. The ruin was our playground. The centrepiece we showed visitors to impress them. By the entrance was a memorial stone embedded in the cobblestones marked 'G. W.,' the spot where the Protestant George Wishart was burned at the stake in 1564 after being tried for heresy. We climbed over the rails, then tumbled into the grassy moat. On the other side, the battlements where Wishart's grieving allies hanged the corpse of Cardinal David Beaton, the man who ordered his death, after they snuck into the castle to seek revenge. By a broken wall, Mike ribbed me about being under my girlfriend's thumb, about forgetting my mates. I said something. Maybe it was funny, maybe it was cruel. Maybe it was both. I can't remember. He swung a half-hearted fist at my stomach. I told him I was going off to drink some whisky. Then he went mumbling into the darkness, and that was that. It must have been in those ensuing minutes that he decided to climb the outer wall of the castle. I don't know for sure. Nobody does. He made his contract with death in private.

I think about him lying in a cemetery on the outskirts of Edinburgh and how I've never been back to visit his grave, even when visiting that city. I think about St. Andrew's and Dover and London, Cardiff, Manchester—all those places where I have lived at some point, yet rarely ever return to. They are memoryscapes for me now. I don't physically walk them. I can't see or touch them. Like many of the rootless class, I've lost that connection to my past. Instead, I roam towns full of other people's memories, other people's dead, other people's narratives. I wonder if all this walking and writing about place is an attempt to make up for my landscape loss. I wonder if the words in this chapter are my own wooden stones as I try to write Mike into the byways, parks and beaches where I walk.

And I wonder if words are enough to bring him back.

Part III

Power and Place

The psychogeographical project, as it was for the Situationists, was to tear down the spectacle and reorder space so as to express the needs and desires of the community. They did this in a number of ways, such as through their unitary urbanism project, which involved redesigning city architecture. But in a practical way, this was carried out through their dérives. By formulating chance routes through the city, the Situationists challenged the domineering nature of urban decor and offered a new approach to the city. By literally chopping out the areas of the city they disliked (for instance, areas dominated by the spectacle or those under redevelopment), they reformed sections of existing city maps into quarters of their own choosing. These quarters reflected their own urban preferences, and they added ambiances to them to express what they would represent in their new city (for example, Happy Quarter). The new maps, the Guides Psychogeographiques or the Naked City maps, suggested a new way of moving through urban space that was counter to the capitalist-dominated city and encouraged people to reconnect with a city they were increasingly being pushed out of through bureaucracy and urban planning.

For many contemporary psychogeographers, even those who would not consider themselves activists, the imposed boundaries that appear in urban space represent power structures that are critiqued as part of their practice. It is the critical act of walking in urban space that enables one to understand firsthand how power operates on the body-politic in subtle and enduring ways. While there have been a number of psychogeographical movements since the disbandment of the Situationist International (SI) in 1972, as there still are today, it is the SI that holds a prominent place in our memory when discussing political urban walking practices. The chapters here offer a historical overview of the activist project of the SI in relation to psychogeography, alongside a subjective account of running an urban walking group in the twenty-first century. These chapters are very different from each other in form and writing style and reflect the heterogeneity of psychogeographic writing today.

EIGHT

Psychogeography Adrift

Negotiating Critical Inheritance in a Changed Context

Christopher Collier

Psychogeography was codified in the mid-twentieth century to explore the effects of spatiotemporal situations on subjectivity and enjoyed a resurgence in the United Kingdom during the 1990s. It has seen further renewal within contemporary culture, particularly in conjunction with the development of its own tentative canon as a literary subgenre. Debate on the 'recuperation' of psychogeography has occurred between various practitioners, partially coloured by the polemical approach of the practice's early avant-garde propagators.

I propose that both sides of such a debate are somewhat problematic. First, the 'literary' conception of psychogeography as an artistic tradition not only tends to disavow its radical Marxist heritage but also fails to account for the conditions of its 1990s reemergence, fundamentally based as they were in social praxis and politicized material culture.

Second, however, decrying psychogeography's fundamentally 'literary' or 'artistic' dimension as recuperation is also unsatisfactory, implying a fall or troubling deviation from definitive, political origins. Such notions of recuperation deploy a neat, stagist narrative at odds with the manner of psychogeography's emergence and proliferation. Focusing on psychogeography as a primarily *critical* practice that has been recuperated potentially fails to acknowledge its immanent, open and prefigurative dimensions. It also glosses over a number of developments since the 1950s and thus risks trapping psychogeography in the ideology critiques of a former age.

By briefly reexamining the conditions of psychogeography's renewal in the 1990s, looking at its embeddedness in contemporaneous social praxis, I argue that psychogeography *is* literary but in an iterative, excessive sense—as what one might tentatively call 'infraliterary,' that is 'literature' as a material, social activity and a condition of possibility for collective subjectivation and resistance. By using this term *infraliterary*, I mean to imply the submerged, amorphous, material basis of communication networks and everyday resistance that, as Stevphen Shukaitis notes, is already apparent in former Situationist Raoul Vaneigem's description of an 'infralanguage,' around which 'declarations of power dance wildly' when they cannot grasp or define its contents (Shukaitis 2009, 194; Vaneigem n.d., 24). This, Shukaitis implies, corresponds with the conception of 'infrapolitics' articulated by James Scott (1990) and Robin D. G. Kelley (2002): '[T]he partially hidden public sphere . . . a space that is somewhat encoded or otherwise made less comprehensible and legible to the view of those in power' (Shukaitis 2009, 209). What I intend is not literature in the sense of a necessarily individualized, commercially or academically published discourse but something more akin to a literary 'dark matter,' to appropriate Gregory Sholette's metaphor, an underground potentiality, an undercommons related to what Stewart Home—deploying the Russian term for clandestine, self-published literature—labels 'samizdat' (Sholette 2011; Home 1991, 102). I propose that this practice has functioned as the material cultural and social basis that nourishes psychogeography's more visible literary or artistic 'tradition.'

Drawing on elements of postautonomist thought and deconstructive critique, I argue that the material form of psychogeographic praxis destabilizes fixed ontologies of enclosure and recuperation, in a sense exceeding ontological questions, whether of origin or of nature, in favour of strategic, de- and recompositional ones. Paradoxically, this might entail looking for origins and definitions if only to disprove their legitimacy.

LOOKING FOR SCHRÖDINGER'S CAT IN A DARK ROOM

The term *psychogeography* travels with baggage: that of its most definitive codification by the French postwar avant-garde. At least for the word's codifiers—the avant-garde group the Letterist International (LI) and its more well-known successor, the 1957–1972 Situationist International (SI)—psychogeography was conceived as a critical strategy, part of a total critique of society, in which specialist activities, such as art or literature, were part of a 'spectacular' regime that had to be abolished. Owing to traces of this codification, psychogeography's operability as an oppositional technique and its political purchase are, therefore, concerns that inhere within the term itself, colouring subsequent considerations on it.

These traces slowly fade over time, but, like radiation, they prove stubborn, powerful and sometimes unpredictable.

Sixty years on, psychogeography has never truly been left behind. If not left, however, perhaps it has often led down a few blind alleys or up various garden paths. As a result, many have criticized the term and its associations. Even those for whom it has proved most lucrative, such as London-based writer, filmmaker and possibly the most famous contemporary 'psychogeographer' Iain Sinclair, have described it as mere branding (Sinclair 2011). To many, contemporary psychogeography's increased visibility is an indication that it has been 'recuperated'—defused and diffused into the 'spectacle' of capitalist cultural discourse and commodity production, incorporated into academia and the cultural industries and thus stripped of critical power. In 1978, the most posthumously prominent Letterist and Situationist Guy Debord claimed, '[T]heories are made only to die in the war of time' (2003, 150). No doubt he would have judged psychogeography, given its proliferation as a cultural artefact, to be well and truly dead.

Except, of course, it isn't. Despite, and perhaps because of, this continual drip-feed of critique, psychogeography refuses to disappear—in the words of artist-psychogeographer Laura Oldfield Ford, 'It goes in cycles, it never really goes away' (Ford 2010, 36). It returns like a recurring apparition, a spectre. As academic and practitioner of psychogeography (or what he reterms *mythogeography*) Phil Smith implies, its practices have become a zombie-like corpse, ambling on, ever in a fruitless process of being remurdered (Smith 2010a; Smith 2010b). Sinclair's books sell more than ever, psychogeographic filmmaker Patrick Keiller recently completed a major retrospective at the Tate, and writer Will Self—onetime author of a newspaper column named *Psychogeography*, along with a book of the same name—as of 2012 leads a module at Brunel University dedicated to psychogeography.

Debord was thus only half right when he suggested that the 'S.I. is like radioactivity: one speaks little of it, but one detects traces of it almost everywhere' (1979). In fact, it seems rather more spoken about than he anticipated, and far from being thought of as dangerous or 'radioactive,' their ideas are now considered a 'national treasure' (Rousell 2009). Yet it is of little surprise that the so-called spectacle should want to 'treasure' radioactive material carefully, interning it in bibliographic bunkers or carefully managing its proliferation for its own ends. As Sadie Plant puts it, '[A]nything which is totally invulnerable to recuperation cannot be used in contestation either' (1992, 180). For Shukaitis, this confirms the proposition of the Situationists' critical interlocutor Jean Barrot (Gilles Dauvé) that 'revolutionary ideas deal with real problems with which counterrevolution is confronted . . . the subversive moment will only reappropriate them by its own practical and theoretical development'

(Barrot 1996, 47; Shukaitis 2009, 201). Perhaps there is life in the old cat yet?

So which is it: dead or alive? Again one is presented with this constant doubling and instability; psychogeography continually seems to present as dialectical, yet remains forever troubled by its own destabilization, the dialectic made unstable by the radioactive traces that haunt it. In this sense perhaps it might actually be better understood as *triolectical*, to follow the notion constructed by onetime Situationist Asger Jorn. For Jorn, building on the theory of complementarity put forward by Danish physicist Niels Bohr, it is the triolectical third point that in quantum physics renders something ontologically (un)decidable between two competing states. To mix physics metaphors somewhat, it is my intention that, in looking again at psychogeography's endurance and reemergence, this chapter will function as just such a triolectical observation point, rendering its dark matter temporarily visible, yet without necessarily stabilizing it.

I propose, therefore, that the apparently vital problem of psychogeography's pulse contains within it the answer, and this answer is the deferral to a different register and in many ways a more profound problem. The register is that of the political, and the problem becomes no longer the binary one of whether psychogeography is dead or alive, recuperated or true to some foundational purity, or even whether art can kill the Situationist International. It is no longer a case of arguing over Schrödinger's cat, locked up in the closet with the SI's decomposing isotope. The question is better posed as whether psychogeography — this playful concept defined by a game designer and self-proclaimed strategist — can be *strategically* operative, or, instead, whether it must concede game over.

ADRIFT BENEATH A SYLLABUS SEA

As far as psychogeography is concerned, traces are indeed detectable everywhere, not least as the proliferation of the term attests. Yet it was always already a trace; psychogeography is literary in a sense that far exceeds the canonical constraints that make up a syllabus at Brunel University. Fundamentally, psychogeography manifests a process of dérive, and yet this statement is not as straightforward as it might appear; words mean different things in different contexts, rendered legible or meaningless by the triolectical third position: their realization — or becoming — in strategy. In many ways, the problem of psychogeography is a problem of definition.

In 1955, Debord selected the term *psychogéographie* to describe the 'study of the precise laws and specific effects of the geographical environment, whether consciously organized or not, on the emotions and behavior of individuals' (Debord 2006, 8). The aim was to understand how power and ideology were sedimented in the city's physical form, thus circumscribing possibilities for autonomous subjectivation beyond the spatial logic of capitalism. Debord claimed the term was the second-language invention of an 'illiterate Kabyle,' whose attraction, he suggests, lay in the fact it was 'charmingly vague' (ibid.). It was perhaps this 'vagueness' that motivated Merlin Coverley (2006) to publish the only sustained attempt at a historicization and consolidation of psychogeography. Debatably, however, this study threw up the term's openness far more than it pinned it down.

Coverley began his study citing the very anecdote recited earlier concerning Debord's attraction to the term's vagueness. It serves to link the origin of psychogeography with Debord and the mid-twentieth-century Parisian avant-garde, while at the same time undermining such origins. Coverley's study was a broadening of psychogeography away from a politicized context, situating it as an ongoing, primarily literary style and, importantly, identifying it with earlier authors who predate Debord's definition and Situationist practice.

Thus Coverley rewrites history, inasmuch as any writing of history is an act of rewriting, and even in their earliest defining texts on psychogeography, the Letterists were drawing many preexisting literary and artistic practices under its umbrella. Coverley rightly shows psychogeography cannot be reduced to the LI's and SI's words or practice, but it always already exceeded their definition. When something called *psychogeography* came into being, it discovered it had already existed for decades, if not hundreds of years. To borrow from E. P. Thompson, like the working class, it did not 'rise like the sun at an appointed time. It was present at its own making' (1964, 9). In as much as Coverley's *Psychogeography* has proved influential, the performativity of any historical account becomes evident. Like the trioletician's eye, perhaps, it determines that which it delineates. Coverley's particular emphasis on psychogeography's *literary* genealogy usefully illustrates, but also somewhat produces, the reorientation of the term as understood in a contemporary UK context.

In this vein, one might cast psychogeography as having been transformed into a fundamentally literary phenomenon, which therefore could be seen as a retreat from political practice—recuperation. In the absence of an explicitly revolutionary, practical orientation, this literary status arguably contains the danger of psychogeography's irrelevance and idealism. To an extent I would agree, and yet I argue that a certain capacity for 'literary' iteration also actually enables psychogeography to evade reification in a singular, static and calcifying definition, offering an *ongoing* radical and strategic potential, as I now outline.

In Debord's early definition, at least, he specifically posits psychogeography as materialist praxis not completely in opposition to, but instead a dialectical sublation of, the 'farcical literary revolutions' (2006, 11–12) of the surrealists. There was thus no total break between surrealism and the SI; the difference was one of strategic orientation. It would be the role of the LI and SI to realize psychogeography's literary heritage in and through a revolutionary praxis—that is, more than simply imagined, it would be taken to, and from, the streets with the ultimate aim of materially transforming them.

In this sense, one might understand psychogeography's 'origins' as neither and both literary and nonliterary. As such, these 'origins' cannot be understood in a definitive, ontologically self-sufficient sense, but rather as the amorphous matter from which psychogeography as praxis diverted, derived and dérived. Paradoxically, therefore, those seeking to return to an originary, 'radical' and purely political psychogeography can only end up disproving the very possibility.

Even if in attempting to evade this literary heritage, the quest for origins leads to Debord, and from him to the 'illiterate' acquaintance who lends an apparent extraliterary immediacy or authenticity of speech, such a task also undermines itself. While the primary orality of the term *psychogéographie* was foregrounded by Debord, in his deferral to its anonymous, illiterate progenitor, I would heed the warnings of Jacques Derrida when he counsels against accepting the apparent primacy and presence of speech. Neither literary nor extraliterary, it is this notion that leads me back to the 'infraliterary' condition of psychogeography I am suggesting.

To heed Derrida's proposition would be to acknowledge that psychogeography, as a neologism grafted onto a literary multiplicity, has always been 'literary' but also excessive and irreducible. The tale of its invention serves to illustrate that it cannot be reduced to a self-contained concept or the political intent of an originating subjectivity. The evasive quality of psychogeography's terminology is testified to by a felicitous coincidence of language; Derrida deploys the same word by which the Letterists described their primary psychogeographic methodology—*dérive*, or drift—to suggest citability, the ability to shift context and to remake context anew (Derrida 1997, 69). Psychogeography appears as praxis for the SI, yet its literary articulation can also be understood as the material condition of its citability, complicating any simple dichotomy between words and practice, original and copy.

When I graft the term *dérive* into English as a French loan word, it equally transforms its context. *Dérive* connotes more than its direct translation, *drift*. *Drift* is passive, to be carried along, whereas *dérive* suggests drive. Thus while still containing the notion of a path constrained by external forces, it also implies a certain insurgent agency, a welling up from below.

Potlatch, the LI journal, in May 1956 contained the following:

'Towards a lettrist lexicon' [1956]

deriver: to divert water (13th cent., Job; gramm. fig. etc.), derivation (1377, L.) -atif (15th cent.), from Latin derivare, -atio, -ativus, in a proper and fig. sense (from rivus, stream).

deriver: to remove from the water's edge (14th cent. B), comp. of rive (water's edge).

deriver: (mar.) to drift (16th cent., A. d'Aubigne, var. of driver), infl. by Eng. drive (push). Der: derive, -atio (1690, Furetiere).

deriver: to undo what is riveted. See river. (Unsigned 1956)

To 'dé-rive' implies, as *Potlatch* notes, a kind of bursting of the banks, an undoing of what is riveted. This places the dérive as the correlate of that other key Letterist concept or tactic—détournement, which is to hijack, to divert. *Détourner*, to 'turn from,' and undoing the riveted are akin. They are about changing a flow of time, of life, of history, into a flood of histories; the dérive breaks the levies, while détournement is 'waiting for you at the turning,' as the SI put it in 1960 (Sadler 1999, 41). This turning is also to dérive, to 'go for a turn,' a walk—that is, in Italian, *in giro*; in Latin, *in girum*—to draw the magic circle, the repeating iteration, the palindrome, we are returned to the start, 'to be gone through again from the beginning,' as the subtitle reads at the end of Debord's masterwork (2003, 193). It is the spectre (re)turning in the night, consumed by fire: *in girum imus nocte et consumimur igni*. Hence, perhaps, dérive is a puzzle that contains within it like a fractal the proliferating radioactive contamination of psychogeography.

Like the river from which it is linguistically derived, dérive contains a sense of flowing from—as in 'to derive a word'—but its river is that of Heraclitus: No one ever steps in the same river twice. In this respect it carries part of Derrida's sense when he uses the word *dérive* to describe an iteration (that is to say, an opening), the impossibility of reducing an entity to a singular, self-contained essence, precisely in the fact that words are not fixed but contain the inherent possibility of drift through infinite contexts, which can be remade by the performative iteration of such words (Derrida 1988, 8). 'Every sign, linguistic or non-linguistic, spoken or written . . . can be cited,' he claims. '[I]n doing so it can break with every given context, engender new contexts to infinity' (ibid., 12). For Derrida, it is precisely the 'essential drift bearing on writing as an iterative structure' that leaves it 'cut off from all absolute responsibility, from consciousness as ultimate authority' (ibid., 243).

It is the citability of language that contains the possibility of difference: that is, the determined and yet indeterminate event, both originary and derived, the decomposing isotope. This informs Derrida's ambition to go beyond a metaphysics of presence; he states, 'Once this parasitism or fictionality can always add another parasitic or fictional structure— what elsewhere I call "supplement of the code"—everything is possible against the language police: for example "literatures" or "revolutions" that as yet have no model' (1988, 243). His linking of 'literatures' and 'revolutions' is important here, as Gayatri Spivak (1980) notes, in that it makes explicit the ambivalent potential that a deconstruction of the oppositional nature of aesthetic and sociopolitical can activate. The supplement here is a familiar feature of Derrida's deconstruction project; it is the spectre, the trace, the pharmakon—poison as well as remedy—that breaks down hierarchical binary oppositions, such as presence and absence, psychogeography's life and death. Perhaps this is akin to the triolectical position of the strategist suggested earlier. Psychogeography maintains a radical potentiality, precisely through a proliferation of infraliterary citations and iterations that keep it open to strategic reconfiguration and recomposition.

UNDER THE (INFLUENCE OF) COUNTERCULTURE, AN INFRALITERARY INFRASTRUCTURE

Psychogeography's 1990s reemergence is more comprehensible when one considers it this way: as part of a proliferating infraliterature. It endures as both poison and remedy, a dark matter that nourishes ongoing recuperation—the enclosure and appropriation of multiple, often indistinct practices into marketable, individualized formats—but also, at given moments, a collectively elaborated strategic coalescence and recomposition for which this continual internal differing provides the social and material infrastructure.

The public literary reprise of psychogeography would unlikely have occurred without the 'countereconomy of creative exchange' that simultaneous to the neoliberal counterrevolution and transforming possibilities for oppositional politics grew within the international Mail Art movement and a burgeoning alternative press between the 1970s and 1990s (Backhouse 2011; Triggs 2010; Dickinson 1997).

Fluxus activities and the parodic New York Correspondence School had provided the extrainstitutional material and social field and conceptual apparatus from which the Mail Art network would develop (Home 1991, 69–70). This blossomed, in turn, into the language games, plagiarism, performative counter- and self-institutions and what Marco Deseriis labels 'improper names' of Neoism and related movements (Deseriis 2012). Likewise, preserving and developing the material, social and conceptual infrastructure of 1960s counterculture, the alternative press and self-publishing continued to cohere around a number of more or less localized but interlinked publications and cultural scenes. This reached new levels of vitality with the growth of renewed DIY, antiauthoritarian social practice in punk and postpunk subcultures.

Former Scottish Situationist Alexander Trocchi had actively disseminated Situationist ideas to key figures in the alternative press during the 1960s through his Project Sigma (Robertson 1995). Likewise, such groups as the onetime English section of the SI — later King Mob — and their publications *Heatwave* and *King Mob Echo* had carried Situationist ideas into the 1970s UK underground. One member, Chris Gray (1974), also published an early translation of key SI writings, illustrated by Jamie Reid, himself involved with the self-published Situationist-influenced *Suburban Press*. These traces received well-documented appropriation by Reid's later collaborator and fellow former King Mob associate — later Sex Pistols manager — Malcolm McLaren as part of the aesthetic identification of punk, but were something that exceeded these individuals in important, if less obvious, ways. What this illustrates is that, while punk might in one way be cast as a recuperation of Situationist concepts, it was also a condition of their continuing vitality. Throughout the 1980s, punk-influenced social networks, often constituted via the circulation and production of independent publications, continued to be central in maintaining, proliferating and transforming traces of Situationist thought, if to a lesser extent psychogeography per se.

As for psychogeography itself, similarly underground, autonomous publishing — perhaps what Deseriis adapting from Gilles Deleuze and Félix Guattari calls a 'minor literature' — also revived its practice (Deseriis 2012, 148). Existing at a third pole between formalized, social subjections of public discourse and individual, private subjectivations, glimpses of such a 'minor literature' are visible during the late 1980s in the works of postpunk self-publisher Tom Vague in his *Vague* fanzine or Stewart Home, active in the Neoist movement, in the *Smile* publications.

It was this form of writing that went beyond the political and artistic inheritance of the SI at the turn of the 1990s, uniting the two into something different and new — that was neither and both — in the form of a psychogeographic revival. On the one hand, it went beyond the very limited engagements with psychogeography undertaken by the UK post- and pro-situ political groupsicles and publishing initiatives of the 1970s and 1980s — including but not limited to Hapt, the Black Hand Gang, *Omphalos*, *Anti Clock-wise*, Pleasure Tendency, BM Combustion, BM Blob, BM Chronos, *The Spectacular Times* and *Here and Now* (Robertson 1995; Goaman 2003). On the other, it also exceeded more mainstream, artistic emergences of SI ideas, such as the 1989 Pompidou/ICA retrospective.

It is worth noting that, in conjunction with the renewed public interest in the SI evoked by the 1989 exhibition, both Home and Vague interviewed the original English Situationist and apparent sole member of the initial incarnation of the London Psychogeographical Association (LPA), Ralph Rumney (Home 1989; Vague 1990). It can be speculated that their renewed interest in Rumney catalysed their attraction to psychogeography at this time. Home, in particular, would have recognized premonitions of his Neoist activities in the dissimulative autoinstitution of Rumney's LPA.

Ultimately it was Home who perhaps did most to both unite and deconstruct these strands of the SI's legacy—the artistic and political—and it was he, and even more so his regular collaborator Fabian Tompsett, who opted to specifically re-cite and re-site psychogeography, initiating its creative reimagining and subcultural proliferation in the early 1990s.

This revived interest in psychogeography inherited from the Neoist experiments a '"mythopoetic" mode of counter-institutional intervention' that, as Jim Backhouse notes, appeared to echo Debord's call for theory to be made 'unacceptable' to capitalist discourse (Backhouse 2011, 7). This was something Home and Tompsett would later articulate directly, as the 'Unacceptable Face of Contemporary Psychogeography' ('Sucked' 1996). Taking on Neoism's collectively elaborated and experimental practices, as well as contemporaneous influences from such occultist experiments as Thee Temple ov Psychick Youth, this nascent new wave of psychogeography integrated this with the SI material circulating through various political groupings. Among these were the London Workers Group and *Workers Playtime*, which in the 1980s had enabled Home to become familiar with a wider Situationist-influenced underground (Home 2001, 58). If Home was more artistically aware, then it was Tompsett who, as part of the London Workers Group and the more politically active of the two, would be still more integral to the psychogeographic revival in the United Kingdom through his performative reincarnation of Rumney's London Psychogeographical Association.

If UK counterculture lived on in alternative publications after 1968, its attempt at wholesale political recomposition appeared cut short. In Italy, however, almost uniquely in the West, such antagonisms were afforded space to expand and develop. Aspects of the emergent Autonomia movement explored possibilities for a direct, immanent politics beyond discredited representational schemas and at a moment of working-class atomization and de- and recomposition. The legacy of Autonomia's Free Radio Alice was an important influence on Italy's own resurgent counterculture during the 1990s, drawing upon creative and autonomous inter-subjectivation from the collectively elaborated media practices of 1977 and their elaboration of 'postmedia' channels following the crackdown on oppositional tendencies by the Italian state (Backhouse 2011, 9). Similar counterinstitutional and internally differing networks, emergent also from punk and Mail Art, developed Neoist ideas on multiple names and produced the likes of Luther Blissett or the Transmaniacs collective.

In turn, throughout the 1990s, these Italian activities cross-fertilized UK-based practices, such as the LPA, through the self-same networks. In London, Tompsett's LPA activities were supplemented by running his own press, Unpopular Books, and his role coediting the short-lived psychogeographical roundup *Transgressions: A Journal of Urban Exploration* (with Alastair Bonnett), along with his participation in print co-ops at Union Place and the 121 Centre in Brixton. This, alongside his background with the London Workers Group—with its proliferation of politicized printers and connection to the Rising Free bookshop, as well as several autonomous publications and social spaces—attests to the importance of an infraliterary infrastructure to the reemergence of psychogeography.

Meanwhile, in Manchester, Manchester Area Psychogeographic likewise emerged from the independent publishing and music scene around such figures as Bob Dickinson, who had himself been heavily involved in the alternative press on such titles as *City Fun*. On the South Coast, the Equi-Phallic Alliance and, later, Proles for Modernism were primarily an elaboration of poet Andrew Jordan, whose desktop-published newsletter, *The Listening Voice*, offered complex meditations on ideology, poetry and landscape. In Nottingham, the Nottingham Psychogeographical Unit also self-published a newsletter and was the product (at least in part, it would seem) of an Italian translator and design student living in the United Kingdom. Even Sinclair, the figure who has become arguably the best-known name in Anglophone psychogeography, had his own practice very much sustained in the early days by self-publishing and an underground poetry scene (Hay 2012). He attributes the revived popularity of psychogeography to the milieu described previously. His books became synonymous with these emergent subcultural streams, and the newly fashionable term *psychogeography* provided a convenient label (Barfield 2008).

Appearing as neoliberalism was cementing its dominance globally, the LPA and related psychogeographical outfits can be understood as examining experimental forms of political recomposition in changing circumstances—seeking revolutions that as yet had no model. Employing the pseudonym Richard Essex, Tompsett and the LPA developed an innovative iteration of psychogeography, reinterpreting the practice through intentionally convoluted occultist narratives, provocatively wedded to a humorous appropriation of revolutionary tropes and language. The result was magico-Marxism—an expression Alastair Bonnett attributes to a review in *Transgressions* in 1996 (Bonnett 2009, 61; Bin 1996, 120–21). This 'mythopoesis' was a 'satirical deconstruction' of both esoteric conspiracies and a dogmatic adherence to leftist political ontologies and grandiose, teleological posturing (Home 1997b, 9). The effect is complex. It appears to concurrently mock the SI's more totalizing rhetorical excesses but also, as Home speculates, to inoculate their practice against academic banalization (Home 1998). In this respect one might cast it as a kind of 'guerrilla ontology,' echoing the style of Robert Anton Wilson, whose conspiratorial narratives provided an ambiguous, if notable, influence on the 1990s psychogeographical milieu (Home 1997a, 57).

The central effect of this 'guerrilla ontology' was a critique of programmatic leftism and the danger of its deterioration into mere metaphysics or stylistic clichés. Arguably, however, endeavours were made by these 1990s psychogeographers to circumvent the risk of individualization and relativism entailed in such a project. These comprised experiments with innovative forms of collectivity consistent with the contemporary capitalist configurations they attempted to oppose. Brian Holmes has designated the tactical use of multiple names, communicative connectivity and collective personalities characteristic of the 1990s psychogeography as the creation of 'collective phantoms.' His formulation indicates how such psychogeographic practices tried to reimagine a resistive post-Fordist political subjectivation without falling back on stable ontologies, such as a metaphysical, humanist idea of the self (Holmes 2002, 32). Holmes understands these manifestations as struggles to resist the contemporary conditions of labour, or what Franco Berardi identifies as the cellular, depersonalized and recombinant fragments, or fractalizations, of microlabour that the networked connectivity and transhuman interfaces of the Internet made possible (Berardi 2011, 35). Much 1990s psychogeography attempted to address the challenge posed to traditional revolutionary agency by post-Fordism precisely through this construction of a networked and transindividual political subject.

Contemporaneous with the so-called organizational, postanarchist 'turn,' which Gavin Grindon among others has outlined, the pursuit of an immanent politics characterized a portion of these 1990s activities (Grindon 2008, viii). It was manifested in attempts at a prefigurative subjectivation and repudiated a programmatic unmasking of ideology. Yet perhaps the risk of such moves, made evident by the collective phantoms and their efforts to found a deterritorialized resistive practice, is the capacity to function simply as a mirror of the networked neoliberalism they attempted to oppose.

MINOR CONFLICTS, MAJOR CONTRADICTIONS — SOME CONCLUDING REMARKS

This consistent tension, as noted by Backhouse, permeated many of the practices touched on earlier (Backhouse 2011, 4). On the one hand, there was the collective elaboration of direct, immanent experiments in collective subjectivation, drawing on the legacies of Autonomia and avant-garde infraliterary activities. On the other, there was the maintenance of a necessary invisibility and instability of such practices in a negative, critical withdrawal—perhaps linguistically suggested in the negative prefix of *dé-rive* and *dé-tournement*—that might offer a structural antagonism to the machinations of capital on a macro level. This went beyond the calcified forms of programmatic leftist representation, attempting to realize

Jorn's demand for 'open creation' as a means of establishing a third pole of subjectivation beyond both public, discursive politics and individual artistic practice (Jorn and Tompsett 1994). Where a Situationist psychogeography had contained both a macrocritical and minor-immanent approach, in keeping with their wider programme, it tended toward the former. The activities of psychogeography's 1990s revival redressed this balance in line with sociopolitical and economic developments, although on occasion arguably tending too far in the opposite direction.

So where now for a practice of psychogeography? I would argue there *is* life in the old cat yet, although it is neither my intention nor my place to teach it any new tricks. The underground that sustained the 1990s psychogeographic revival is now more or less decomposed. Once it was the very invisibility of this underground that sustained the open possibility of strategic recomposition. Now perhaps the imperative lies in making visible its traces and the way in which it did sustain recomposed practices in order to enable future recompositions. I have suggested that the renewed visibility of the SI and the activities of Ralph Rumney around 1989 and 1990 potentially catalysed the recomposition of a strategic psychogeography but ultimately, also, its recuperation from the proliferation of minor, infraliterary instances. So, too, a renewed visibility of 1990s practices and their own proliferation of infraliterary developments could produce, if not a revitalized strategic orientation for psychogeography—were this to occur, it would necessarily be a collective project—then at least a renewal of the conditions of its possibility. The problem becomes, therefore, not how to reinvent or revive psychogeography, but rather how to maintain and sustain the increasingly fragmented and enclosed social and material base from which not just psychogeography but a variety of other, perhaps more urgent, political recompositions might emerge.

BIBLIOGRAPHY

Backhouse, James. 2011. 'The "Collective Phantom": Convergent Networks, Counterculture and the Recomposition of the Radical Political Subject.' Master's thesis, Kingston University.

Barfield, Steven, ed. and introduction. 2008. 'Psychogeography: Will Self and Iain Sinclair in Conversation with Kevin Jackson.' *Literary London: Interdisciplinary Studies in the Representation of London* 6 (1). http://www.literarylondon.org/london-journal/march2008/sinclair-self.html.

Barrot, Jean. 1996. 'Critique of the Situationist International (1979).' In *What Is Situationism? A Reader*, edited by Stewart Home, 24–62. Edinburgh: AK Press.

Berardi, Franco. 2011. *After the Future*. Oakland, CA: AK Press.

Bin, Dusty. 1996. 'Review of London Psychogeographical Association Newsletter and Manchester Area Psychogeographic.' *Trangressions: A Journal of Urban Exploration* (2/3): 120–21.

Bonnett, Alastair. 2009. 'The Dilemmas of Radical Nostalgia in British Psychogeography.' *Theory, Culture and Society* 26 (1): 45–70.

Coverley, Merlin. 2006. *Psychogeography*. Harpenden: Pocket Essentials.

Debord, Guy. 1979. 'To Michel Prigent.' Not Bored! www.notbored.org/debord-7December1979.html.

———. 2003. 'In Girum Imus Nocte et Consumimur Igni.' In *Guy Debord: Complete Cinematic Works*, translated by Ken Knabb, 133–205. Edinburgh: AK Press.

———. 2006. 'Introduction to a Critique of Urban Geography.' In *Situationist International Anthology*, edited and translated by Ken Knabb, 8–12. Berkeley, CA: Bureau of Public Secrets.

Derrida, Jacques. 1988. *Limited Inc*. Evanston, IL: Northwestern University Press.

———. 1997. *Of Grammatology*, translated by Gayatri Spivak. Baltimore: John Hopkins University Press.

Deseriis, Marco. 2012. 'Improper Names: Collective Pseudonyms and Multiple-Use Names as Minor Processes of Subjectivation.' *Subjectivity* 5 (2): 140–60.

Dickinson, Bob. 1997. *Imprinting the Sticks: The Alternative Press beyond London*. Aldershot: Arena.

Ford, Laura Oldfield. 2010. 'Laura Oldfield Ford: Interview.' *Tough Crowd* (Spring/Summer): 34–36.

Goaman, Karen. 2003. 'The Old World Is Behind You: The Situationists and Beyond in Contemporary Anarchism.' PhD thesis, University of London.

Gray, Christopher, ed. 1974. *Leaving the 20th Century: The Incomplete Work of the Situationist International*. London: Free Fall.

Grindon, Gavin. 2008. Introduction to *Aesthetics and Radical Politics*, edited by Gavin Grindon, vii–xvii. Newcastle-upon-Tyne: Cambridge Scholars.

Hay, Duncan. 2012. 'Form, Place and Memory: Materialist Readings of Iain Sinclair's London Writing.' PhD thesis, University of Manchester.

Holmes, Brian. 2002. 'Unleashing the Collective Phantom (Resistance to Networked Individualism).' *Mute* 1 (24). www.metamute.org/editorial/articles/unleashing-collective-phantom-resistance-to-networked-individualism.

Home, Stewart. 1989. 'Interview with Ralph Rumney.' *Art Monthly*, no. 127 (June): 3–4.

———. 1991. *The Assault on Culture: Utopian Currents from Lettrism to Class War*. Stirling: AK Press.

———. 1997a. *The House of Nine Squares: Letters on Neoism, Psychogeography and Epistemological Trepidation*. London: Invisible Books.

———. 1997b. 'Mondo Mythopoesis.' *Variant* 2 (2): 9.

———. 1998. 'On the Mind Invaders Anthology: A Talk Originally Entitled "Mind Bending, Swamp Fever and The Ideological Vortext: How Avant-Bard Satire Blisters the Cheeks of the Aparatchiki."' Stewart Home Society. http://www.stewarthomesociety.org/ga/swamp.html.

———. 2001. *Jean Baudrillard and the Psychogeography of Nudism*. London: Sabotage Editions.

Jorn, Asger, and Fabian Tompsett. 1994. *Open Creation and Its Enemies: With Originality and Magnitude (on the System of Isou)*. London: Unpopular Books.

Kelley, Robin D. G. 2002. *Freedom Dreams the Black Radical Imagination*. Boston: Beacon Press.

Plant, Sadie. 1992. *The Most Radical Gesture: The Situationist International in a Postmodern Age*. London: Routledge.

Robertson, George. 1995. *The SI: Its Penetration into British Culture*. Edited by Stewart Home. San Francisco: AK Press.

Rousell, Fredrique. 2009. 'Debord, A Treasure.' Translated by Not Bored! *Liberation*. www.notbored.org/national-treasure.html.

Sadler, Simon. 1999. *The Situationist City*. Cambridge, MA: MIT Press.

Scott, James C. 1990. *Domination and the Arts of Resistance: Hidden Transcripts*. New Haven, CT: Yale University Press.

Sholette, Gregory. 2011. *Dark Matter: Art and Politics in the Age of Enterprise Culture*. Marxism and Culture. London: Pluto Press.

Shukaitis, Stevphen. 2009. *Imaginal Machines: Autonomy and Self-Organization in the Revolutions of Everyday Life.* London: Minor Compositions.

Sinclair, Iain. 2011. 'Once upon a Time in the Fields, Vol. 3 Feat. Iain Sinclair.' London Fields Radio. Accessed March 14, 2014. http://www.londonfieldsradio.co.uk/2010/05/20/from-the-archive-once-upon-a-time-in-the-fields-vol-3-feat-iain-sinclair.

Smith, Phil. 2010a. 'The Contemporary Dérive.' *Cultural Geographies* 17 (1): 103–22.

———. 2010b. *Mythogeography: A Guide to Walking Sideways.* Axminster: Triarchy Press.

Spivak, Gayatri Chakravorty. 1980. 'Revolutions That as Yet Have No Model.' *Diacritics* 10 (4): 20–49.

'Sucked.' 1996. Unpopular Books.

Thompson, E. P. 1964. *The Making of the English Working Class.* New York: Pantheon Books.

Triggs, Teal. 2010. *Fanzines.* London: Thames and Hudson.

Unsigned. 1956. 'Towards a Lettrist Lexicon. Potlatch: Bulletin of the Lettrist International.' *Not Bored!* May 7. http://www.notbored.org/lexicon.html.

Vague, Tom. 1990. 'On the Passage of a Few People through a Brief Moment in Time: Ralph Rumney: The Vague Interview.' *Vague* (June): 27–41.

Vaneigem, Raoul. n.d. [1979]. *Collection of Desires.* Richmond, VA: Paper Street.

NINE

Confessions of an Anarcho-Flâneuse, or Psychogeography the Mancunian Way

Morag Rose

THE LOITERERS RESISTANCE MOVEMENT

This chapter explores my experiences as a founding member, and continued participant in, the Loiterers Resistance Movement (LRM), a Manchester-based psychogeographical collective. The first time I heard the word *psychogeography*, I had a minor epiphany because it seemed to me to give a shape (albeit an amorphous one) to something I could feel on the streets but not quite define. It was 2005, and I was involved in running an autonomous, anarchist social centre that we constructed in a disused warehouse in Manchester as an attempt to create a noncommercial alternative space in the rapidly expanding neoliberal city. Around this time, I drew a Venn diagram to explain my conception of psychogeography (see figure 9.1).

I still believe this to be a good illustration of contemporary psychogeography's seductive interdisciplinary qualities, although it misses the vital all-encompassing circle of embodied experience. By this I mean the multisensual interaction produced through walking and its capacity to generate a relationship between self, space and left-behind traces: the reason I believe walking has terrific power as a kinaesthetic learning tool. At the time the LRM was founded, I was somewhat disillusioned and burned out from conventional activism and frustrated by what I felt was the limited impact of shouting (and indeed writing) about spatial justice and inequality. I wanted to explore the use of psychogeography as a

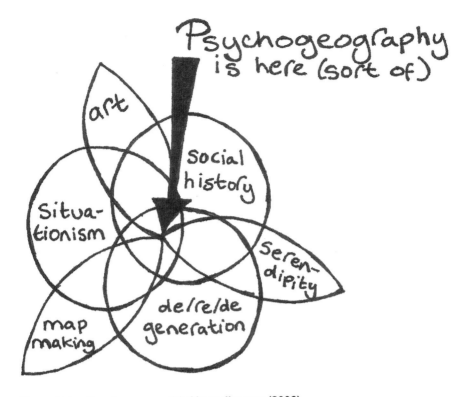

Figure 9.1. Psychogeographic Venn diagram (2006)

participatory tool to disseminate radical theories and stimulate critical debate. It was crucial to me that loitering was a form of stealth politics that hid its intention under ludic joy, inspired in part by the imperfect avant-garde neo-Marxism of the Situationists. It is important to acknowledge here that other Loiterers have different influences, motivations and memories. Early members included artists, activists, academics and a heterogeneous treasury of moochers who were curious about their environment. We wanted to be as open and welcoming as possible, and our fluid structure still reflects this ideal; people float in and out and define their own level of commitment. Some see loitering purely as an aesthetic or social activity, and, indeed, the convivial atmosphere during the post-dérive debrief, almost always held in the pub amid a cacophony of shared experiences, is very enticing. Many new, enduring and often unexpected alliances have formed during the course of our walks. For me, psychogeography primarily offered a form of public engagement with radical theory that was fun, irreverent and active, a praxis developed out of a desire to find appealing methods to critique the hegemonic view of the city.

Loiterers all have our own preoccupations, and I should also acknowledge a crucial personal influence. A key reason I felt alienated by much direct action is because I have a neurological disorder that limits my mobility. An affordance of my disability is an inability to walk fast, and I am unable to drive or cycle, meaning I spend a lot of time wandering the streets observing, absorbing, marking changes and developing a heightened sense of curiosity and attachment to the city. I am not a flâneur in the pure sense because a working-class, queer, disabled woman does not have the affordances of Benjamin's privileged subject, but I have adopted some of his habits, perhaps because at the birth of the LRM I had read very few key texts and was unaware they were not designed for the likes of me. Furthermore, I wanted to disrupt the activities of the street and playfully subvert them, and the social centre the LRM initially coalesced around provided a supportive environment encouraging cross-pollination, radical thinking, optimism and experimentation. It is worth mentioning here how the LRM got its name. An early compadre was returning to Australia because 'if you loiter in Brisbane you get a suntan, loiter in Manchester and you get an ASBO.' This encapsulated, lightly, something intrinsic to our spirits; we were fully aware of the many connotations loitering has but wanted to celebrate mindfulness and subversive leisure. Walking and playing should not be radical, but they can become so in a city designed for commerce and speed.

Loiterers love Manchester, but, like all cities, it is contradictory, chaotic and in constant flux. The city is made from a rich tapestry of intertwined stories created by a diverse cast of characters, human and otherwise, that have passed through. However, the palimpsest leaks and is messy; a dérive can begin to break through habit and convention to decode complex place narratives. Frederick Engels walked here, and later Ewan McColl spoke of using 'The Condition of the Working Class in England' as his Baedeker guide. Although the street layout may have changed somewhat, their metaphorical ghosts, and those of a million unnamed workers, continue to haunt Manchester, while the injustices they documented still prevail. How can we begin to unravel the stories they can tell? We could perhaps start by meeting outside the Harvey Nicholls, located in the shiny postbomb nirvana of Manchester City Centre, and think about whom we can see using the space and who is absent. Then we could walk for just twenty minutes, absorbing myriad changes in architecture, texture and emotional temperature before stumbling on a volunteer-run food bank within a community, where, according to Salford City Council's ('Ending Child Poverty' 2010) own website, around 60 percent of children live in poverty. Perhaps through observant, open-minded wandering, we can begin to see and feel more connected to our environment, more conscious of its complexities, to *know our place* and think about how we can (re)create it. More than any lecture or printed text, I believe walking as a methodology offers powerful impact and relevance, affording us a deeper appreciation of the nuances of our city. Place marketing can never do justice to this diversity and often actively seeks to avoid exploring the city's liminality and decay. Instead, regeneration policies seek to create an illusion of progress, of smoothness and comfort. For example, when CityCo (the quango responsible for managing Manchester City Centre) stated that its key aims included moving young people on from the Millenium Square and challenging begging on Market Street, they did not appear to care where people were transported to, as long as it did not affect commerce. In the wake of the 2011 riots, the most visible response from the council was an 'I Heart Manchester' marketing campaign to encourage shopping; the cause of the riots was complex, but this solution was risible and misplaced.

After our first expedition, the LRM issued the following communiqué on its website and via a series of flyers. It has gone through several iterations but remained substantially the same:

> We can't agree on what psychogeography means, but we all like plants growing out of the side of buildings, looking at things from new angles, radical history, drinking tea and getting lost; having fun and feeling like a tourist in your home town. Gentrification, advertising and blandness make us sad. We believe there is magick in the Mancunian rain. Our city is wonderful and made for more than shopping. We want to reclaim it for play and revolutionary fun. On the first Sunday of every month we go for a wander of some sort and we also organise occasional festivals, exhibitions, shows, spectacles, silliness and other random shenanigans. Please come and join us, everyone is welcome. (Loiterers Resistance Movement 2006)

The LRM website states, 'The LRM embark on psychogeographical drifts to decode the palimpsest of the streets, uncover hidden histories and discover the extraordinary in the banal. We aim to nurture an awareness of everyday space, (re)engaging with and (re)enchanting the city' (Rose 2012). I have worked professionally as a community development worker in local charities for more than fifteen years. This has led me to a passionate belief in encouraging grassroots cooperative and collective action, coupled with a strong desire to blur the boundaries between activists, academics and artists. For me, this is a key strength of the Situationist International's philosophy and fundamental to a politicized psychogeography, an integrated approach to Vaneigem's *The Revolution of Everyday Life* ([1967] 1983). I have a deep desire to democratize the practice of the dérive and reclaim it from the occult and for all classes and genders; an activist class or an artistic elite is as damaging as a cabinet full of millionaires. An uncomfortable undercurrent of misogyny and neocolonialism lurks within much psychogeography and has since its inception. The LRM intends to both challenge this idea and provide a walkable alternative.

Our dérives are always coproduced by participants, and although they may be initiated by an individual, the practice is nonhierarchical; as the walk progresses organically, positions fluctuate, conversations flow and movement is directed by consensus. Of course, we are not the first or the only people to do this, and I was directly influenced by the work of such artists as walkwalkwalk, Lottie Childs, Laura Oldfield Ford, Phil Smith and many others. Although psychogeography is most frequently associated with London and Paris, we also wanted to demonstrate its mutability and to tap into a rich history of walking the Mancunian Way. From the escape of a young De Quincey to the march of the Suffragettes, Peterloo participants trekking from the outer boroughs, the Kinder Tres-passers, Sebald's teaching, Morrissey's modern flânerie and Tony Wilson building Chtcheglov's Hacienda on the Rochdale Canal, the cultural practice of walking has shaped our genus loci. There have been overt psychogeographers, too, most prominently the poetic agit-prop of Man-chester Area Psychogeographic (MAP), which levitated the Corn Ex-change and left a rich archive to inspire the LRM. There are also many local artists and groups, including the Zedders, Manchester Modernist Society, Jane Samuels, Maureen Ward and Roger Bygott, for whom walk-ing is central to their aesthetic praxis.

In a most un-Situationist fashion, the LRM has welcomed this, never intending to compete and encouraging mutual support by declaring there is room enough for us all and our different psychogeographies within the myriad stories written on the streets through wandering. Col-laboration has always been important to us, and so we became involved in jointly organizing 'Territories Reimagined: International Perspectives' (TRIP; 2008), an ambitious conference and festival that took place at Man-chester Metropolitan University in 2008. TRIP and 'Get Lost!' are both community-facing fringe programmes that aim to bring together diverse psychogeographers from across the world, despite (and because of) the contradictions and conflict inherent in that mission. Conversations and controversies ignited by that gathering still resonate within the LRM to-day, although, tellingly, we have not attempted to work on that scale since. However, we do relish a sense of comradeship, albeit diffused, among contemporary psychogeographers and radical walkers. This is nurtured online, and we have enjoyed many inspiring, generous and occasionally heated debates via Facebook, Twitter and e-mail. These metaphysical dérives help illuminate and shape the action we care about most that happens, of course, on the street.

Loitering theory takes shape, and flight, on the first Sunday of every month, when we organize some kind of public dérive. The tactics differ every time, but this consistency and dedication has helped build a Man-cunian walking community, and I would like to express my heartfelt thanks to everyone who has contributed to this. I see the dérive as a tool for questioning, for opening dialogue, for exploring space: a tactic, not a solution, and I do not claim we will smash the spectacle simply by drifting through it, but together we can create a temporary autonomous zone, a space of inspiration, imagination and emergent possibilities.

THE PRAXIS OF LOITERING

The LRM uses a variety of methods to facilitate dérives on a first Sunday, including algorithmic walks, transposing maps, throwing dice, concentrating on specific senses and the use of what Phil Smith calls 'catapults' as stimuli (Smith 2010b). Sometimes there are more formal ludic interventions, such as the game of CCTV bingo (see figure 9.2), which was invented to explore the proliferation of surveillance in the city in a nondidactic way. The purpose was to provoke mindfulness and ask questions rather than simply condemn. The construction of fear and the dominance of the modern panopticon has been a recurring theme emergent through my walking, and I have become increasingly concerned with the psychological impact of the robotic all-seeing eye. As Jacobs's (1961) eyes on the street become nonhuman, it feels to me that the sidewalk ballet is diminished and the spectacle becomes ever more consuming. I am not suggesting loitering can solve this, but it can ask questions and provoke debate. I want to be playful rather than pedagogical, so I developed a game to be played anywhere. Find a camera, let its gaze direct your wandering, turn when you see another camera and take notes on your card when you spot certain varieties of apparatus, in the spirit of a subversive 'I-Spy' spotter's guide.

The camera is a conduit for wider discussions on the form, function and construction of public and private space in contemporary cities, epitomizing Foucauldian notions of decentralized, subtle forms of social control. However, these conversations need to be nuanced, as the spectacle seduces with pleasurable experiences, and perceived security is a priority for many when thinking about quality of place. Sousveillance (that is, the subversion of the gaze to watch the watcher) echoes the spatial détournement of the Situationist International and de Certeau's (1988) individual resistances subverting space. SI-style tactics have been utilized (knowingly or not) by a range of protest groups and artists, and CCTV bingo can be placed in this tradition. The game can be as unsettling as it is fun, raising awareness of the cameras and provoking questions about their ownership, effectiveness and efficacy. Common responses from participants include shock at their proliferation and a mild paranoia that stimulates a rich and nuanced conversation about privacy, ethics and surveillance. Contrasting issues of spatial justice are raised as we play together; however, I am not sure ludic interventions change perception or affective responses among the communities that coinhabit the space we wander within, especially as our intervention is so subtle.

The LRM invite you to play with no prize every time all new

CCTV BINGO

How to Play: Go for a walk anywhere you fancy. When you have found a good place to start look around you and find a CCTV camera. Follow its gaze and let it guide your wandering until you spot another one, then head in the direction it points you in until you see another camera showing you the way to go. Carry on in this manner until you have had enough or you have filled in every square on the game board with details of appropriate cameras, including when and where you spied them.

Please note: We have been playing this game for a while now and no harm has befallen us. We believe an open mind and curious nature are good things; the city is our playground to have fun in. However, we must always take care and be mindful of our environment. Don't be scared; it's common sense really. Always watch out for traffic, trip hazards and other people on the street. Please stay polite to everyone; respect other's boundaries and keep out of trouble! It is perfectly legal to take photographs in public places but be sensible and don't be intrusive. No loitering is worth putting yourself at risk. **Have fun and know your rights**

CCTV Bingo is bought to you thanks to a **Cornerhouse Micro Commission, supported by Paul Hamlyn Foundation**

CORNERHOUSE ARTFILMBOOKSFOODDRINK

phf Paul Hamlyn Foundation

Love from the loiterers resistance movement twitter@thelrm www.nowhere-fest.blogspot.com email loiter@hepzombie.co.uk on the first Sunday of every month we go for a walk...

Figure 9.2. CCTV bingo card, version 3 (front side; 2012)

The LRM does not always require a theme for first Sunday dérives; sometimes an aimless drift will reveal its own desire lines and secrets through synchronicities and open-minded observation. One recent intervention involved mapping our course by throwing metal discs with arrows on them. The game pieces were made from aluminium slugs produced through the manufacture of battery housings for electric sports cars. As an unfunded group that wants to encourage noncommercial activity and reduce consumption, we are always keen to repurpose materials, and there was a particularly delicious resonance to reclaiming automobile byproducts to celebrate the pedestrian. Like many psychogeographers, we tend to gravitate to edgelands and liminal spaces, to seek out blurry and forgotten places where cobbles peek out from under tarmac and buddleia (surely every postindustrial city's patron plant) blooms triumphantly after breaking through concrete and rust. Interestingly, on this occasion, the game kept dragging us back into the centre of retail activity and the bustle of commerce. With no key theme, our attention was repeatedly drawn to the absurd, anomalous and fantastical, finding the curious in the midst of the mundane. Even on Market Street (Manchester's core retail area), we found strange corners of buildings, hidden spaces, runic signs and mythological animals. We also find an abundance of revanchist architecture: newly erected walls to stop homeless people from taking shelter, subtle fortresses secured by design and street furniture too uncomfortable to sleep on. The uncovering of power structures, interrogating the everyday, conjuring the invisible into view and asking how we can make things better feels to me to be the very essence of loitering.

We have occasionally attempted to use a psychogeographical ontology to subvert heritage walks. Our approach is to make clear that history is permeable, plural and open to contestation. We seek to explore stories rarely told and invite contributions from participants. An example of this approach was the Manchester Modernist Heroines project, a collaboration between the Manchester Modernist Society; the LRM; and *Shrieking Violet*, a local arts and culture magazine. It rose out of our frustration about the lack of women in public narratives of Manchester. I conducted research into heritage tours of the area and found an almost total lack of female presence in terms of landmarks (statues, buildings, etc.) and the individuals featured (whether vernacular tales or the great and the good). We issued a public call for nominations of remarkable twentieth-century women and for advocates to celebrate them in a special edition of *Shrieking Violet*. We selected ten women with Manchester connections who excelled in fields not traditionally seen as female, such as aviation, architecture and modernist design. Most are relatively unknown to a general audience. My interest in walking as a cultural practice and a public engagement tool led to the curation of a tour based on the work of these ten women. It visited locations chosen for their symbolic value because in most cases there was no obvious memorial or anchor point, such as a blue plaque or home. By emphasizing resonance, memory, absence and affect, the tour complicated received notions of heritage trails by revealing history to be a subjective and affective construction. This multifaceted approach somewhat echoes the conception of space in the writing of Doreen Massey. One of our featured heroines, she was born in Wythenshawe, South Manchester, and her theories around gender, space and power permeated the walk, giving it an explicitly feminist emphasis. Another heroine, Marie Stopes, afforded the opportunity to complicate notions of achievement and celebrity; while acknowledging her important work in sexual health, I focused on *why* she advocated family-planning clinics, which included a belief in eugenics underpinned by classism, racism, anti-Semitism and hatred for disabled people. I made it clear on the tour that I do not celebrate someone for their biology. I also paid tribute to local women who cooperatively launched initiatives in working-class neighbourhoods to empower others and share knowledge about contraception. Their individual names are now largely lost to history. I have repeated the walk several times through popular demand, each iteration incorporating suggestions and stories from previous participants until it has evolved into something akin to an immersive theatrical performance.

REFLECTIONS ON LOITERING

Every loiterer's map becomes annotated by stories generously shared on expeditions. On the 'Heroines' walk, these were deeply touching reflections on inspirational women or the pernicious effects of sexism. Other wanders become richly embellished with memories provoked by encounters, comic observations, retelling/reappropriating 'official' narratives, streams of consciousness and vernacular folklore. The latter includes enthralling reports of Manchester's mysterious (and elusive) canal monster—something amazing, uncanny and unknowable lurking tantalizingly beneath the surface. We treat each tale respectfully; they influence future explorations and help construct our contribution to Manchester's palimpsest. However, the ephemeral nature of our dérives and an emphasis on the sensual, experiential and 'authentic' has made documentation and understanding the impact of the LRM a challenge, although many participants take photographs or audio recordings, collect paraphernalia, write personal reflections or produce other artefacts inspired by each walk. After organizing a series of three dérives for the Cornerhouse Arts Centre, I e-mailed a short survey to all the participants. Perhaps not the most robust methodology, but the response was encouraging. One hundred percent of people said they learned something new, and 75 percent said that it changed their view of the city. Everyone stated they would use the techniques learned in the future. Survey comments reinforced positive feedback during the dérives, and respondents explained how:

> I visited parts of the city I've never been to before, seeing how certain areas of the city connected together.

> I noticed new details and sensations; it was stimulating and inspiring, I enjoyed seeing it as a palimpsest.

> I experienced my route into work in a different way.

> It was a great experience sharing the walk with someone who knew the city differently; I saw it with pride and new eyes.

> When you walk like this, you readjust your focus and see things differently.

> Fascinating. I learnt some new streets of Manchester and thought about more than the surface, not just focusing on sight.

The dérives revealed several recurrent themes, including a ludic tendency waiting for release, suggesting many adults are secretly longing for permission to play out on the streets; a pleasure in edgelands and glimpses of the 'natural' incongruent with expectations of the urban environment; and an ambivalence toward the city and a fascination with place memory. These emerged organically, and I view this as a testament to the reflexive nature of the methodology. Further, comments provide a polyvocal account of the dérives, echoing the crystalline and multifaceted nature of the walks, making clear the embodied, subjective experience of participants and reflecting their agency.

The dérive offers a creative response to Massey's 'chance of space' (2005, 11) by temporarily rewriting the city, revealing its multiplicities and complicating the power relationships implicit in conventional cartography. Objectively knowing the city remains an impossibility; the dérive champions' localized attempts to (re)map the territory afford creative acts of self-determination reminiscent of de Certeau's (1988) small resistances. However, this elusive and contested practice raises many difficult questions, including a structural conundrum: Is the organized dérive an oxymoron? To acknowledge the drift and announce its starting point is surely to lose an element of unconsciousness, and so the pure dérive must be a mythological creature. Smith makes clear 'such a tension between an "aimless stroll" and an instrument of urban transformation is not a problem within the dérive; it is the work of it' (2010a, 107).

I suggest while the dérive has, in many ways, become detached from the overt political intent of the SI, this is a positive. Free from didactic and revolutionary polemic, it enables personal epiphanies and imaginative working more suited to our postmodernesque age. Debord (1955) made it clear that the SI were practicing 'not subordination to randomness but complete insubordination to habitual influences.' Psychogeography was initially intended to be a quasi-scientific method despite the subjective nature of the data, and I believe it can yield valuable evidence when seeking to interpret the underlying power structures of capitalism. The city is not deterministic, as de Certeau (1988) and others suggest; walking interprets and animates place, and the dérive does so using its own unique language, which triggers freedom to explore beyond the everyday, to break through the paradox of aimlessness with a purpose.

Bassett encapsulates the contradictions of utilizing dérive as a methodology with students as inevitably 'something of a compromise with Situationist principles, which were, after all, linked to forms of radical transgression' (2004, 403). However, my experience leads me to concur with Bassett's conclusion that the dérive has merit as a pedagogical tool; the work of Richardson (2013) reiterates this and suggests enticing new directions. Psychogeography as radical practice has mutated; it has a role enacting 'demands for the rights to the city, [which] require the production of an appropriate space' (Pinder 2005, 400). This raises bigger questions around the role psychogeography can and should play in regeneration while resisting recuperation, but this contested Floridian creativity that accelerates gentrification and widens social divide must be addressed elsewhere. Psychogeography does not have to be, and should not be, didactic, as it requires an abandonment of functional rules and an openness to *sense* the city and experience its flows. The conversations generated on the LRM's dérives demonstrate how powerful and beautiful this abandonment can be.

My work demonstrates the accessibility of psychogeography, which still remains an esoteric methodology with a reputation for being arcane and difficult. I believe this is a fallacy based on misunderstandings. The first of these arises from the SI themselves; some of their writing can appear abstracted and impenetrable. Solnit gives little space to Debord's 'pugnacious treatises' (2006, 212) and appears to take exception to combining cultural activity with radical intent. Nicholson is scathing, saying psychogeography is a 'nice idea, a clever idea, an art project, a conceit, but it had very little to do with any real experience of walking' (2011, 150). Both appear to suggest the dérive is an introspective indulgence, linking to wider suspicions of high art, but I want art that is accessible to everyone. It is disingenuous to remove practice from theory regarding psychogeography, as since its inception 'at the same time as being a form of action, it is a means of knowledge' (SI member Khatib, quoted in Andreotti and Costa 1996, 73). However, contemporary writers, such as Sinclair and Self, work to retain their claim to expert status through linguistic skill and other forms of cultural capital, exemplified by their rallying against the popularization of psychogeography while still building their personal profiles. There is an implicit irony in celebrity criticism of the spectacle, an oxymoron best challenged by a democratization of the

technique, a dismantling of barriers and a struggle to break through cognitive dissonance and mediated messages. The elite will always resist this
and raise alarm at the dangers of devaluation through proliferation; however, at the heart of this concern appears to be a tacit assumption that the
proletariat cannot be trusted with the power of the dérive. I dismiss this
and believe we should welcome an increased interest in spatial analysis;
I want a psychogeography that is accessible to everyone and truly becomes part of Vanegiem's *Revolution of Everyday Life*. The collective dérives that I coproduce with participants not only uncover power structures in the landscape but also dissolve group hierarchies and enable
individual agency, strength in the methodology Smith (2010a) celebrates.

This opening-up of wandering echoes debates revolving around the
(im)possibility of the flâneuse. Presently the dérive remains an esoteric
methodology, but I believe it has great potential. Massey criticizes the SI
for their pursuit of 'laddish thrills' (2005, 47), and it is true the language
and practice of masculinity still dominates the psychogeographic canon
and indeed other forms of geographical investigation. Mott and Roberts
(2013) provide a stimulating and resonant critique of this tendency within urban exploration. Without dismissing the embodied, and therefore
gendered, experiences of sexism and space (and to reinforce my call,
voiced loudly elsewhere, for a more explicitly feminist psychogeography), contemporary dérive practice can provide alternatives. The psychogeographer is not necessarily synonymous with the flâneur; group dérives in particular democratize the practice and destabilize power structures. Issues of safety, respectability and eroticism are depressingly still
valid, but the women I walk with are adamant they can, and will, embrace flânerie despite (and, indeed, sometimes because of) the challenges
and oppressions. Scalway (2002) identifies the fear of embarrassment and
the consequence of transgressing social roles as a key reason women may
not wish to wander, but she also describes the pleasure that can be had
when that fear is conquered. The communal walk itself breaks down
social barriers and elicits both sensations and conversations that can be
far reaching. I suspect participants become so embedded in their affective
experience, so entangled with the city, that the disinterested, haughty
label of the flâneur is not appropriate for either gender; however, such a
semantic debate distracts from the bigger issue. The flâneur and the
flâneuse are best seen as archetypes, conduits, inspirations and provoca-
tions rather than literal figures.

THE LOITERERS' ATTEMPTS TO DEFINE THEIR DÉRIVE

My methodology challenges the authority and exclusivity of the privileged flâneur. It demonstrates, as so many artists have done in their work
(see, for example, Heddon and Turner 2010 and much of the Walking

Artists Network n.d.), that the female walker does not only exist for the benefit of the male gaze. The collective dérive provides opportunities, which deserve deeper analysis, to explore sousveillance and alternative perceptions of place. The group has its own ecology and embodies unpredictability, risk and freedom, disturbing normality, transforming the mundane and encouraging embodied learning and spatial knowledge. These affordances are provided by other walking methodologies, but the dérive has unique qualities, creating its own space of resistance and joy. As Massey contests, space is the sum of its trajectories. The LRM suggests an alternative, more empowering practice, where walking creates new possibilities and a transformation of place. Through my praxis, I have identified five key characteristics of a dérive. This was written for the LRM website and thus intends to convey the potentialities and the pleasures afforded to a wider public, seeking to reconcile the divergent strands of political engagement and poetic enchantment. As a work in progress, it will doubtless evolve, but I am confident my research validates my practice. It succeeds in attracting around eight hundred people to LRM events each year, suggesting that, as a tool to engage wider audiences to critical (psycho)geography, the dérive has a powerful attraction.

1. It should be spontaneous, directionless, aimless, but also mindful: Who is sharing the streets with us, and who is absent? Why is this? We follow lines of desire, curiosity and coincidence but also invisible threads of power and the whispers of ghosts under the pavement.
2. Loitering is participatory, and everyone has a collective responsibility to look after themselves and each other. We are open to all, and anyone can become involved; we are always up for collaboration and will never claim to be offering a definitive version of the city. (How could we when we walk on such a rich tapestry of stories?)
3. Our walks are noncommercial; no one makes a monetary profit. We will never charge because the streets are free and belong to everyone.
4. And yes, this may contradict point 1 a little bit, but so what? We aim to disrupt the banal and find new views; to glimpse the magic in the Mancunian rain and the universes swirling around the city. We want to see remarkable sights, and with the right frame of mind, we can all do so frequently.
5. First Sundays are for fun, and we want to bring pleasure and convivial company. Stop if you are not happy. (Some walks, of course, investigate uncanny or dark atmospheres but still should be a positive experience.)

Bodies are both materially and socially constructed, always in a state of becoming, constantly (re)configured in relation to their environment.

The act of walking lays this bare and emphasizes the embodied and gendered nature of experience, providing a vehicle to promote an inter-disciplinary, expanded psychogeography. There is particular potential in exploring the methodology with different groups and specific bodies, many of which remain underrepresented in (psycho)geographies. For ex-ample, my own personal experiences of walking are shaped by engage-ment with impairment and the associated pain, including a tendency to fall, as well as enabling technologies (sticks, orthotics, calipers, etc.), what the social model reveals as a disabling environment and, of course, other intersectional dimensions of my experience.

THE POTENTIALITIES OF THE DÉRIVE

Each walk produces what Heddon and Turner term a *toponarrative*, a 'collaborative, partial story of place constructed by at least two walkers' (2010, 15). These narratives are provocative, contradictory and heteroge-neous, illustrating the thick atmosphere of place, the nuance of embodied experience and a transformative remapping 'provoked by an affective and sensual encounter with materiality that promotes empathy with oth-er times, people, events and non-human agents' (Edensor 2012, 2). The artistic turn that the dérive offers can promote both personal liberation and a sense of community; the minor epiphanies offered and new paths created not only transform the space traversed but also make Jacobs's (1961) sidewalk ballet into a new kind of dance, uninhibited by time or convention. The banal can become fascinating on close inspection, and the dérive provides an insight into mundane practices while also offering a form of enchantment. Walking offers a direct, multisensory way to (re)engage with the city, which can be echoed, and enhanced, by the interventions of artists and activists. In turn, artistic and activist methods can be adapted and integrated into geographical methodologies that ex-plore the relationship to place. The dérive values every participant's agency, extending an implicit invitation to become an active, inquisitive citizen as opposed to a passive consumer (though I appreciate that many daily interactions resist and complicate this binary). Interventions in memory and imagination and opportunities for subversive play can en-gage all senses and rewrite the city for their duration, producing a form of concrete art and poetry. Binaries are dissolved, at least temporarily, and, as envisioned by the SI, leisure and work combine. The body be-comes a tool for exploration and kinaesthetic learning; to walk together uncovers and creates new traces, tracks, connections and stories that par-ticipants can share, debate and solidify. I believe developing these tech-niques contributes to a revived psychogeography and an accessible, po-litical and engaging form of psychogeographical enquiry.

Debord's spectacle is still pervasive today, and Massey (2013) suggests the key task of contemporary intellectuals and cultural activists is to create an ideological crisis, to trigger imaginations and to inspire new ideas to break the hegemony. The dérive is a mental and physical tool that can contribute to this work toward a more equitable society, which surely must be a goal of an engaged social psychogeography. If we consider psychogeography as an evolving practice rather than a theory (and surely, due to its embodied nature, we must), then the reality is infinitely richer, more diverse, accessible and inclusive, and its potentialities are more breathtakingly beautiful than the established canon would lead us to believe. It is in the plurality, the minor epiphanies, that we find possibilities to create a truly revolutionary spatial awareness. The potential for diverse groups of people to engage in experimental walking should be developed as it affords the opportunity to rupture the banal and disrupt the monotony of capitalism, (re)connecting with space, (re)mapping according to personal affect and (re)creating with multitudinous new stories. I warmly invite you to experience this by joining the LRM for a wander whenever you desire.

BIBLIOGRAPHY

Andreotti, L., and X. Costa, eds. 1996. *Theory of the Dérive and Other Situationist Writings on the City.* Barcelona: Museu d'Art Contemporani de Barcelona.

Bassett, K. 2004. 'Walking as an Aesthetic Practice and a Critical Tool: Some Psychogeographic Experiments.' *Journal of Geography in Higher Education* 28 (3): 397–410.

Debord, G. 1955. ' Introduction to a Critique of Urban Geography.' Translated by Ken Knabb. *Les Lèvres Nues* 6. Bureau of Public Secrets. http://www.bopsecrets.org/SI/urbgeog.htm.

de Certeau, M. 1988. *The Practice of Everyday Life.* Translated by Steven Rendall. Berkeley: University of California Press.

Edensor, T. 2012. 'Vital Urban Materiality and Its Multiple Absences: The Building Stone of Central Manchester.' *Cultural Geographies.* http://cgj.sagepub.com/content/early/2012/06/15/1474474012438823.abstract.

'Ending Child Poverty in Salford: Position Statement.' 2010. Salford City Council. https://services.salford.gov.uk/solar_documents/CBNT270710A3A.PDF.

Heddon, D., and C. Turner. 2010. 'Walking Women: Interviews with Artists on the Move.' *Performance Research* 15 (4): 14–22.

Jacobs, J. 1961. *The Death and Life of Great American Cities.* New York: Random House.

Loiterers Resistance Movement. 2006. 'Untitled Flyer.' Manchester: Self-published. http://www.nowhere-fest.blogspot.co.uk/2012/05/hello.html.

Massey, D. 2005. *For Space.* London: Sage.

———. 2013. 'Vocabularies of the Economy.' In *After Neoliberalism? The Kilburn Manifesto,* edited by S. Hall, D. Massey, and M. Rustin, 3–17. London: UK Soundings.

Mott, C., and M. Roberts. 2013. 'Not Everyone Has (the) Balls: Urban Exploration and the Persistence of Masculinist Geography.' *Antipode* 46 (1): 229–45. http://onlinelibrary.wiley.com/doi/10.1111/anti.12033/full.

Nicholson, G. 2011. *The Lost Art of Walking: The History, Science, Philosophy, Literature, Theory and Practice of Pedestrianism.* Chelmsford: Harbour Books.

Pinder, D. 2005. 'Arts of Urban Exploration.' *Cultural Geographies* 2 (328): 383–411.

Richardson, T. 2013. *Concrete, Crows and Callouses: Dispatches from a Contemporary Psychogeographer*. Leeds: Particulations Press.

Rose, M. 2012. 'About the LRM.' The LRM. http://nowhere-fest.blogspot.co.uk/2015/03/about-lrm.html.

Scalway, H. 2002. 'The Contemporary Flânuese: Exploring Strategies for the Drifter in Feminine Mode.' Helen Scalway. http://www.helenscalway.com/wp-content/uploads/2013/01/The-Contemporary-Flaneuse.pdf.

Smith, P. 2010a. 'The Contemporary Dérive: A Partial Review of Issues Concerning the Contemporary Practice of Psychogeography.' *Cultural Geographies* 17 (1): 103–22.

———. 2010b. *Mythogeography: A Guide to Walking Sideways*. Axminster: Triarchy Press.

Solnit, R. 2006. *Wanderlust: A History of Walking*. Second edition. London: Verso.

Territories Reimagined: International Perspectives. 2008. www.trip2008.wordpress.com.

Vaneigem, R. (1967) 1983. *The Revolution of Everyday Life*. Translated by D. Smith. London: Left Bank Books and Rebel Press.

Walking Artists Network. n.d. www.walkingartistsnetwork.org.

Part IV

Practicing Psychogeography/ Psychogeographical Practices

Debord wrote *The Theory of the Dérive* in 1959, setting out instructions on how to drift through the city in such a way that the participants are in tension between a relaxed state of being open to what may arise on the walk and a conscious awareness in regard to the controlling force of urban decor. Recommending it as a group practice (even specifying the number of participants), suggesting the duration of the walk and discussing the logistics of the area under observation, Debord's text unfolds the genesis of a methodology. He tentatively describes psychogeography as a methodology under development at the time of writing his essay and tells the reader how the dérive can be used as a springboard to further the purposes of the Situationists' wider project, later laid out in *Basic Programme of the Bureau of Unitary Urbanism* (1961).

Formulating a methodology for philosophical (or scientific) inquiry is often necessary for an academic in order to propose potential work and to validate the results of findings. There are a number of situations where this might be required—for instance, when presenting one's work to a particular body (such as an ethics committee) in order to validate a prospective research proposal.

The three chapters in this section represent the academic work of three individuals from three different fields: performance, urban planning and cultural studies. The authors have developed a methodology for their walking-based practices and named the methodology in order to distinguish their form of walking from other psychogeographical practices. These chapters show the development and evolution of a methodology over time, the fleshing out of a process for a specific project and the practical aspects of applying a methodology to walking-based research.

TEN

Psychogeography and Mythogeography

Currents in Radical Walking

Phil Smith

The mythogeography project was not planned. It emerged from particular circumstances that still mark it: a transition within artists' collective Wrights & Sites (Stephen Hodge, Simon Persighetti, Cathy Turner and myself) from making site-specific performances to making interventions in everyday life. What it then became is more a result of emerging opportunities for dispersal than of any coherent strategy—an interwoven set of terms, theory-tales and praxis-narratives made available as far as resources allow to that assemblage of ambulatory and 'resistant' practitioners who escape the more popular and literary summaries of psychogeography (Coverley 2006).

Mythogeography is a theorization of multiplicity and mobility that hangs on the texture, grit, sweat and emotion of individual journeys. Its promotion of its own ideas stems partly from a painful awareness of how quickly actions can melt into air and partly from a grudging admiration for those, like the postmodern performers Forced Entertainment (Etchells 1999), who have created a critical-theoretical scaffolding around their own activities (getting their retaliation in first).

ORIGINS OF MYTHOGEOGRAPHY

Walking became the central practice of Wrights & Sites in response to tensions around the use of theatricality in our site-based performances. Searching for performance sites united us in pleasure; what we performed in them divided us. So we decapitated theatre from the process and began exploring together. After our first expedition in December 2001, Wrights & Sites began to regularly invite guests on daylong forays around our city (Exeter, UK). Sometimes we used 'catapults' to start these walks, random bus rides or blindfolded rides in taxis. Often we began at unfamiliarly early hours of the morning.

These explorations generated rewalkings of routes and 'interventions,' forays into the rural hinterland, mapping projects, a series of walking-video experiments (*4 x 4 Screens*, 2005–2007, released on DVD in 2013 by the Live Art Development Agency), ambulatory dialogues about the future of a forest (*Possible Forests*, 2006–2007), misguided tours and a *Three Minute Wonder* film for Channel Four, and they led to our curating programmes of ambulatory events for the Wiener Festwochen in Vienna (2007) and the Belluard Bollwerk International in Fribourg (Switzerland, 2008).

In order to engage beyond the limited numbers who walked with us, we created two handbooks—*An Exeter Mis-Guide* (Hodge et al. 2003) and *A Mis-Guide to Anywhere* (Hodge et al. 2006b)—and 'A Manifesto for a New Walking Culture' (Hodge et al. 2006a). The books were used far more widely than we expected, selling well in the United States, Canada and Australia, even reaching India and Scandinavia. They were used extensively on theatre and fine arts courses and by informal therapeutic and activist groups. They fed into a growing practice of ambulatory arts. A number of academic geographers adopted them in their work, and the Transport Department of Trondheim City Council ordered ten copies (why, and with what effect, we never found out).

From the very start of our exploring, we were at least dimly aware of psychogeography, referring to our first planned day of walking as a 'drift' or 'derive' [*sic*]. While still in my teens, I had read Richard Gombin's *The Origins of Modern Leftism* (1975) and enthusiastically devoured passages on the Lettrist International (LI) and Situationist International (SI) and their critiques of everyday life and the society of the spectacle. In 2000, I used the word *mytho-geographical* in a publication about the first Wrights & Sites performance project, *The Quay Thing* (1998; see Hodge et al. 2000), which was almost certainly a misremembering of 'psychogeographical.' This mistake became useful to us as we sought to distinguish ourselves from certain hegemonic aspects of the SI—'traces of a desire to maintain a monopoly on the radical' (Jappe 1999, 97)—and the functional role assigned to 'drifting' in their project.

In 2004, when we introduced our work to the Walk 21 Conference in Copenhagen, we described how:

> [W]e have been exploring the potential of an approach to place through the lens of mytho-geography that places the fictional, fanciful, mistaken and personal on equal terms with the factual, municipal history. It suggests performance through the participation of active spectators as researchers of the city, allowing authors and walkers to become equal partners in ascribing significance to place. At its simplest we are interested in findings ways of experiencing the built environment of the city in a creative or, more specifically, a re-creative manner. (Hodge et al. 2004)

By 2004, many of the key elements I would elaborate on later (Smith 2010b) were already adhering to our concept of mythogeography: attention to a multiplicity of layers, equal status given to the subjective and the fanciful as to the public and the political, and the walk itself as a making and changing of meanings rather than as a service function for a later process of change or representation. At Copenhagen, psychogeography and the Situationists were mentioned in passing, but two years later our anxiety around creating a distinguishable identity had waned and our study of psychogeographical practices deepened, sufficiently for us to place them much closer to our core practice (now using a solipsistic and interiorized flânerie as our point of difference):

> Rather than the 'transient passage' (often translated as 'rapid passage') of the situationists, we usually proceed at a slower than normal walking pace: tracing and retracing routes; discovering deadends; following existing desire paths; creating new routes; stopping to talk to people, or to reconfigure detritus. . . . [The walks] are still resistant to the flâneur's stroll, and certainly open to 'playful-constructive behaviour and awareness of psychogeographical effects.' In addition to psychogeography . . . Wrights & Sites draw on 'mythogeography.' Rather than looking inwardly towards the self, mythogeography draws on collective data relating to site and landscape: on myths, rumours and lies; on unrealised architectures; on collectively held desires, etc. (Hodge 2006)

This formulation of mythogeography now specifically addressed the play of ideology, adding apparently missing layers of contestation between the 'geographical environment,' 'emotions,' and 'behaviours' engaged by existing psychogeographical practices. These missing layers were addressed as the 'myths' of a place and then engaged playfully, parodistically, destructively, or deconstructively. In Copenhagen, the conference delegates were asked to make a Kierkegaardian 'leap' on their way to lunch; on the outskirts of Vienna we curated a 'safari' (with alpine guides) across the city's mountainous waste dump to visit its herd of huge, endangered mountain goats (Smith 2009). Our misguided tours were devoted to engaging, dismantling and remaking the 'myths' of their routes (Crab Man & Signpost 2012, 73–78), a seeking for mythogeographical terrain that intertwined with our aspiration to re-create the experiencing of place.

After 2007, following the publication and dissemination of models we had developed during five years of sporadic walking, the four members of Wrights & Sites increasingly devoted themselves to their own projects: expanded dramaturgies (www.expandeddramaturgies.com), walking in Second Life, publishing books and journal papers and teaching. Since 2009, we have been slowly developing 'ambulant architectures,' transient physical interventions in cities. As part of the turn to our own practices, I made my own misguided tours, developed the dispersed practice of 'countertourism' (Smith 2012; see figure 10.1) and conducted two pilgrimage-like walks: one following the 1910 route of an acorn-planting engineer, and the other the 'route' of W. G. Sebald's *The Rings of Saturn* (1998). The latter provided the overarching narrative for my book *On Walking* (2014), and the former gave me the core of *Mythogeography* (2010b).

Although the project of mythogeography grew within Wrights & Sites, it escaped it. It has not coagulated around any other group since, which gives it a useful flexibility when it comes to dispersal but also, in common with other neopsychogeographies, a susceptibility to theoretical dissolution. There is no detailed theoretical account of, or practical manual for, systematic psychogeographical praxis. Certainly not in the texts of the LI or SI. With the exception of McKenzie Wark's (2008; 2011; 2013) vivid excavations of a meshwork of practices, relationships and ideas from the milieu of the LI and SI, it is often difficult to find the contexts through which to understand the dérive. Such is this difficulty, indeed, that many come to psychogeography through its negation in the form of literary novels and art movies. The problem was exemplified in a 2007 interview with former SI member Jacqueline de Jong, who characterized 'drifts' as 'something you have to initiate yourself by doing' (de Jong 2011, 187) but then could only describe banal features; they were 'like a tourist stroll . . . mostly ended up in cafés' (ibid.). Having defended the agency of dérive against nostalgia and commodification, de Jong struggled, like many dérivistes, to articulate dispersible principles or tactics.

Springing from performance practice, mythogeography was informed by its originators' awareness not only of the inadequacy of documentation to capture affect and liveness (Phelan 1993, 146), and of documentation's poisonous transformation of actions and experiences into critical artefacts, but also of the alternative possibility of a repertoire of actions (Taylor 2003) supported less by descriptions of practice than by practice as recycling and by toolkits and handbooks.

Figure 10.1.   Walkers with Phil Smith on a 'Refrains for Uncertainly Sacred Spaces' walk for Airspace Gallery, Stoke-on-Trent (Courtesy of Glen Stoker, director at Airspace Gallery)

DISPERSAL OF TACTICS

Couched within an arcane structure and apparently consisting of the 'found' documents of a lost walking conspiracy, *Mythogeography* (Smith 2010b) attempts to lure its users into a performative reading in order to inculcate them into mythogeographical thinking as much as into thinking about mythogeography. Frustrated by the superficiality of many accounts of drifting and psychogeography, I set out to create a book that would be an initiatory and educative ordeal as granular and structural as the drifts themselves: 'resisting the traditional mapping of a book, it becomes a maze' (Broomer 2012). *Mythogeography* contains a toolkit of practical tactics and a manifesto of ideas but resists the temptation to draw these together into a unified theory, advocating instead the mobilization of multiple ways of thinking (embracing the 'and and and' assemblages championed by Gilles Deleuze and Félix Guattari [1987, 108–9]) around the trajectories of walking.

By 2012, I became aware that the book, the work of Wrights & Sites, Cathy Turner's article 'Palimpsest or Potential Space?' (2004), an essay-length discussion of mythogeography in *Walking, Writing and Performance* (Mock 2009) and a website that carried similar materials (www. mythogeography.com) were being increasingly cited as influences on a range of practices. I started to keep a record of these references, and they included a student in Cornwall making 'mis-guides around my mythoge-ography'; a new magazine, *The Pamphlet*, 'inspired by Mythogeography and pioneers like Sinclair'; and a 'Myth-guided tour of Aberystwyth.' Bio-art projects, a number of books, workshops, lectures, theatre re-search, therapeutic walks, alternative tourism, manifestos, gallery exhibi-tions, community arts projects, films of drifting, blogs, dance projects and sonic walks all cited mythogeography. Among specific examples were John Davies's *Peculiar Pedestrian Pilgrimage in Cheltenham*, Morag Rose's 'Art of Walking' course at Manchester's Cornerhouse and *The Great Walk* feature-length film directed by Clive Austin (2013), and Zoe Young wrote to me that 'your postings also helped inspire my recent tour to the ends of the earth, guided by the ancestors' (her grandmother was the widow of Scott of the Antarctic).

The variety of these practices, in tune with the mythogeographical principle of multiplicity, is consistent with a growing variegation of dé-rive-influenced activities, both in Britain and beyond, in the last decade (Smith 2010a). Just as mythogeography has escaped its organization, so these practices resist centralization. The Walking Artists Network (WAN), probably the only organization with a sizeable membership to offer radical walkers connectivity with each other, operates a steadfastly 'open' policy around 'walking' and 'art.' The loose and informal but spreading meshwork that now seems to characterize radical walking in Britain is very different from the network of small 'revivalist' psychogeo-graphical groups that emerged in cities like Toronto, New York, Wash-ington and Manchester in the 1990s and early 2000s. In their journals, in their occasional rancour with each other and in their sporadic antistatist actions, there hung about them a legacy of leftist party organization that, even at the SI's founding in 1957, was a shell of the mass revolutionary parties of the first half of the twentieth century. While these revivalist groups continued to invoke Debord (intensifying an exclusion of the wid-er Situationist milieu), occultism, conspiracy theory and flânerie helped to fill the void left by dialectical materialism.

It is easy to deride these small groups and their orientation to activ-ities ('drifting in search of what some of my comrades fondly imagined were occult energies' [Bonnett 2014, 5]) and producing journals, as op-posed to strategy and organization. Yet it may have been their fuzziness ('Is there a schism? Was there ever a "movement"? And what's all this psychogeographic stuff actually about anyway?' [Dickinson n.d.]) and their scattergun approach to action that has cleared the ambulatory ter-rain of the exhausting and self-replicating theoretical disputes and ambi-ence of threat that sometimes hung about the Situationists' legacy (Hus-sey 2002, xi). Rather than raising the ghost of the SI—in effect, if not intention (although Stewart Home and Fabian Tompsett's LPA [East Lon-don Section] may have had this in mind)—they erased it. What emerges from their granular, embodied and empirical adventures is fourfold: a multiplicity that embraced occultism and a street-level human-shaped reformism, a reliance on doing rather than being (shedding the burden of having to *be* revolutionary), the preponderance of friendly and informal links between people rather than organizations ('[O]ur mailing list covers these islands from Lands End to John O'Groats' [Dickinson n.d.]) and an exorcism of the ghost of 'the party.'

A key argument for party organizations was the need for a 'memory.' During the feudal period, so the argument went, the bourgeoisie created their own institutions (like university colleges) in which to prepare their ideologies, but the severity of exploitation under capitalism prevented the working class from generating and sustaining their own ideas except on the 'war footing' of a revolutionary party. Capitalism, however, is not what it was. Under the conditions of the integrated spectacle (Debord 1998, 8–11), with the digitization of information; the looting of libraries (Baker 2002); the rapid expansion and globalization of access to universities on a paying basis; and the part-proletarianization, part-managerialization of university educators, there is no longer a vital, institutional memory for *anyone*. Courting shock and disaster (Klein 2008) as integrated economic tools, the dominant ideology is no longer one of structural and ideological conservatism but of 'starting from scratch' and 'wiping the slate clean.' Under conditions of atomization and amnesia, the battleground now shifts from insurrectionary praxis (disaster capitalism has co-opted that) to the more basic one of interiority; everyday life becomes an ever more tactical practice as 'essential processes of social communication and production . . . escape[d] the capacities of human knowledge and control' (Berardi 2012, 26).

The downside of stripping psychogeography from détournement and construction of situations has been depoliticization. The upside has been its freeing from functionalism—servicing future events—in favour of a dispersed autonomy and agency. Intentions, similar to those expressed by Wrights & Sites, of 'find[ing] ways of experiencing the built environment of the city in a creative or, more specifically, a re-creative manner' (Hodge et al. 2004) have increasingly suffused the activism and arts around walking without any perceived need for overarching organization. Territorial gains and strategic plays on the fields of affect, subjectivity and embodiment are shared in (mostly noncommercial) digital and real-world exchanges rather than passed down through an organizational hierarchy.

The dominant orientation of the artefacts in the recent exhibition *The Walking Encyclopaedia* (2014) at Airspace Gallery (Stoke-on-Trent) was toward action and exchange, suggesting that radical walking's textual and visual arts outputs are less about dialogic engagements with other arts and more about talismans, mappings and handbooks for ambulatory engagement with terrains. A crafted book like Nick Papadimitriou's *Scarp*

(2012) attracts a readership of users as much as literary consumers, while Gareth E. Rees's *Marshland* (2013), a blend of firsthand accounts of drifts around East London's marshes and destabilizing fictions, comes with copious appendices to aid readers in their own wanderings and sonic-assisted dérives. The growing habit of reenacting rather than passive consuming (Heddon 2002) infects the reception of existing texts, turning Sinclair's books and Alan Moore and Tim Perkins's live 'workings' into exemplary toolkits.

In 2010, I sought to propose a response to these shifts: 'The key lies not in reproducing romantic urban nomadism . . . but in generating "any-wheres," not as an alternative meta-theory with a new narrative of origins, but as a conceptual (and mutable) tool kit . . . both an art of memory and an actual, physical, memorialised landscape' (Smith 2010a, 120).

In other words, the subjective act of psychogeographical drifting and the objective, Situationist action of place making could and should be one and the same thing. One side of the equation need not retreat into a hard politics of objectless, relational distributions and activisms while the other immerses itself in affect, subjectivity and aesthetics. Instead, as the conditions of social hypercomplexity and info-acceleration (Berardi 2012, 96–98) intensify, and as an integrated spectacle that 'now permeates all reality . . . the absolute master of memories' (Debord 1998, 9–10) looks ever more aggressively for new, more intimate and more intangible terrains with which to integrate, radical walking's entanglements with anti-spectacular interiority-battlefields and affect-impregnated anti-identity terrains ('anywheres' [Hodge et al. 2006b, 110]) become all the more time-ly and strategically apt.

However, even though such tendencies in radical and mythogeography-influenced walking can be both fortuitous and efficacious, there are wrinkles and contradictions. In Wrights & Sites, we developed a model of participation—full individual creative autonomy within shared, collectively chosen structures and themes, very like the compartmentalization of Happenings—and a model of activity based on dispersal rather than coalescence. These were not in themselves prescriptions for autonomy but just as firmly integrated within the spectacle as the inside and outside work in institutions, such as that of tutors I found using mythogeography in university courses at Cardiff, Northumbria, Central Lancashire, Edinburgh, Lincoln, East London, St. Mary's, Roehampton and Plymouth, or of those ambulatory artists who receive public funding or private sponsorship.

While Anselm Jappe has described the Situationists' own balancing of gains and losses in this respect in optimistic terms, 'to be at once "in and against" a decaying cultural sphere obviously exposed one to the risk of regression, yet it also opened up the prospect of a broader based project of supersession' (Jappe 1999, 63), Mikkel Bolt Rasmussen's formulation is probably far more accurate, both for the Situationists' historic prospects and for our own: '[T]he odds were stacked massively against the Situationists, but they threw themselves into the battle fully aware that there was no other world to escape to. They had to fight the spectacle from *within* the spectacle using whatever means they could find along the way' (Rasmussen 2011, 106).

Even on the terrains of protected autonomy and interiority, the odds continue to be stacked against us, but there are means to be found 'along the way,' including desire and pleasure, imagination and enjoyment. Such affective and subjective means became 'severely problematic' within the LI and SI project due to their 'aggressive superiority' (Rasmussen 2011, 87), closing their own subjectivities to the critique they turned on others. The possibility for deploying such means is returning now as radical walking becomes increasingly reflexive and self-reflective.

THE EXEMPLARY TALE OF THE *GEOQUEST*

During informal walks in 2008 and 2009, composer Hugh Nankivell, writer and performer Tony Lidington and I formed an idea for a performance journey, manifesting in 2010 as *GeoQuest*: a week of daily workshops, roadside encounters, disintegrating costumes, misguided tours, evening feasts, talks and performances:

Layer One: We are walking away from a care home. I have been sitting with an elderly man as he showed me his paintings of Stonehenge. He painted each image from a photograph, reliving the biography of each stone.

Layer Two: Along narrow roads, we cross from Permian sandstone piled up in hot deserts 300 million years ago, the soil red from oxidized iron, onto silvery grey limestone cliffs made of billions of tiny corpses that sank to the bottom of warm, shallow seas.

Layer Three: We pass through a village. Robert Graves wrote *The White Goddess* here. In the shadows of a lawn, we glimpse the double inauthenticity of reproduction neoclassical statues (pagan dreams of the Renaissance).

Layer Four: With fifty walkers in a lay-by, we dance the collision of Gondwana and Laurasia to form Pangaea.

Layer Five: The landscape is bathed in movies; here it is *The System* (1964), which used a nearby beach for an unexplained ritual, waving flaming torches in the 1960s where they had begun to build a modernist village in the 1940s.

Layer Six: On the way up to the promontory, Tony's geological costume falls apart. Hugh plunges into a swimming pool and plays his Melodian, catastrophically, underwater. It wheezes a few notes of Reverend Lyte's 'Abide with Me,' written in the house here: 'Change and decay in all around I see, but Thou who changest not . . . o yes, o yes you do . . . the last fart of breath. . . . In the caves beneath us, closed now, the key finds that upset Biblical time and pricked the timid Darwin, writing in a house across the bay, to break his two decades of silence and share his blasphemy with a world of apes.'

As the week of the *GeoQuest* unfolded, its various elements became ever more interconnected and interwoven. At first we had, conservatively, kept aesthetic and everyday elements apart, but internal tensions and spontaneous encounters on the road began to feed the more prepared elements. This in turn fuelled our greater willingness to be spontaneous. A virtuous flow began to gain momentum, and we increasingly shifted from an aesthetic mode to a heightened and aesthetically bathed everyday, to an 'art of living' (Smith 2012, 168–69), not a 'way of living' but an art of moving from intense moment to intense moment through changes of pace, abrupt turns, juxtapositions and surprises. This immersive interlacing of art and the everyday—improvised rituals of feasting and washing and shaving, sleeping in hotels and caves, a growing 'community' of daily returning participants, street arts and autobiography—during which 'any point . . . [could] be connected to anything other' (Deleuze and Guattari 1987, 7) was complementary to a developing hypersensitization to the terrain, to the layering of a multiplicity of themes and histories and to a reparative reconstituting of a tourism landscape.

I was unprepared for this 'leap.' We were not an experienced neopsychogeographical group. We were unexpectedly reconnecting with a politics of 'situations' in mythogeography's deep background. Despite the *GeoQuest*'s institutional links, funded by Torbay Council and supported by English Riviera Global Geopark (or perhaps because of a certain savvy inside-outside method of 'open infiltration' [Smith 2012, 181–83]), its 'art of living'—a living that 'frees time from its binary form of work time and leisure time . . . [so that a] dérive then becomes the practice of lived time, time not divided and accorded a function in advance' (Wark 2011, 25)—offered the political aesthetics necessary to bridge a gap between mythogeography's tactics for an attractive, exploratory-looking and more active (consuming-producing) multiplicitous remaking of the bounded and homogenized production of meanings of place and space.

I wrote up this model for my *Counter-Tourism: The Handbook* (2012), but it was refined by developments within the broader 'countertourism' project (Smith 2013). As that project shifted in focus from specialist performers and interpreters to the agency of ordinary tourists, I returned to questions about organization I have tentatively evoked previously, had fictionalized in *Mythogeography* (Smith 2010b, 207–12) and explored in detail in 'Tourists/Terrorists: Useful Ambiguities in a Search for Models' (Smith 2010c). In the latter, I had sought, speculatively, to wed the multiplicity and limited nomadism that had coalesced in the *GeoQuest* and qualities I had observed in drifting groups (leadership and initiative from the margins, rhythms of dispersal and concentration, the development of narratives, the fraying of purpose, collective self-education) to the cellular structures of small covert or subversive organizations (Smith 2014, 75–80). This model evaporated the moment I attempted to share it; proposed as a cellular structure to the sixty volunteers helping with my countertourism research, it was ignored.

I was missing the point in more than one way. First, I learned that the volunteers were already assembling their own groups of friends and using my tactics on drift-like wanders and reperforming my misguided tours. They were quite capable of organizing themselves once equipped with tactics. Second, I realized that what was so vital and exemplary about the *GeoQuest* was its *transition* from its various parts to an 'art of living,' not the imposition of that 'art of living' as a structure. It became clear that, rather than disseminating organizational models into which others were expected to fit their tactics, what was needed for a transition to an 'art of living,' or any other assemblage emerging from the 'and and and' of tactics, were more and more tactics and an advocacy for setting these tactics in motion about each other in hypersensitized, limited nomadism.

At last, practising what I had preached in *Mythogeography*—the deferring of any synthesis of tactics into organization—I stopped searching for ways to organize others and concentrated on dispersing tactics and theorizations of resistant walking, leaving users and participants to decide on their own forms of organization.

The *GeoQuest* was exemplary in another respect. The characteristics that helped it make a qualitative transition conform to some important general trends emerging within radical walking in Britain: the influence of newcomers, the multiplicity of practices and approaches, geographical dispersal, tension between mobility and place, and the return of 'art.'

NEW CURRENTS

Perhaps the most significant force driving radical walking in Britain at the moment is the participation of women. In terms of numbers and impact, both have increased significantly in the last decade (Smith 2014, 160–65). Dee Heddon and Cathy Turner (2012), in a rare acknowledgement of this fact, speculate on how this is already starting to shift the 'scales and tales' of radical walking from heroic ordeals to the construction of social relationships.

Not only is there now a growing multiplicity of resistant ambulatory practices in Britain—from Laura Oldfield Ford's *Savage Messiah* zines explicitly reviving the political radicalism of the 'drift,' via Amy Sharrocks walking on shoes of butter and the regular forays of Manchester's Loiterers Resistance Movement (LRM), to the choreographic walks of Vanessa Grasse, plus organizations like WAN and Making Routes in Glasgow/ Ayr—but, compared to just a few years back, there is also now a far greater range of impressively written nonliterary sources for the walker to consult (e.g., Coverley 2012; Papadimitriou 2012; Richardson 2013; Rogers 2013).

Apart perhaps from mainstream publishing on psychogeography, there is no evident weighting of activity to London; radical and aesthetic walking are as likely to be practised in Falmouth, Norwich, or Cardiff as in the English capital. Edinburgh's Artlink creates description walks for visually impaired audiences, the Parlour Showrooms produced *Walking in the City* (2013) in Bristol and Sunderland hosted the 2013 *On Walking* conference.

Despite this regional dispersal, there is little evidence of 'revolutionaries . . . bound to place' (Bonnett 2014, 205). While many aesthetic, disrupted, or radical walkers (the difficulty in finding a suitable collective term is a welcome one) pay close attention to the fine details and textures of their terrains, among such walkers there is more often a sense of connections, mobilities and trajectories than of identities bound exclusively to locations. Alastair Bonnett has recently attempted, in undoing his psychogeographical past, to challenge the 'rapid transit' of the mobilities paradigm (Urry 2007) and the academic preference for transitory space over located and bounded 'real places' (Bonnett 2014, 285). Nothing in mythogeography requires such a choice, practising both a disruption from everyday life and a disruption of that disruption (Smith 2010b, 139), embracing a limited nomadism as well as an obsessive site-specificity that can place a disruptive torque on seamless flows of information and objects.

Finally, there seems to be a return of art to radical walking in Britain. Within the LI and SI tradition is a tension between an 'art . . . to be realized directly in life' and an art only 'to be realized through its destruction' (Rasmussen 2011, 105). The revival associations of the 1990s often followed punk (Marcus 2011, 408–9) in the artless, handmade quality of their outputs, at odds with the highly wrought textual works of literary psychogeographers. However, there is a problem for those following the classic formulation of détournement, in which two moribund art products are combined, destroying both but producing a new, vivid, third artefact: the law of diminishing returns. Where do the skills or materials continue to come from to create that third artefact if they are broken or rejected in the process?

In Wrights & Sites, we moved away from theatrical product, but we retained and deployed our dramaturgical skills. Too often, accounts of drifts have been empirical, linear and tending more toward the bureaucratic report than the refrains of poetry made through flesh (Berardi 2012,

20–22)—at best, souvenirs for those who were on the walks. Transforming ambulatory experiences into dispersals of usable tactics or inspirational representations requires a détourning of arts based on a facility with their techniques, using the anachronism of the aesthetic (just like the specificity of place or the slowness of walking) to create a distorting defamiliarization that disrupts and reveals the routine processes of the ideological noosphere, springing open the bonnet of the techno-linguistic machine while at the same time celebrating and enjoying something like the original symbolist deregulations and reassemblages of language and meaning.

As walkers of many kinds who, by analysis or instinct, stand in some psychogeographical tradition, the odds are more than ever 'stacked against us.' Such is the 'rapid transit' of forms, images and ideas that little of any substance—let alone radical traditions—can be preserved for very long, by either organizations, markets or inspirations. Fuzzy activity will mostly have to do. We can trust nothing and so have to trust 'everything' and 'anywhere,' plunging both pleasurably and fearfully into the 'and and and' of multiple narratives and trajectories, stitching together new subjectivities and traditions in ruins in a reparative and depressive interweaving (Sedgwick 2003, 123–51), under cover of our individualities, paranoias and disruptive anachronisms.

BIBLIOGRAPHY

Austin, Clive. 2013. *The Great Walk*. DVD.

Baker, Nicholson. 2002. *Double Fold: Libraries and the Assault on Paper*. London: Vintage.

Berardi, Franco 'Bifo.' 2012. *The Uprising: On Poetry and Finance*. Los Angeles: Semiotext(e).

Bonnett, Alastair. 2014. *Off the Map: Lost Spaces, Invisible Cities, Forgotten Islands, Feral Places, and What They Tell Us about the World*. London: Aurum Press.

Broomer, Stephen. 2012. Review of *Mythogeography: A Guide to Walking Sideways*, by Phil Smith. *Journal of Cultural Geography* 29 (1): 129–31.

Coverley, Merlin. 2006. *Psychogeography*. Harpenden: Pocket Essentials.

———. 2012. *The Art of Wandering: The Writer as Walker*. Harpenden: Oldcastle Books.

Crab Man & Signpost. 2012. *A Sardine Street Box of Tricks*. Axminster: Triarchy Press.

Davies, John. 2011. 'Peculiar Pedestrian Pilgrimage in Cheltenham.' Public talk, Greenbelt Festival, Cheltenham, UK. http://johndavies.typepad.com/blog/2011/05/cheltenham-peculiar-pedestrian-pilgrimage.html.

Debord, Guy. 1998. *Comments on the Society of the Spectacle*. Translated by Malcolm Imrie. London: Verso.

de Jong, Jacqueline. 2011. 'A Maximum of Openness.' In *Expect Everything Fear Nothing: The Situationist Movement in Scandinavia and Elsewhere*, edited by Mikkel Bolt Rasmussen and Jakob Jakobsen, 183–204. Copenhagen: Nebula/Autonomedia.

Deleuze, Gilles, and Félix Guattari. 1987. *A Thousand Plateaus*. Translated by Brian Massumi. London: Continuum.

Dickinson, Bob. N.d. 'Creatures of the MAP.' Accessed 15 April 2014. www.twentythree.plus.com/MAP/creatures.html.

Etchells, Tim. 1999. *Certain Fragments: Contemporary Performance and Forced Entertainment*. London: Routledge.

Gombin, Richard. 1975. *The Origins of Modern Leftism*. Harmondsworth: Pelican.

Heddon, Deirdre. 2002. 'Performing the Archive: Following in the Footsteps.' *Performance Research* 7 (4): 64–77.

Heddon, Deirdre, and Catherine Turner. 2012. 'Walking Women: Shifting the Tales and Scales of Mobility.' *Contemporary Theatre Review* 22 (2): 224–36.

Hodge, Stephen. 2006. 'Situations.' Unpublished notes.

———. 2007. *Possible Forests*. Devon: Haldon Forest. DVD-ROM.

———. 2013. *4 x 4 Screens* (Wrights & Sites). London: The Live Art Development Agency. DVD.

Hodge, Stephen, Simon Persighetti, Phil Smith, and Cathy Turner. 2000. 'The Quay Thing.' In supplement, *Studies in Theatre and Performance*.

———. 2003. *An Exeter Mis-Guide*. Exeter: Wrights & Sites.

———. 2004. 'Mis-Guiding the City Walker.' Wrights & Sites. Accessed 5 April 2014. www.mis-guide.com/ws/documents/citywalker.html.

———. 2006a. 'A Manifesto for a New Walking Culture.' *Performance Research* 11 (2). Reprinted 2010 in *Performance and the Contemporary City: An Interdisciplinary Reader*, edited by N. Whybrow, 69–86. Basingstoke: Palgrave Macmillan.

———. 2006b. *A Mis-Guide to Anywhere*. Exeter: Wrights & Sites.

Hussey, Andrew. 2002. *The Game of War: The Life and Death of Guy Debord*. London: Pimlico.

Jappe, Anselm. 1999. *Guy Debord*. Translated by Donald Nicholson-Smith. Berkeley: University of California Press.

Keynes, Milton, and Daniel Edelstyn. 2005. *Subverting the City: Mis-Guide to Milton Keynes*. Channel 4/Optimistic Productions (*Three Minute Wonder*). Film.

Klein, Naomi. 2008. *The Shock Doctrine: The Rise of Disaster Capitalism*. London: Penguin Books.

Marcus, Greil. 2011. *Lipstick Traces: A Secret History of the Twentieth Century*. London: Faber and Faber.

Mock, Roberta. 2009. *Walking, Writing and Performance: Autobiographical Texts by Deirdre Heddon, Carl Lavery and Phil Smith*. Bristol: Intellect.

Papadimitriou, Nick. 2012. *Scarp*. London: Sceptre.

Phelan, Peggy. 1993. *Unmarked: The Politics of Performance*. London: Routledge.

Rasmussen, Mikkel Bolt. 2011. 'To Act in Culture while Being against Culture: The Situationists and the "Destruction of RSG-6."' In *Expect Everything Fear Nothing: The Situationist Movement in Scandinavia and Elsewhere*, edited by Mikkel Bolt Rasmussen and Jakob Jakobsen, 75–113. Copenhagen: Nebula/Autonomedia.

Rees, Gareth E. 2013. *Marshland: Dreams and Nightmares on the Edge of London*. London: Influx Press.

Richardson, Tina. 2013. *Concrete, Crows and Calluses: Dispatches from a Contemporary Psychogeographer*. Leeds: Particulations Press.

Rogers, John. 2013. *This Other London: Adventures in the Overlooked City*. London: HarperCollins.

Sebald, W. G. 1998. *The Rings of Saturn*. London: New Directions Books.

Sedgwick, Eve Kosofsky. 2003. *Touching, Feeling: Affect, Pedagogy, Performativity*. Durham, NC: Duke University Press.

Smith, Phil. 2009. 'Burning the Box Office.' *Performance Research* 14 (3): 90–101.

Smith, Phil. 2010a. 'The Contemporary Dérive.' *Cultural Geographies* 17 (10): 103–22.

———. 2010b. *Mythogeography*. Axminster: Triarchy Press.

———. 2010c. 'Tourists/Terrorists: Useful Ambiguities in a Search for Models.' *Rhizomes* 21 (Winter). Accessed 12 April 2014. www.rhizomes.net/issue21/smith/index.html.

———. 2012. *Counter-Tourism: The Handbook*. Axminster: Triarchy Press.

———. 2013. 'The Volatile Virtues of the Guided Tour: Live Performance and the Journey to Counter-Tourism.' In *Conference Proceedings, Third International Research Forum on Guided Tours*, edited by Dineke Koerts and Phil Smith, 27–40. Breda, the Netherlands: NHTV Breda University of Applied Sciences and NRIT Media.

————. 2014. *On Walking*. Axminster: Triarchy Press.

Taylor, Diane. 2003. *The Archive and the Repertoire: Performing Cultural Memory in the Americas*. Durham, NC: Duke University Press.

Turner, Cathy. 2004. 'Palimpsest or Potential Space? Finding a Vocabulary for Site Specific Performance.' *New Theatre Quarterly* 20 (4): 373–90.

Urry, John. 2007. *Mobilities*. London: Polity.

Wark, McKenzie. 2008. *50 Years of Recuperation of the Situationist International*. New York: Princeton Architectural Press.

————. 2011. *The Beach beneath the Street*. London: Verso.

————. 2013. *The Spectacle of Disintegration*. London: Verso.

ELEVEN

Developing Schizocartography

Formulating a Theoretical Methodology
for a Walking Practice

Tina Richardson

WHAT IS SCHIZOCARTOGRAPHY?

My interest in psychogeography began in 2009 on a master's module that included the work of the Situationist International (SI). At the same time, I set up the Leeds Psychogeography Group and also decided to develop my own specific form of psychogeography as a critical method of urban walking. This was because I wanted to differentiate the urban walking I did from that of others and at the same time to add nuance to a seemingly vague term. Also, I needed to think through my own type of critical walking as a more formulated methodology that could stand up to critique, to the extent it would be credible as part of a PhD.

By applying Félix Guattari's theoretical critique to the practice of psychogeography, I formulated the term *schizocartography* from his terms *schizoanalysis* and *schizoanalytic cartography*.[1] In its combining with psychogeography, what schizoanalysis does is enable alternative existential modes for individuals in order to challenge dominant representations and power structures as they appear in urban space. This provides an opportunity for multiple ways of operating in and reading the environment; it critiques the conventional ways of viewing, interpreting and mapping space. In this chapter, I detail the theoretical aspect of schizocartography, explain the comparisons with Guattari's work and that of the walking practices of the SI and describe the methodology of schizocartography by providing examples. The following is my own definition of *schizocartography*:

> Schizocartography offers a method of cartography that questions dominant power structures and at the same time enables subjective voices to appear from underlying postmodern topography. Schizocartography is the process and output of a psychogeography of particular spaces that have been co-opted by various capitalist-oriented operations, routines or procedures. It attempts to reveal the aesthetic and ideological contradictions that appear in urban space while simultaneously reclaiming the subjectivity of individuals by enabling new modes of creative expression. Schizocartography challenges antiproduction, the homogenizing character of overriding forms that work toward silencing heterogeneous voices.

Schizocartography challenges the ossified symbols of hierarchical structures through the act of crossing the barriers (concrete or abstract) of a particular terrain. This enables a process whereby something other is accessed, something that might normally be hidden behind the veneer of the dominant spectacle of urban space. Schizocartography is the walking practice, the observation and the critique of a particular space. It includes the archival, historical and theoretical analysis attributed to that space and the form of output that this research might take. It is a process that appears as a drift through the physical space under inspection, the psyches of those involved in the walk and the literature available on that space. It culminates in a form of expression that is offered as an alternative to more dominant histories of a place, highlighting ideological processes that might be in operation within the terrain. Schizocartography is an ongoing process that demonstrates that place is complex and fluid, with an identity that is heterogeneous and an unconscious that can be excavated. Schizocartography, as a form of psychogeography and urban critique, challenges the status quo in order to question a 'capitalist subjectivity [that] always leans in the same direction, that of the neutralization and expulsion of processual singularities' (Guattari 2013, 44). In the act of walking, the body can trace a new map, one that escapes the rigid hierarchies of an imposed order: 'Freed from a pretense of objectivity that reduced it to the passivity of observation, the map can be restored to the instrumentality of the body as a whole' (Wood 1997, 183).

THE ORIGINS OF SCHIZOCARTOGRAPHY

In 1984, Guattari's *Molecular Revolution: Psychiatry and Politics* (*MRPP*) was published. Based on essays from two earlier texts, it is a compilation of politically based articles that provide an institutional critique of psychiatry in the 1960s and 1970s. Following his training, Guattari worked at La Borde psychiatric clinic until he died in 1992. While he never considered himself part of the antipsychiatry movement, he nevertheless shared many of the same concerns that the antipsychiatrists had in terms of challenging the concretized attitudes of established psychiatric approaches. As David Cooper says in his introduction to *MRPP*, Guattari's 'aim is to destructure a consciousness and a rationality over-sure of itself and thus too easy prey to subtle, and not so subtle, dogmatisms' (1984, 3). Guattari's institutional analysis is deconstructive in the sense that it is concerned with repeating neither triadic structures (such as Oedipal relations) nor dyadic ones (such as hierarchical binary oppositions). It is concerned with 'the other' to dominant voices and constructions and explores the heterogeneity that is often sidelined in arrangements of hierarchical power. Therefore, Guattari's assessment of psychiatry lends itself to being adapted for critiquing other hierarchies and other institutions. In the instances where institutions and organizations are concretely manifest in urban space—which they invariably are in their administrative form—using Guattari's analysis of patriarchal bureaucratic arrangements in conjunction with psychogeography allows one to critique outward-facing physical structures in the form of the buildings that belong to them and the urban settings in which they arise.

In 1986, Guattari's book *Molecular Revolution in Brazil* (*MRB*) was published, which he wrote with Suely Rolnik. It was the culmination of the work that they carried out in examining totalitarian political structures at a period of Brazil's transition. In their discussion on the effects of globalization (what they call Integrated World Capitalism), Guattari and Rolnik say, 'The state fulfils a basic role in the production of capitalist subjectivity,' and it is 'this set of ramifications, this kind of rhizome of institutions that we call "collective facilities"' ([1986] 2008, 208). They go on to explain that these collective facilities are designed in order to 'accelerate [the] process of entry into capitalistic flows, promoting "progress" in accordance with a particular conception' (ibid., 209). However, what makes *MRB* especially significant in the formation of schizocartography as an aesthetico-spatial practice are the 'molecular revolutions against the production of capitalist subjectivity' (ibid., 291) that appear in the text as discussions on how individuals or creative collectives can become 'producer[s] of new realities' (ibid., 404).

I mention these *Molecular Revolution* texts in order to orient schizocartography in those texts of Guattari's that specifically involve a geospatial aspect: the geographical space of a country (*MRB*) and the urban spaces in which institutions or organizations appear in their administrative materialization (*MRPP*). While schizocartography is underpinned by Guattari's theories in general, these two texts analyse dominant structures, discuss the effect of capitalism on individuals and also provide examples of how people find a way to operate outside (or alongside) these overriding forms. It is primarily these concepts, used in conjunction with a critical form of urban walking, that make up schizocartography.

The urban walking involved in schizocartography is based on the psychogeography of the Situationists.[2] For the SI, psychogeography can be summarized as the 'study of the specific effects of the geographical environment, consciously organized or not, on the emotions and behavior of individuals' (Andreotti and Costa 1996, 69). They walked European cities as a way of highlighting the subjective impact that urban architecture had on the lives of those living and working there. At the heart of this project was the critique of the spectacle, capitals' obfuscating modus operandi: 'The spectacle is not a collection of images, rather it is a social relationship between people that is mediated by images' (Debord 2005, 4). Guy Debord, the leader of the SI, did not see the spectacle as being something that was opposed to material reality; he saw it as the simulacrum-like form that capital actually takes.

CAPITAL AND DESIRE

What makes Guattari's *Molecular Revolutions* relevant to psychogeography is its critique of capitalism. For the Situationists, capitalism was not just a politico-economic system concerned with market forces but also a system that permeated people's everyday lives. Guattari saw capitalism in a way similar to the SI: as a prevalent form of consciousness that took consumption as the norm. Capitalist consciousness considers that consumerism is all-pervading, infiltrating every aspect of society and postmodern life, forming a large part of the identity of individuals. Guattari believed that there are many subjectivities available, but the prevailing one is a capitalist one. For Guattari, 'capitalist subjectivity' (2013, 44) is a worldview that not only pervades the daily lives of people but also orients them according to a singular form of desire that predominantly involves the attainment of mass-produced consumer goods. While it might appear that capitalism is simply an economic system, even if we do choose to accept that it can influence our consciousness, what has capital got to do with the way the city is manifest; the way it is formed out of buildings, routes and spaces; and the effect it has on individuals who move about it?

David Harvey explains, 'An event or a thing at a point in space cannot be understood by appeal to what exists only at that point. It depends on everything else going on around it' (2006, 124). The process of urban development arises from a number of forces, such as through the zoning of cityscapes by urban planners in order to optimize geographical space. Areas within cities are concentrated into specific functions—housing, shopping, retail and industry—with transport routes being oriented around them. It also occurs through capital accumulation because, as an economic activity, it concentrates wealth in order to generate more capital, such as through reinvesting profits. This capital can appear in the form of land or property, is included in the capital base of a company (or any organization) and is part of what the company or organization is financially worth. This has a geographical effect whereby wealth becomes concentrated in different areas—on both a worldwide and a local level, especially in regards to real estate.[3]

There are administrative, economic and political processes behind the way urban space looks, with these processes having a historical lineage that appears in the form of an audit trail of particular spaces. Urban space can often hide the social impact that its development has on the lives of people, either directly or indirectly. Once the geographical landscape is 'established,' it has the effect of appearing to have always been that way. This is the homogenizing effect capital has on urban space, with urban landscaping creating a tabula rasa effect, which Guattari sees as the 'goal of the production of capitalist subjectivity' (2008, 276).

An article by the Situationists' Attila Kotanyi and Raoul Vaneigem provides a harsh critique of urbanism; they state, 'The development of the urban milieu is the capitalist domestication of space. It represents the choice of one specific materialization, to the exclusion of other possible ones' (1996, 116). It was this domineering appropriation of space that troubled the SI so much: 'For in fact one doesn't live somewhere in the city; one lives somewhere in the hierarchy' (ibid.). When looking at this quote by Kotanyi and Vaneigem, the similarities in the object of study for both the Situationists and Guattari become apparent: totalizing modes of power that have the effect of removing alternative choices that might deviate from a set mission. This means a historical and archival analysis is often required to reveal the history of a place in its present conglomeration because urban space often obfuscates heterogeneity. This analysis may also require a psychogeographical aspect because inserting the body into the space enables one to disclose a social history that may not be apparent on a cursory viewing of that space, nor be accessible in the more readily available literature on that place.

The concept of desire was significant to Guattari as well as to the Situationists. The Situationists believed that city buildings were characterless and had become a threat to any sense of freedom or playfulness. They thought any new approach to architecture should enable desire to be freed up and for it to be injected into the process of creating buildings. Urban walking became part of this undertaking in an effort to question and make claims on urban space. The SI's plan was to reroute desires back into the urban setting and alter how the end product appeared in order to highlight an alternative aesthetic value that opposed the intended one, a détournement.

Guattari explains that the success of capitalism is contingent on its ability to reroute any wayward desires back into the capitalist process: 'There is always an arrangement ready to prevent anything that might be of a dissident nature in thought and desire' (2008, 58). Capital's ability to redirect deviant flows and turn them to its advantage is part of its success, not only as an economic model but also, and more importantly, as a mode imposed on individual consciousness. The SI felt that desire could be usefully redirected into a new approach to architecture and wanted it to be injected into the process of creating buildings under the umbrella of what they called *unitary urbanism*.

AESTHETICS AND AFFECT

The psychogeography I employ is used in a critical way to examine a number of factors: the social history of a place, the sense of place (the affect as it is for a specific group or individual), the contradictions between the discourse on place and the actual space itself, how dominant forms can override other aesthetics within a particular space and how people find ways to sidestep these prevailing structures. The terms *affect* and *aesthetics* are important psychological responses to Guattari and the SI. I am using the word *aesthetics* in the psychic sense in regards to the response the individual has to a cultural object—in this context, that of urban space. This response is not necessarily an explicit reaction to space and might be partly unconscious or subconscious, but, either way, it is affective.

Affect is not the same as emotion or mood. Emotion has an apparent stimulus, and mood is a rather more generalized feeling, often without an obvious cause. In psychology, *affect* is mostly seen as positive or negative, involving an interactive process of some sort, and is considered to be an instinctual reaction. In philosophy, *affect* is a term used by a number of theorists, including Gilles Deleuze and Guattari when they write together and also Brian Massumi. Massumi describes affect as 'intensity owned and recognised' (1996, 221). I use the terms *affect* and *aesthetics* (often interchangeably) as a way to promote the heterogeneity of subjectivities, a central theme of my practice.

While *aesthetics* has traditionally been used for the philosophical study of beauty within the sphere of the arts, I use it as a response to a sensory event as it pertains to the reaction a person has to a specific spatial setting. It has a personal, individual and subjective effect on the person that is not necessarily objective in nature and also involves what that particular individual brings to the moment. The response may well not be a judgement on what is 'good' or 'bad' about that particular space, and binary oppositions might be irrelevant. The aesthetic just *is*, as it is for that person, even if there may be some contradictions in the material space being studied or within the psyche of the observer. Also, the individual's response to a space will not necessarily be the same at a different moment in time or upon another visit.

Guattari, in his essay 'Ritornellos and Existential Affects,' discusses affect within the framework of the aesthetic, explaining how expressions of an aesthetic nature can become catalysts for the individual. In *Chaosmosis* he uses the phrase *poetic-existential catalysis* to explain a trigger operating within a particular enunciative domain (1995, 19). This catalyst can become a personal denotation that serves to 'put emergent subjectivity to work' (ibid.). This affective reaction forms a 'molecular rupture, an imperceptible bifurcation capable of overthrowing the framework of dominant redundancies . . . the classical order' (1995, 19–20). Aesthetics and affect are used as a way to promote the heterogeneity of subjectivities, a central theme of schizocartography in regard to the experience of a particular terrain and to the output that can result from that encounter.

CREATING SITUATIONS

The walking practice of the SI was known as the *dérive*. In 'Theory of the Dérive,' Debord (1996) provides extensive instructions on how to partake in a dérive (drift). The SI describes a dérive as a 'mode of experimental behavior linked to the conditions of urban society: a technique through varied *ambiances*. Also used to designate a specific period of continuous dériving' (Andreotti and Costa 1996, 69). The dérive involves moving through the city in a new way by creating different paths by chance. Despite the fact that a playful element was deemed essential for the dérive, those taking part were expected to be conscious of the environment, especially in the way it tied in with a critique of capitalism. Walkers were encouraged to be aware of 'fissures in the urban network . . . microclimates . . . administrative districts, and above all the dominating action of centers of attraction' (Debord 1996, 22). In terms of the practice itself, Debord says, 'Progress is nothing other than breaking through a field where chance holds sway by creating new conditions more favorable to our purposes' (ibid., 23). This purpose was to challenge capital as it appeared in the form of the spectacle. While the SI's form of psychogeography is the basis of that employed in schizocartography, the walking aspect of it is not necessarily an overtly activist or political one. It might appear in the form of a chance discovery of a piece of street art when walking with friends in the city, or a solitary expedition examining the signs that appear in a specific space, such as a graveyard, shopping mall or suburban neighbourhood cul-de-sac.

For the SI, dérives became 'moments' or 'situations': 'The "moment" is mainly temporal, forming part of a zone of temporality, not pure but dominant. Articulated in relation to a given place, the situation is completely spatio-temporal' (Andreotti and Costa 1996, 101). The SI's project was about seizing a moment in time and space and attempting to change its aesthetics for a short time by diverting it away from the project of capital. They were conscious of the effects that the environment had on the individual and wanted those participating in dérives to be aware of this and at the same time attempt to let notions of the dominance of the capitalist city to be temporarily stemmed (Debord 1996, 22).[4] Dérives were considered a process of surveying space and, consequently, enabling a narrative to arise from it (ibid., 24). However, as a method of urban walking critique, schizocartography does not just limit itself to the various ways of carrying out a dérive as part of its walking practice. It can also take a number of different formats (for instance, a questionnaire that participators might be asked to complete about the aesthetics of a new urban development, a mapping exercise based on one's memory of a specific place or the exploration of a piece of land in order to look for something specific).[5] None of these requires the chance quality that the dérive demands, but they do involve the presence of the body in space, subjective reactions to place, or a search for something that may reveal 'the other' of a place.

DÉTOURNEMENT AND TRANSVERSALITY

Détournement was a significant part of the work of the SI. They saw it as a way of continually reworking the past in order to resituate it in the form of the new. Détournement was '[s]hort for: détournement of preexisting aesthetic elements. The integration of present and past artistic production into a superior milieu' (Andreotti and Costa 1996, 70). This description demonstrates how the process of détournement can be utilized within any form of production and is not something solely associated within an overt act of challenging capitalism. The act or process of détournement is not something that has only been used in a utopian project, such as that of the SI, but can also be employed for any political end or, indeed, artistic means. In relation to the power invested in the term *détournement*, in essays by many members of the group, including Debord's 'Détournement as Negation and Prelude' (1959), it is clear that the Situationists used the process in a practical sense. The SI states, 'The use of détournement in architecture . . . signifies the reinvestment of products abstracted from the ends contemporary socio-economic organization gives them' (Andreotti and Costa 1996, 107).

The relationship between détournement and the schizoanalysis of Guattari is apparent in Guattari's questioning of overriding forms and how they can become reappropriated, enabling a reformulation (a reterritorialization) to occur that appears as a translation of certain structures. Guattari's schizoanalysis is a process that enables other forms of representation to be made available (1998, 433). He states that schizoanalysis has the 'potential for reading other systems of modelization' (ibid.). Schizoanalysis challenges dominant powers and offers a process for remodelling their structure, not only to suit heterogeneous voices but also to reflect a history that may be counter to the dominant one. The output of a schizocartography often introduces some form of reappropriation (détournement). This is a way of highlighting how controlling forms appropriate minority structures, but it also shows how inventive avenues can be closed off due to what could be called creative protectionism (or, indeed, antiproduction).

Along with détournement is a concept of Guattari's that is an integral part of schizocartography: transversality. Transversality is a particular form of communication that forms a bridge that takes unconventional routes between systems (Guattari 1995, 23–24). Gary Genosko describes Guattari's transversality as the 'tool used to open hitherto closed logics and hierarchies' (2008, 54).[6] In a section of his book *Félix Guattari: An Abberrant Introduction* entitled 'Extension,' Genosko discusses urban space and walking. He explains that a 'transversal territory' that operates within unconventional power structures is the 'site of pure potentiality and marked by such valorized terms as "transgress" — "deviate" — "defy" — "cut across" — "disorganize" — "smooth space"' (2002, 57). He says that this mode of operating in space offers an alternative form of articulation, providing one with a different self to that which is expected by the dominant powers in the capitalistic city (ibid., 58). These elements of transversality can be translated into how one can operate in urban space through psychogeographical means (for instance, in public performance art) but also in more subtle ways.

During a weekend walk in an area of the University of Leeds campus called St. George's Field, I came across a student who was traversing the base of a building on the periphery of the landscaped park (see figure 11.1). The act of traversing is a good example of a physical act of transversality. In mountaineering, *traversing* is the term used to describe how one moves sideways across a rock face. This building, a hall of residence, is actually built on a wall that used to be the border of the cemetery, which is now the park known as St. George's Field. The student probably did not realize he was traversing a cemetery wall and may well have seen it as in integral part of the building, which it now is. The cemetery has a controversial past because of the university taking the area over during its major development period in the 1960s. To acquire the cemetery, the university had to apply for an act of Parliament in order to change the use of the land and remove the gravestones. At this time, a pressure group was set up by local people, who were distressed by the prospect of losing the gravestones that located their family members who were still interred there.

Traverse is described in the *Oxford English Dictionary* as 'to pass or journey across, over, or through; to pass through (a region) from side to side, or from end to end.' However, it is further described as a type of writing ('To trace . . . continuously without lifting the pen or pencil'), as a

Figure 11.1. Student traversing the cemetery wall

way of negotiating life ('To "go through" life [life, time or anything fig-
ured as extended space or region]') and as a form of reading ('to read
through or consider thoroughly') (Simpson and Weiner 1989). While the
traversing student may not intentionally be acting defiantly, he does
challenge the use of the space and also provides a new route that is
inspired by his own subjective desire to respond to the environment in an
unconventional way: 'Transversality in the group is a dimension opposite and complementary to the structures that generate pyramidal hier-
archization and sterile ways of transmitting messages' (Guattari 1984, 22).
For Guattari, it is desire that enables creativity to be expressed and challenge the accepted, dominant logic of a given situation.

The act of traversing by the student questions the permissions and
power attached to allowing, and preventing, certain behaviours in particular spaces. It also enables one to question the underlying logos of the
space in the sense that individuals have certain 'common sense' actions
expected of them. Desire finds a route through transversality, allowing it

to be released from overriding social forms that attempt to regulate the subjectivity of the individual and their behaviour within a given setting. In specific circumstances, Guattari says, individuals or groups of individuals can 'crystallise complementary segments of subjectivity' and hence 'release social alterity' (1995, 98). It is this that he describes as 'ethico-aesthetics' and occurs when enunciation is 'caught up in the movement of processual creation' (ibid., 107). An ethico-aesthetic approach offers something other than the 'technical and institutional apparatuses,' and it allows alternative subjectivities to flourish that respond to a heterogeneity of psychic drives and produce a 'multiplicity of cartographies' (ibid., 11). This means the act of traversing becomes a schizocartography, whether intentionally or not, in its rewriting of the space.

CONCLUSION: IS SCHIZOCARTOGRAPHY A METHODOLOGY?

This chapter has presented schizocartography as a formalized system with a specific trajectory that takes up archival, historical, theoretical and practical elements in order for it to be considered an acceptable methodology. Nevertheless, I would like to stress that it should not be considered in such rigid terms. A methodology suggests many things that are counter to the heart of schizocartography. The origins of the word *method* might suggest something is 'rational' or perhaps 'systematic.' As well as my own use of schizocartography as a process of exploring and writing about place in an academic setting, I attribute it to the work others might do in a particular space, and they may well be operating in the absence of knowledge of the term itself.

Schizocartography can be any one, or all, of the parts of the process that make up a given situation. But what they have in common is that they involve a process of revealing to take place through a remapping and a re-presenting of voices and places that otherwise may remain hidden. Schizocartography enables the topophilic relationship between space and its inhabitants to become a creative process whereby those spaces can be rewritten.

While it does not propose to be the authority on a particular place under observation, nor can it possibly provide every counterstrategy or mapping event that has occurred there, it does offer a process that goes further than an archival exploration by offering a psychogeography of place that can add something that might be undiscovered, were it not for the act of placing the physical body in space as a critical tool. Of affect, in regard to walking and the body, Massumi states, 'You can think of affect in the broadest sense as what remains of the potential after each or every thing a body says or does—as a perpetual bodily remainder. Looked at from a different angle, this perpetual remainder is an *excess*. It's like a reserve of potential or newness or creativity that is experienced alongside every actual production of meaning in language' (Massumi 2002, italics original).

Schizocartography is not a classical cartography in the sense of a straightforward mapping of space; it is a series of tracings in the form of readings and writings of place. They appear as a reframing that attempts to contest the dominant semiotic of a situation. They can be thought of as 'de-territorialized *jouissance*' (Guattari 1984, 95), where individuals react to space as sign and allow meaning making to run free, thus enabling what Guattari describes as the releasing of transversality (ibid., 103). In this sense, schizocartography might be better thought of as a 'line of flight' (in the Deleuzo-Guattarian sense of the word), whereby a communal group is able to make momentary connections: 'When an element is deterritorialized, when it escapes from an apparatus of capture and begins to construct its line of flight, it does not have to do so alone. It has the potential to connect up with other lines of flight, to link up with other deterritorialized elements and remain distinct but move together in a shared project to evade recapture' (Purcell 2013, 27). These lines of flight are performative inasmuch as they are transversal—taking untraditional routes—and they execute actions. The schizocartographies highlighted here operate against the grain, counter to the well-trodden urban path, while at the same time recognizing the dominant structure for what it is, what it does and what it represents.

NOTES

1. While the term *schizoanalysis* is derived from *schizophrenia* (as discussed in depth in the *Capitalism and Schizophrenia* collaborative series of Guattari and Gilles Deleuze), it does not promote mental illness; rather, it is used as a way of offering up the possibility of multiple voices and alternative worldviews, among other factors.

2. The SI was a group of activists based in Europe from 1957 to 1972. It was made up of writers, artists and theorists who were politically oriented around a predominantly Marxist agenda. Their concern was with the rise of consumerism after World War II and the way that it infiltrated everyday life, particularly the urban spaces in which people moved and lived.

3. This process can also include expropriation, which is the power that a public body has to acquire property and land for the purposes of 'public interest,' even against the will of the current owner.

4. The SI believed that urban planners saw the city as being divorced from the needs of humans, and that therefore planners made practical choices about housing and transport based on other criteria.

5. The list of what one might be examining in urban space is endless and often specific to a particular agenda. It might involve looking at the boundaries between public and private space, examining the material remnants left over on a site of demolition, or photographing or writing about a space predevelopment.

6. In 'The Life and Work of Félix Guattari,' Genosko explains that Guattari's term *transversality* is complex and has changed over time; it was developed out of the term *transference*, used in psychoanalysis (Genosko 2008, 46–49).

BIBLIOGRAPHY

Andreotti, Libero, and Xavier Costa, eds. 1996. *Theory of the Dérive and Other Situationist Writings on the City* . Barcelona: Museu d'Art Contemporani de Barcelona.

Cooper, David. 1984. Introduction to *Molecular Revolution: Psychiatry and Politics*, by Félix Guattari, 1–4. Translated by Rosemary Sheed. Harmondsworth: Penguin Books.

Debord, Guy. 1959. 'Détournement as Negation and Prelude.' Translated by Ken Knabb. Situationist International Online. Accessed 26 February 2015. http://www. cddc.vt.edu/sionline/si/detournement.html.

———. 1996. 'Theory of the Dérive.' In *Theory of the Dérive and Other Situationist Writings on the City*, edited by Libero Andreotti and Xavier Costa, 22–27. Barcelona: Museu d'Art Contemporani de Barcelona.

———. 2005. *The Society of the Spectacle*. Detroit: Black and Red.

Deleuze, Gilles, and Félix Guattari. 2007a. *Anti-Oedipus: Capitalism and Schizophrenia*. Translated by Robert Hurley, Mark Seem, and Helen R. Lane. London: Continuum.

———. 2007b. *A Thousand Plateaus: Capitalism and Schizophrenia*. Translated by Brian Massumi. London: Continuum.

Genosko, Gary. 2002. *Félix Guattari: An Aberrant Introduction*. London: Continuum.

———. 2008. 'The Life and Work of Félix Guattari.' In *The Three Ecologies*, translated by Ian Pinder and Paul Sutton, 46–78. London: Continuum.

Guattari, Félix. 1984. *Molecular Revolution: Psychiatry and Politics*. Translated by Rosemary Sheed. Harmondsworth: Penguin Books.

———. 1995. *Chaosmosis: An Ethico-Aesthetic Paradigm*. Translated by Paul Bains and Julian Pefanis. Bloomington: Indiana University Press.

———. 1996. 'Ritornellos and Existential Affects.' In *The Guattari Reader*, edited by Gary Genosko, 158–71. Oxford: Blackwell.

———. 1998. 'Schizoanalysis.' *Yale Journal of Criticism* 11 (2): 433–39.

———. 2008. *The Three Ecologies*. Translated by Ian Pinder and Paul Sutton. London: Continuum.

———. 2013. *Schizoanalytic Cartographies*. Translated by Andrew Goffey. London: Bloomsbury.

Guattari, Félix, and Suely Rolnik. [1986] 2008. *Molecular Revolution in Brazil*. Translated by Karel Clapshow and Brian Holmes. Cambridge, MA: The MIT Press.

Harvey, David. 2006. *Spaces of Global Capitalism: Towards a Theory of Uneven Geographical Development*. London: Verso.

Kotanyi, Attila, and Raoul Vaneigem. 1996. 'Elementary Program of the Bureau of Unitary Urbanism.' In *Theory of the Dérive and Other Situationist Writings on the City*, edited by Libero Andreotti and Xavier Costa, 116–18. Barcelona: Museu d'Art Contemporani de Barcelona.

Massumi, Brian. 1996. 'The Autonomy of Affect.' In *Deleuze: A Critical Reader*, edited by Paul Patton, 217–39. Oxford: Blackwell.

———. 2002. 'Navigating Movements.' Brian Massumi. Accessed 13 January 2014. http://www.brianmassumi.com/interviews/NAVIGATING%20MOVEMENTS.pdf.

Purcell, Mark. 2013. 'A New Land: Deleuze and Guattari and Planning.' *Planning Theory and Practice* 14 (1): 20–38.

Simpson, J. A., and E. S. C. Weiner, eds. 1989. *Oxford English Dictionary*. Oxford: Clarendon Press.

Wood, Denis. 1997. *The Power of Maps*. London: Guilford Press.

TWELVE

Route Planning a Sensory Walk

Sniffing Out the Issues

Victoria Henshaw[1]

Sensory walks have emerged since the late 1960s as one form of psycho-geography with a focus on environmental characteristics, experiences and perceptions gained through one or more of the senses. Their emergence as a research method was a consequence of the coming together of a range of philosophical and theoretical thought and debate, influenced predominantly by feminist and ecological movements where the investigation and analysis of everyday experiences are argued important and necessary in gaining insights into the physical and social environment.

In the 1970s, R. Murray Schafer (1994) and colleagues on the World Soundscapes Project introduced sound-walking as a means of studying soundscapes, undertaken 'as a practice, an activity in and of itself, whether alone or in groups, and the main aim was educating others about the nature of soundscapes' (Adams 2009, 6). Sensory walks have subsequently been adapted and utilized in different ways by researchers, adopting the virtues of the varieties of philosophical thought to which each research discipline or researcher subscribes. In 1969, Southworth explored the sonic environment of cities and interactions between senses (primarily the visual and auditory) by taking participants, in groups and on an individual basis, on a set route in Boston and in various states of sensory deprivation. Some participants were blindfolded and pushed in wheelchairs; others had their ears covered; and some, both. Participants were provided with portable voice recorders and encouraged to record their impressions of the sites through which they travelled. Following the walks, participants were asked to draw maps of the sequence of spaces as they remembered them and to recall and describe their most memorable and least- and most-liked sites. In contrast, Semidor (2006) explored urban soundscapes by undertaking sound-walks alone on a predetermined route on either side of La Rambla in Barcelona. The study evaluated what is pleasant and relevant in urban sound environments in accordance with activities in the area. Semidor documented the soundscape using sound-recording equipment, accompanied by analysis commentary and photographs. The resulting data was analysed and presented using quantitative tabulations, including 3-D spectrum or acoustic imaging.

These two examples highlight very different approaches to sensory walks, both situated within differing epistemological and analytical frameworks. The research undertaken by Semidor focuses on the sensory environment as being a measurable and physical entity, whereas Southworth's study centres on human perception of sensory stimuli within certain environments, albeit within a state of sensory deprivation.

Despite the increasing use of sensory walks as a research method, little has been written about the practical considerations and decisions to be made by the researcher during their planning and implementation. In order to promote and inform the continued use of sensory walks as a method, further debate and discussions are therefore required. In this chapter, I examine the decisions faced in selecting the environments through which a sensory walk might travel and, in doing so, highlight the implications of research site selection on such factors as the nature of the data collected and participant reflections on the research design.

SENSE-WALKING AND SITE

The choice of the environments selected for inclusion in a sensory walk are influenced at a practical level by a range of issues. Perhaps of most influence are the epistemological beliefs and disciplinary norms of the researcher or research team, with these reflecting directly in the selection of the environment(s) within which the research is implemented. Route selection impacts the data collected in a sense-walking study, with the physical components of the selected environments (e.g., materials, form, topography) all having influence whether recorded via electronic or digital devices or through researcher or participant observations. In a more human-centred study, the physical environments through which a walk passes can provide many layers of meaning influenced by social and cultural norms, memories, experiences, expectations and power relationships. Elwood and Martin highlight the importance of selecting appropriate sites in such studies, explaining 'the interview site embodies and constitutes multiple scales of spatial relations and meaning, which construct the power and positionality of participants in relation to the people, places and interactions discussed in the interview' (2000, 650–52).

The selection of a route for a sensory walk presents a range of opportunities and challenges for the constitution of meaning, with potentially shifting relations of power as the environment changes throughout the process of the walk. The balance of power between the researcher and participants will be influenced by such factors as *where* the route starts, travels through, pauses and ends, and *who* participates in the study and determines the length of the walk and the various sites visited as part of the journey. In research exploring the dynamics of social networks, neighbourhoods and communities in the city of Leeds, Clark and Emmel (2008) asked participants to identify their own routes and timescales for walks through their own neighbourhoods, with the aim of situating experiences of place, space and neighbourhood within 'everyday' practices and knowledge. This approach was grounded in the nature of the data these researchers wanted to collect, reflecting an interplay between epistemology and methods, and was further illustrated in the research questions asked. The resulting length of time taken to undertake the walks was unpredictable as a result of the open nature of the approach, with walks ranging from forty-five minutes in the shortest interview to six hours in one case. In such an example, participants play an active role in determining the experience of the sensory walk as influenced by the environments through which it passes, assisting in a coproduction of knowledge between researcher and participants.

In contrast, many sensory walks follow predetermined routes through city spaces and environments with the intention of exploring people's sensory perceptions of those particular environments or learning more about the nature of sensory experience itself. The study of experiences of smell environments in particular has posed particular challenges for the research community, given low societal value placed on the sense of smell (Vroon 1997), the limited number of previous studies on urban smell experience (Henshaw et al. 2011), difficulties faced when attempting to record smells using mechanical or electronic devices (Henshaw 2014, 15–19), the limited olfactory vocabulary in most Western societies (ibid.) and the lack of a universal smell classification system (Classen et al. 1994, 109–11). As such, studies that utilize sensory-walking methods as a means of exploring human smellscape perception have emerged in recent years. In this chapter I draw from my experiences gained in organizing and implementing 'smellwalks' in towns and cities in the United Kingdom, mainland Europe and North America.

SMELLWALKING CASE STUDIES

This chapter draws from two distinct smellwalking studies. The first and primary study of focus was implemented in Doncaster, South Yorkshire (UK), in 2009 as part of my doctoral research investigating the role of the sense of smell in the perception and design of towns and cities (see Henshaw 2014). This study incorporated semistructured interviews and smellwalks, individually carried out along a predetermined route with each of the fifty-two participants, including built-environment professionals, pub and club licensees, retailers and other local businesspeople. The methodology was predominantly qualitative in its design, drawing from and adapting methods used within the Vivacity2020 Project in Sheffield; Manchester; and Clerkenwell, London, between 2004 and 2005 (Adams et al. 2009) and the Positive Soundscapes Project (see Davies et al. 2013).

The second ongoing study is more quantitative in nature, commencing in 2011 and including group smellwalks within four English cities (Birmingham, Manchester, Sheffield and London), two European cities (Barcelona and Istanbul) and three North American cities (Seattle, Montreal and New York) as part of the Smell and the City Project (see www. smellandthecity.wordpress.com/about/). In each of these cities, a partial or complete route was preplanned, and participants were asked to record and map the smells detected while undertaking the walk and to rate their liking of these smells on a scale of 1–5 as they walked through the environments.

In both of the examined studies, the routes of the smellwalks were predetermined, although in the latter study, these were occasionally changed en route due to unforeseen opportunities to explore additional smell environments or because of time constraints. In both studies, walks incorporated a number of different stopping points, with the aim of collecting more detailed data from participants regarding their perceptions of those areas and their urban smellscapes. Participants were asked to undertake the walks in silence, enabling them to focus in greater detail on the smells detected, although this was less strictly applied during group smellwalks. Silence was broken during the stopping points when on-site questioning or smellscape-liking ratings took place. In asking all participants in the Doncaster study to undertake the same walk and to visit the same stopping points, I aimed to gain a more detailed understanding of a number of different locations and routes around the town. This facilitated the exploration of difference and similarity of experiences, related judgements made and the influence of a variety of temporal factors, such as the time of day, day of the week, different weather types and temperatures and the related changing flows of activity and movement in the experiencing of those specific smellscapes. Similarly, group smellwalking sessions provided the opportunity for participants to compare their smell experiences while undertaking and following the walks.

SELECTION OF CITY AND ROUTE

The town or city selected for inclusion in a sensory walk provides a dominating factor in influencing the related experiences to be gained during the walk. That said, the majority of urban environments are marked by their 'city-ness,' including the characteristics one might expect of any gathering together of large numbers of people into one urban site, including roads, food outlets, markets and waste.

Doncaster is a large town located in South Yorkshire's ex-coalfields area in northern England, serving a population of almost 300,000 for the wider metropolitan borough of Doncaster and situated within the Sheffield city region. The town was selected as the primary site for inclusion in my doctoral research for a variety of reasons, the main being that it offered access to a range of different urban sites within relatively close proximity to one another and thus potential to access data on different kinds of smell experiences. Additionally, I aimed to target built-environment professionals for inclusion in the study in attempting to understand the paradigms upon which existing practices of the design and management of sensory urban environments are conducted. Key potential participants included architects, urban designers, planners and engineers, with these supplemented by walks with pub and club licensees, retailers and other businesspeople.

The key criteria considered while planning the route and stopping points within each of the previously outlined smellwalks can be categorized into three areas: suitability for purpose, practical considerations of site and the personal safety of researcher and participants. I started the process of selecting a route for the more detailed smellwalking study in Doncaster with a refamiliarization visit to the area, where I marked on a map any notable smells I detected in and around the core of the town. I supplemented this mapping exercise with a photographic record of potential stopping points and smell sources, guided by key smell themes identified from the literature and previous sensory studies. These themes included pollution (specifically traffic pollution), food sources (with a particular emphasis on markets and international cuisines), cigarette smoke and other smells associated with the evening economy, and scenting practices.

Once the initial assessment was complete, I considered the different areas visited and their characteristics: smell, environmental quality and notable built or typographical forms. I also thought about the distances between the areas. I devised a resulting draft route, including a number of identified stopping points. I was keen to accommodate as many areas as possible within the walk but was aware that the time required to undertake the walk and the questioning at the various stopping points had to be factored in. This timing was crucial, given that many target participants would be limited in the amount of time they would be willing and able to take out of their working day, and I made the decision to limit the total walking time, and time taken questioning at the various stopping points, to a maximum of one hour. Following this decision, I undertook a lengthy process of route testing and revision. The final selected route took a maximum of thirty-five minutes walking time, allowing up to twenty-five minutes stopping time, and incorporated six distinct areas: a new mixed-use leisure and retail development, a secondary local authority–owned and –managed outdoor shopping precinct, a strip of evening-economy-related businesses located on a busy road and bus route, an ethnically diverse residential neighbourhood with high concentrations of international restaurants and businesses, a large and historical market area and a primary shopping street. These specific sites offered opportunities for participants to detect, or fail to detect, stereotypical smellscapes associated with such areas, including the smells of smoke, alcohol, vomit and take-aways on the evening-economy strip or fish, meat, fruit and vegetables, and waste in the markets area.

PRACTICAL CONSIDERATIONS:
LAYOUT, TERRAIN, ACCESS AND SERVICES

A range of practical considerations were also included in the selection of each of the walking routes. Along with the length of the walk, it is important to consider the suitability of the terrain to accommodate participants of a range of ages and abilities. This is of particular importance when seeking to gain insights into the experiences of people with a wide variety of personal characteristics we know to be of influence in sensory perception, such as age, gender, ethnicity and sensory impairments. Doncaster's town centre has a very flat terrain, and this presented very few issues relating to access and walkability. However, in some of the Smell and the City sites, such as Seattle and Istanbul, there are many steep hills and stepped areas, and thinking through and planning for related issues of accessibility was important.

Another key consideration is access to site and the identification of any related permissions or restrictions that might be required while conducting research in specific areas or on particular routes. Two of the areas considered as part of the original route through Doncaster were a privately owned local indoor shopping centre and the indoor markets owned by local authorities. These areas were both relevant to the themes I wanted to explore within the study, although I subsequently narrowed the study focus down to the examination of outdoor spaces within the city and decided to exclude these sites, both for this reason and relating to permissions required. Experiences shared by colleagues who have undertaken other sense-walking studies have highlighted that the planning of routes through privately owned areas can be potentially problematic, with researchers frequently being approached by security staff and asked to refrain from making recordings or taking photographs or asked to leave entirely. In a detailed study involving many repeat smellwalks along the same route, prior permission should therefore be sought from the managing organizations of any private areas before commencing, with written evidence that such permissions are in place be carried by the researcher(s) while on-site. Similarly, in the case of less frequent smellwalks, such as those included in the Smell and the City study, efforts should be made to inform store or building managers that the walks are occurring and that people might be 'poking their heads' through the doors. In such cases, I usually visit the premises on the day of the group smellwalks to inform managers of the walks and ask for their permission, and so far I have been lucky with all premises being willing to allow this.

Other practical considerations to think about include the identification of suitable places to stand at each of the stopping points on a walking route in order to provide shelter in inclement weather and to protect recording equipment from getting wet or from the howl of the wind, which can ruin voice- or sound-recording quality. Access to other facilities, such as public toilets, should also be evaluated.

PERSONAL SAFETY OF THE PARTICIPANTS AND RESEARCHERS

The safety of participants is a key consideration when evaluating any potential risks prior to undertaking a research study. Less commonly thought about is an evaluation of the risks presented to the safety of the researchers, but it is important to include both of these elements when planning the route and timing of a sensory walk. Undertaking solo walks can be particularly problematic when entering unfamiliar environments, as I have found in my own research while conducting a solo smellwalk in the city of Grasse, France, and finding myself isolated and surrounded by a group of locals, some attempting to grab my bag. The identification of a standard route for the Doncaster study allowed me to build in a high degree of participant and personal safety. I planned a route that I believed was safe to walk, and I informed local agencies that I would be undertaking the walks prior to commencing the study. Group walks pose slightly different issues, for although a certain degree of safety is gained by the larger numbers, the group can also be more conspicuous and potentially intrusive when entering specific environments, so care must be taken to find out about the sites to be visited beforehand and from a native of the city where feasible.

The nature of sensory walks also presents a very specific safety risk in that by asking people to focus on one specific aspect of the environment—in this case, smell characteristics—I have found that people frequently seem to 'tune out' or fail to notice everyday environmental risks and, in particular, road traffic. The situation is exacerbated in group walks when large groups frequently attempt to cross the road at pedestrian crossings, even when the pedestrian signals turn to red. In all of the sensory walks I undertake, I therefore ask participants to be aware of the risks presented by the traffic and, while on-site, I pay additional attention to the risks posed and stand and wait at the lights if only half of the group is able to cross at any one time.

IMPLICATIONS OF THE IDENTIFIED ROUTE

An inherent consideration when route planning a sensory walk as part of a research project, and central to decisions and discussions of site, is that the selection of a specific route has direct influence on the experience, and therefore the resulting data, to be gained from the walk. In selecting a route, the research team is in part designing a sense-walking experience, and this has implications that should be acknowledged when analysing and drawing conclusions from the resulting data collected.

In the case of fieldwork carried out in Doncaster, the desire to explore identified themes from contextual literatures and previous studies (e.g., markets, ethnicity and air pollution) resulted in those themes being over-represented and reinforced through both the route selected and related questioning. This exploration and prioritization of particular aspects of the smellscape had clear benefits, as it facilitated data collection on these themes, enabling more in-depth understanding to be gained as a result; however, in doing so, there were implications for the overall findings. It is likely, for example, that had the participants selected the smellwalking routes, other potential themes might have emerged of relevance to smell-scape experiences, perceptions and design. One example of this is that Doncaster town centre has very few animals, specifically dogs; as a result, it is very uncommon for people to experience any animal-related smells in the town, particularly dog excrement. In contrast, data collected as part of the Smell and the City group smellwalks highlighted dog faeces as posing a significant smell issue for urban residents.

The identification of a preselected route can also increase participant awareness of the focus of the research enquiry, potentially influencing behaviour and response as a result. Consider, for example, the information that Doncaster participants were provided with prior to the walks commencing. They were informed that the nature of the walk was to explore the role of smell in experiences of urban environments and that they would be taken on a predetermined route, shown on a plan illustrating the various stopping points. With access to this information, it is likely that participants might consider, either immediately or while undertaking the walk, the rationale for selection of that identified route and its relationship to topic. Some participants displayed a resulting awareness within their responses. Consider, for example, the reflections of this participant at the end of the smellwalk when asked whether there had been a range of different smellscapes:

> As you go around the town? . . . So on my walk, I was supposed to be able to smell the different smells? . . . I think we're too early in the morning, but I would have loved to have been able to have walked around today and gone past a curry house and smelt that. Around the market I would have liked to have smelt the vegetables, smelt the fish in the fish market, and then come up and smelt the bread in Subway. That would have been a really interesting walk for different smells. Yeah, that would have been nice. . . . I think we're too early in the morning, or I've got too much hay fever. I have smelled it before, all those smells in all those places, particularly the fish market.

This participant observes the smellwalk as being designed to provide a specific experience and to explore participant response to it. Although this was not my intention, the participant's comment is a valid and astute observation of the implication of preidentification of route.

REFLECTION

The physical site within which a research study is implemented is clearly indicative of the epistemic values of the profession or academic discipline to which the researcher belongs. Just as the laboratory has served as an important location for the overriding priority to achieve objective results within positivist studies, the sites within which a sensory walk is carried out also play a highly influential role in determining what will be found. In fact, with the introduction of sensory walks as a method aimed at examining sensory aspects and human experiences of visual, acoustic, haptic and olfactory aspects of environmental experience, issues of site become even more crucial, as the environment takes on a dual role, providing both the location and the stimulus of the enquiry. As a result, it is important to think through the various decisions made in route planning a sensory walk, such as those I have outlined earlier. In an attempt to illustrate the sequencing of these varied considerations and the relationships between them, I have summarized these factors in figure 12.1.

Sensory walks have been used to gather data of varied types and formats, with data-collection methods ranging from the use of electronic data-capturing techniques, such as that approach adopted by Semidor

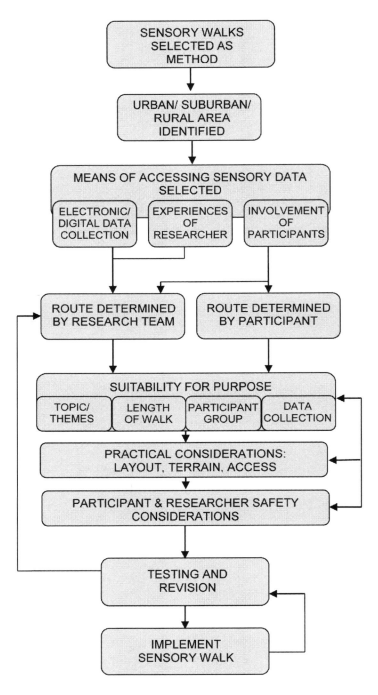

Figure 12.1. Model of site-related decision making in sensory walks

(2006), to more human-centred approaches, such as those included within my outlined case studies, involving participants in the research on an individual or group basis. Although sensory walks have to date focused on characteristics or perceptions of a range of predominantly urban environments, it is not necessarily the case that all environments included within such studies should be urban in nature. Depending on the focus of the enquiry, the physical location of the walk might include different types of areas, be centred within rural or agricultural land or occur in places that fall in the grey area between urban and rural areas.

Once the type or categorization of the appropriate general area within which the walk will be implemented has been selected, attention should turn to the walking route. Depending on the focus of the study and the selected means for evaluating or recording the environment (electronic/ digital, researcher insights or via participants), a decision must be made on whether the route should be determined by the research team or, if involving others, by the participants themselves. In fieldwork where there are no participants other than the researcher, in most cases the route will be determined by the research team either before commencing or while undertaking the study. One exception to this case would be a sensory walk following the traditional dérive method of the Situationists, where a researcher might use specific sensory stimuli to determine the walking route (for example, by heading in the direction of the strongest smells detected).

In the case of sensory walks including participants, a decision must be made regarding whether the route is to be predetermined by the research team or by the participants themselves. This latter option can provide useful insights into the participants' relationship with and experiences of the environment itself but does have implications that should be considered in relation to the planning of the study, the data collected and participant and researcher safety. If a predetermined route is to be selected by the research team, then a range of interrelating factors will contribute at this point as part of the planning process. In reflecting on my own experiences of route planning sensory walks, I identify these as being the suitability of the route for purpose, practical considerations and participant and researcher safety.

The suitability of the route toward exploring the topic of enquiry is a crucial factor in determining the route of the walk, and the criteria by which the research teams make related decisions of site should be identified and acknowledged while analysing and drawing conclusions from the resulting data. In the case study examples of smellwalking studies outlined previously, the identification of predetermined routes in order to accommodate and further investigate specific themes and variety of smellscapes had two key effects. First, in selecting a specific route that included opportunities for participants to potentially experience aspects of the preidentified themes of pollution, food, smoke and other evening economy–related smells and artificial scenting, other olfactory experiences were potentially excluded from the research findings, leading to an abnormal environmental experience. Second, in selecting a preidentified route, research participants displayed a resulting awareness of the relationship between that route and the topic of enquiry, with this reflected in responses and, to some degree, the data collected.

In predetermined walks, consideration can also be given to practical issues of site, such as the layout, steepness of terrain and access to site and services, reducing the likelihood of problems being faced once the research commences in earnest. In cases where participants determine the route, the research team can provide criteria that will ensure the suitability of the resulting walk and the data collected in illuminating the research question. In predetermined walks, careful consideration can be given to the ideal length of the walk (in both distance and time), the expectations of any target participants or participant groups and the suitability of site to the method of data collection. This latter factor might include, for example, consideration of the impact of site on sound-recording quality.

Researcher and participant safety considerations are important in both scenarios of research team– or participant-determined routes; however, the actions that can be put into place to remediate risks will vary, with predetermined routes providing more opportunity for the reduction of risk through environmental choice.

Once research teams have considered and made decisions on these variety of factors and have determined the preferred route of the sensory walk, if this approach is selected, then detailed testing and revision of the route and other related aspects of the methodology should be undertaken, where possible, on-site. Where problems and a lack of suitability of site are identified through testing, the research team might go back and reconsider all aspects of route; however, and more likely, a series of revisions to the route will take place prior to the sensory walks commencing on site.

In drawing from my own experiences of route planning a range of sensory walks, I hope to assist and guide future researchers in a very practical way while planning and undertaking studies that explore characteristics or human perceptions of the sensory environment. Decisions are made by researchers throughout the planning and implementation stage of sensory walks that are of influence on the nature of the data collected, the observations made and the resulting conclusions to be drawn. In undertaking a systematic consideration of a range of issues relating to the site of the sensory walk, researchers and research teams are able to respond to the opportunities presented by this research method as well as avoid some of the pitfalls that might otherwise be presented as part of the journey. The model I have introduced in this chapter is based on some of those decisions and related issues that I have encountered while exploring human perceptions of smell environments and is further supplemented by observations made regarding the implementation of sense-walking studies by other researchers from other disciplinary perspectives and with different epistemic values than mine.

NOTE

1. I would like to thank Dr. Andrew Clark of the University of Salford, for his much-valued comments on a very early version of this paper, and Professor Trevor Cox and Dr. Mags Adams, also of the University of Salford, who acted as supervisors for the Doncaster study, which was supported by an EPSRC bursary.

BIBLIOGRAPHY

Adams, Mags D. 2009. 'Hearing the City: Reflections on Soundwalking.' *Qualitative Researcher* 10: 6–9.

Adams, Mags D., Trevor Cox, Ben Croxford, Gemma Moore, Steve Sharples, and Mohamed Rafaee. 2009. 'The Sensory City.' In *Designing Sustainable Cities*, edited by Rachel Cooper, Graeme Evans, and Christopher Bokyo, 75–85. Chichester: Wiley-Blackwell.

Clark, Andrew, and N. Emmel. 2008. 'Connected Lives: Understanding Networks, Neighbourhoods and Communities.' *Vital Signs: Researching Real Life*. Manchester: ESRC Real Life Methods. http://eprints.ncrm.ac.uk/800/1/2009_connected_lives_methods_emmel_clark.pdf.

Classen, Constance, David Howes, and Anthony Synnott. 1994. *Aroma: The Cultural History of Smell*. New York: Routledge.

Davies, William, Mags D. Adams, Neil S. Bruce, Rebecca Cain, Angus Carlyle, Peter Cusack, Deborah A. Hall, Ken I. Hume, Paul Jennings, Melissa Marselle, Christopher J. Plack, and John Poxon. 2013. 'Perception of Soundscapes: An Interdisciplinary Approach.' *Applied Acoustics* 74 (2): 224–31.

Elwood, S. A., and D. G. Martin. 2000. '"Placing" Interviews: Location and Scales of Power in Qualitative Research.' *The Professional Geographer* 52 (4): 649–57.

Henshaw, Victoria. 2014. *Urban Smellscapes: Understanding and Designing City Smell Environments*. New York: Routledge.

Henshaw, Victoria, Andrew Clark, and Trevor J. Cox. 2011. 'Smell and the Urban Environment.' In *The Proceedings for the Soundscapes and Urban Planning Conference*, 61–65, Stockholm, Sweden, 30 September–1 October 2010.

Semidor, C. 2006. 'Listening to a City with the Soundwalk Method.' *Acta Acustica United with Acustica* 92: 959–64.

Schafer, R. Murray. 1994. *Soundscape: Our Sonic Environment and the Tuning of the World*. Rochester, VT: Destiny Books.

Southworth, Michael. 1969. 'The Sonic Environment of Cities.' *Environment and Behavior* 1 (49): 23.

Vroon, Piet. 1997. *Smell: The Secret Seducer*. Translated by Paul Vincent. New York: Farrar, Straus and Giroux.

Part V

Outsider Psychogeography

Psychogeography has always had to deal with its detractors, from the criticisms aimed at the Situationist International's hankering for a lost past to the contemporary disapproval levelled at it in its current incarnations. This is especially prevalent today with the proliferation of online forums, blogs and zines. For example, a post entitled 'How Could Psychogeography Come to This?' appeared in June 2012 on the blog *Cosmopolitan Scum*, which criticized the psychogeography carried out on the London Olympic site in 2012.

Some disciplines can be very welcoming to psychogeography, but this is not necessarily the case in all academic fields. When attempting to justify one's own practice in what may be a somewhat 'hostile' environment, it is easy to come across as apologetic or overly defensive. While the vagueness of the term *psychogeography* enables it to be an inter- or transdisciplinary tool, as a field in itself (if we choose to call it that) it is considered unscientific, even if some of the practices employed within it might be used in a scientific way elsewhere and might appear under a different label. For instance, the Recitoire project run by the Grenoble Computer Science Lab looks at qualitative surveys that involve citizens in their local urban-planning projects. While this is not labelled *psychogeography* at all, nor is the term used in the documentation, the comparisons are apparent.

The two chapters that represent this section reflect the work of two academics who use psychogeography in their own field. They both draw on walking-based literature and philosophy and demonstrate how psychogeography can be used as an interdisciplinary tool that can be incorporated in a discipline in which it might not usually be considered.

THIRTEEN

Rewalking the City

People with Dementia Remember

Andrea Capstick

PSYCHOGEOGRAPHY AND DEMENTIA

Do you know what's going on in the past? You don't know, do you?
Wait here and see what's going to happen.
—Meg, quoted in Bryce et al. 2010, xxxii

Within the dominant biomedical discourse, late-life dementia is regarded as a pathological condition characterized by short-term memory loss, word-finding difficulties and such 'problem behaviours' as 'wandering' and 'repetitive questioning.' As its title suggests, one of the main purposes of this chapter is to shift the focus from what people with late-life dementia forget to what they remember, particularly as this relates to places they have known much earlier in life. A central part of my argument is that dementia, often somewhat crudely represented as wholesale memory loss, might better be regarded as a form of spatio-temporal disruption, a disruption that intersects with the theoretical territory of psychogeography.

People with dementia are often regarded as unreliable narrators, and I first became interested in psychogeography when searching for archival and historical evidence that the places people with dementia referred to in stories they told about their lives actually existed. Or, at least, that they once had, as the changes that have taken place in the outer built environment during a lifetime of eighty or ninety years are often extreme. The first section of the chapter, 'Locating Narratives,' discusses narrative biographical work carried out with people with dementia as part of the Trebus Projects (www.trebusprojects.org). Many of the narrators were people whom staff in the care homes where they now lived believed could no longer communicate meaningfully, and often their stories were dismissed as mere invention or attention seeking. It was noticeable, however, that very often they appeared to use quite precise geographical markers to 'signpost' memories from earlier life. I found that, although many of these places either had disappeared or were altered beyond recognition in the intervening decades, the references themselves were almost always accurate and verifiable. In one care home, for example, two women both referred independently in conversation to 'black cat.' While this could easily have been taken as a reference to a former pet or a superstitious belief, it emerged that in fact each woman had worked at the Black Cat cigarette factory in Camden. In working with people with dementia, there is often a need to suspend our disbelief and resist what Russell Jacoby (1996) has described as 'social amnesia': the societal tendency to undervalue, and therefore to forget, the past. This resistance is in itself a form of psychogeographical détournement (Debord and Wolman [1956] 2006) in that an existing concept—that of the amnesiac—is 'liberated' from its usual meaning and relocated in wider society. The destruction of memory lies as much in the outer world with its demolition sites, road-widening schemes, bomb damage, slum clearance and gentrification as it does in the 'damaged' brain of the person with dementia. The tendency for people with dementia to 'wander,' get lost or become anxious in places that have changed significantly is better understood when we consider it as a correlate of change in the external world as well as internal cognitive impairment.

The second aspect of my work discussed here is the use of walking interviews to facilitate communication with people who have dementia. This was a method I adopted during a series of participatory film and photography studies. Here the concept of 'wandering'—typically viewed as a behavioural symptom of dementia—is also 'turned' or liberated to recognize the active agency of the wandering person, in something more akin to the Situationist *dérive*. Persisting in autonomous movement may, for example, be one person's way of subverting the expected sick role of the 'dementia patient' or another person's way of seeking escape from confinement. The walking interviews discussed here were carried out, among other reasons, in order to ascertain what Debord describes as the 'effects of the geographical environment, consciously organised or not, on the emotions and behaviour of [those] individuals' (1958, 22).

Finally, I became increasingly interested in Mikhail Bakhtin's (1981) concept of the chronotope (or 'time-space') and its application to the organization of spatial and temporal elements in the stories told by people with dementia. The last section of the chapter describes an unaccompanied urban walk that I undertook in Dalston in northeast London, which had been mapped out using the words of Sid, one of the Trebus contributors, who died with dementia in 2012, having lived there eighty years earlier.

Using a process that David Serlin (2006, 206) refers to as 'recoding the possibilities of disabled experience,' the chapter draws on a series of real, remembered and virtual walks with people diagnosed with dementia, in order to explore their constructions of time, space and place. What follows is not a discussion of walking as a therapeutic activity for people with dementia, a subject that has been written about elsewhere (e.g., Mapes 2010). It is, rather, an attempt to use some of the theoretical tools provided by psychogeography to analyse their remembered journeys. More in the spirit of grounded theory than experimental research, I have drawn on the work of key thinkers in psychogeography, including Benjamin and Debord, to suggest where I think the links between psychogeography and dementia might lie and to begin to explore them.

LOCATING NARRATIVES: THE TREBUS PROJECTS

Everything that the big city has thrown away,
everything it has lost, everything it has scorned,
everything it has crushed underfoot,
he catalogues and collects.

—Walter Benjamin, 1938

Named after Edmund Trebus, a Polish war veteran who became famous for hoarding things other people believed to be rubbish in his Crouch End council flat (BBC 1999), the work of the Trebus Projects has been collected in two anthologies, *Ancient Mysteries* (Brown and Clegg 2007) and *Tell Mrs. Mill Her Husband Is Still Dead* (Bryce et al. 2010). Part of the founding ethos is that it is important to rescue stories told by people with dementia—stories that might otherwise have been consigned to the 'dustbin of history'—and to write them down while there is still time. In his introduction to the first volume, director David Clegg notes, 'Just how close to the edge we came is clear from the fact there are half a dozen stories here that include the last ever spoken words of the contributors' (Brown and Clegg 2007, 9).

To demonstrate, first of all, the regularity with which these narrators foreground geographical markers when invited to talk about themselves: Out of forty-four contributors to the most recent volume (Bryce et al. 2010), only two make no reference at all to a specific named place, while more than half refer to a specific area, street or building. This suggests a strong and consistent tendency to locate themselves and their stories in geographical space; as Habib Chaudhury (2008) has also noted, telling about self is telling about where we come from. References to place that come early in a narrative are generally also more precise (for example,

'Nayland Road . . . opposite the off-licence' [Nelson, line 1]; '17 Alcroft Road' [Mabel, line 2]; 'a farm called Dungary' [Mrs. Mill, line 2]; 'Heide, Germany' [Eva, line 4; all quoted in Bryce et al. 2010, 21–157]).

A further consistent finding is that these were not places where the narrators had lived recently. Rather, they are hometowns and birthplaces often left decades earlier. This is consistent with findings about autobiographical memory in dementia, in which it has been shown that memories of events that take place between around six and thirty years of age remain well preserved, often for a considerable time (Thomsen and Berntsen 2008). Indeed, many of the narratives appear to be 'fastened onto' geographical markers to such an extent that they appear to have been constructed as remembered journeys through geographical space. For example, within the first paragraph of her story, Meg says, 'Where is this? Is it Harrow Road Nursery? I was brought up in a children's home on the King's Road. Bridestone Court? Just off George Street . . . Central London District School, Hanwell, Middlesex' (Brown and Clegg 2007, 139). Here it seems that Meg is sifting back through a series of internalized images of places around which she might structure her story.

Following these threads often leads to moments of what Walter Benjamin in 1929 described as 'profane illumination'—that is, a 'materialist, anthropological inspiration' (1999, 179). A little further research tells us, for example, that Central London District School, the children's home Meg refers to, was originally opened as a pauper school in 1856 and closed down in 1933, when Meg would have been a teenager. One of its earlier alumni was a certain Charles Chaplin. A present-day map of a town in County Limerick called Newcastle West fits precisely with Niamh's story (Bryce et al. 2010, 185–88) of walking up and down Maiden Street and across the 'water bridge.' Digging a little deeper reveals that Niamh shares the street of her birth with the noted poet Michael Hartnett (1941–1999), among whose other works is *Maiden Street Ballad* (1980). One verse of this ballad refers to Hartnett waking up in the morning to the sound of 'John Kelly's forge music . . . the sparks flying out like thick, golden sleet, from the force of his hammer and anvil,' an image strikingly similar to the following extract from Niamh's story: 'Did you see the forge where they done the horses? The horseshoes, my son, my brother, he used to mend the shoes. . . . [O]h, and when they put it onto their feet, the smell and the smoke. . . . [O]ne of the tallest men . . . he was a smith putting horseshoes on' (quoted in Bryce et al. 2010, 187). By making these connections, we become more aware that people with dementia have lived not just in a homogeneous 'past' but also in a real, historical time that intersects with social and national events.

Interesting, too, from a psychogeographical perspective are the connections made by the Trebus narrators between home, place memory and emotional affect: 'I've got to remember my road so I can get back,' says Christina, while Janet notes, 'All my memories are at home.' Asked to describe his first memory, Aidan says it is a 'slight memory only . . . like a short dream, of the house in Liverpool.' As these extracts indicate, people with dementia often cease to make the distinctions between past and present that are usual in contemporary Western thought, although not in many other worldviews. We are so accustomed to the idea of time as linear progress that it is easy to pathologize a version of reality in which past and present coexist and interpenetrate. Psychogeography is, however, very much at ease with this standpoint, consistent with Benjamin's notion that 'it isn't that the past casts its light on what is present, or that what is present casts its light on what is past; rather the Then and the Now come together in a constellation like a flash of lightening' (cited in Cohen 1993, 10).

The figurative 'wandering' of people with dementia through remembered landscapes is also reminiscent of what has been described as the occultist tendency in psychogeography. Merlin Coverley, for example, draws attention to Peter Ackroyd's 'recognition of zones within the city which display chronological resonance with earlier events, activities and inhabitants' (cited in Coverley 2010, 124). Cohen draws attention to the Gothic Marxism of much of Benjamin's work, including his description of the 'promenade into the past,' where the 'street leads the strolling person into a vanished time' and the 'haunting' of present-day places by archaic place names (Cohen 1993, 202). As demonstrated further in the section about Sid's story, 'Places in the Heart,' all of these are also features of the narratives of people with dementia. First, however, I want to explain a little about the use of walking interviews with people with dementia as a method for creating research data.

WALKING INSIDE: EXPLORING THE 'GO-ALONG'

Conducting social research with people who have dementia in ways that enable their active participation in data creation presents specific challenges. Due to the very nature of the subjects' disabilities, traditional methods, such as 'sit-down' interviews, are unlikely to be successful and can cause significant distress. For several years now, the focus of much of my research activity has been on methodological innovations that offer alternative ways of participating for people with dementia. Here there is a need to identify, explore and focus on faculties that remain relatively intact in dementia, such as procedural (or embodied) and emotional memory. Film, music and photo elicitation are among these methods, as are walking interviews.

In recent years, walking interviews have become popular in studies related to place, community and the urban environment (Clark and Emmel 2010). As Phil Jones et al. (2008, 1) point out, there is likely to be a significant connection between 'what people say and where they say it';

there is, however, scant literature on the use of walking interviews with people who have dementia, even though it is a method that seems particularly appropriate for this participant group. Participant-led walking interviews are described by Margarethe Kusenbach (2003) as the 'go-along' because the research participant directs the route and the researcher follows. Kusenbach suggests that this method is particularly suited to five areas of enquiry: exploring environmental perception, spatial practices, biographies, social architecture and social realms.

The first walking interviews I carried out with people with dementia were during participatory filmmaking projects carried out in two day centres for people with dementia, between 2009 and 2011 (Chatwin and Capstick 2010; Capstick 2011; Capstick and Chatwin 2012). I had noticed that people were often more communicative while on the move and that physical movement seemed to jog memories, promote narrative flow and reduce anxieties related to what the person 'ought' to be doing. For example, Brian, like many people with dementia, had a spontaneous inclination to walk, which was connected with his previous career or day-to-day life. In his case, this had been as a member of the Transport Police and was something he rarely spoke about except when actually on his feet (Kusenbach 2003).

In another walking interview, Norma led me straight to a Christmas tree in the window of the lounge (social realm) and pointed out specific decorations, showing that she was aware that it was the focal point of the room (environmental perception). After a few minutes, she became concerned that the cameraman was getting left behind and started to look round for him (spatial practices). She then led me out of the lounge into the hallway, turning right to show me a postbox in the shape of a snowman (social architecture) and pointing out the different-coloured buttons down his front. This is a small example but nevertheless significant. As Norma rarely spoke, it was difficult, for example, to know how much of what was being said she actually understood. From her response to the invitation to show us around, however, it was evident that her comprehension was at a significantly higher level than her expressive language. Walking interviews may therefore be one way of avoiding what has been termed 'excess disability' for people with dementia.

Walking necessarily involves passing by a different range of objects and scenes than can be seen from any static position and as a result often seems to trigger novel observations. Cyril, for example, voluntarily left a quiz game in the main lounge, where he had been sitting, looking abstracted and slightly worried. Walking along the day centre corridor, he stopped to look at some framed pen-and-ink sketches on the wall and then told us that he had won a scholarship to art school, which he had always regretted not being able to take up. Here we see a move from a static activity involving cognitive skills that Cyril knew were deteriorating to active walking and engagement with artwork that reminded him of a talent he possessed.

Most of the walking interviews referred to here were carried out inside the day care environments in question, but, for the final one, we accompanied Cath back at the end of the day to the inner-city smallholding where she kept goats with her daughter. At the day centre, Cath often seemed bored and sleepy, and she had a tendency to be self-deprecating, referring to herself as a 'silly old woman.' Out in the open, feeding the goats, however, her demeanour was completely different, and this was one of the things that first alerted me to the possibilities of 'walking outside'—that is to say, carrying out walking interviews, such as the one outlined in the next section, in places that have particular meaning for the person taking part.

WALKING OUTSIDE: FROM FRENCHGATE MALL TO FISHPOND LANE

To lose one's way in a city,
as one loses one's way in a
forest, requires some schooling.

—Walter Benjamin, 2006

In 2012, John Chatwin and I recorded three film clips with Dennis Jubb, who was born in 1942 and has lived in the same street in Scawthorpe on the outskirts of Doncaster all his life. At the age of fifty-nine, Dennis was diagnosed with dementia. A lifelong trade union activist, he went on to set up the People Relying on People (PROP) group in Doncaster and in 2010 was awarded an MBE for his work on behalf of people with dementia. The aim of the film was to record a pilot walking interview that contrasted 'static' communication with communication in response to an external environment that had emotional meaning for the person taking part and that included sensory triggers, such as recovered sights and sounds. Dennis helped us with this pilot work in the role of a coresearcher rather than a research participant (Capstick, Chatwin, and Jubb 2012).

When asked to think of a place he would like to revisit, Dennis chose Castle Hills, a place where he used to play as a boy. Located southeast of Adwick-le-Street, just off the Great North Road, Castle Hills is the original site of an eleventh-century earthwork motte and bailey fortress founded by Nigel Fossard. Although it was within easy walking distance of his home, Dennis said he hadn't been there for more than sixty years.

The first film clip shows Dennis sitting in the porch of his home and answering questions in standard 'sit-down' interview format. His speech is quite hesitant, and he pauses and asks whether there is anything else I want him to say. Asked about a place he dislikes, he talks about the Frenchgate Shopping Centre in Doncaster. He explains that the layout made him very confused; once inside, he found it difficult to get out again and had to ask for help, which he found embarrassing. In his 'Theory of the Dérive,' Guy Debord notes that 'cities have psychogeographical contours, with constant currents, fixed points and vortexes that strongly discourage entry or exit from certain zones' (1958, 22). Shopping malls have been consciously designed to keep people circling within them for as long as possible, but, due to his cognitive disability, Dennis had a heightened, and somewhat ironic, awareness of this form of manipulation.

In the second clip, we walk through the housing estate where Dennis lives and pass through a grassed-over area that used to be a quarry where he remembers lighting bonfires with his friends and trying to cook things on them: 'We'd try to cook anything; even a cabbage or summat.' He starts to become more animated at this point, using hand gestures to explain how the area has changed over time. Later, back at home, he drew us a diagram of how the quarry used to look with its steep stone walls, in contrast with the new landscape-designed contours.

In the final clip, we walk down a narrow lane toward Castle Hills ('And this takes you into Castle Hills itself, this does'). The site is now overgrown, and although it doesn't look quite as Dennis remembered it ('It weren't overgrown like this, then'), there were other sensory triggers. It had been raining heavily earlier in the day but brightened up while we were walking. There was an evocative smell of damp foliage, the texture of mud underfoot, a rather steamy atmosphere and periodic dappled sunlight through the leaves.

What happened at this point was more than we had bargained for. Dennis became enthusiastic about the prospect of finding a stream where he used to catch sticklebacks in a jam jar as a boy. The film shows him run down a bank ahead of me and begin to plough his way through dense overgrowth, talking excitedly ('Oh, hang on! We've got a stream here! Look!'). The stream, although heavily overgrown, was still where Dennis remembered it, in a place that we discovered used to be known locally as Fishpond Lane. Here it seemed that Dennis was not merely 'drawn by the attractions of the terrain' (Debord 1958, 22) but almost bodily impelled by them. 'So we found the stream, didn't we? Yeah, yeah,' he says, as the film ends.

PLACES IN THE HEART: WALKING WITH
CHRONOTOPIC NARRATIVE

There is a place in the heart that will never be filled
and we will wait
and wait
in that space.

—Charles Bukowski, 1986

Sid was born in Dalston, London, in 1918 and died in November 2012, aged ninety-four, just a few months before the 'walk in his shoes' that I am about to describe took place. Sid's story appears in both Trebus anthologies and was recorded twice, four years apart. He was the youngest of seven children, and his upbringing was, as he put it, 'rock-bottom, working class . . . no money' (quoted in Bryce et al. 2010, vi). The memories Sid returns to time and again in his final years are those of his childhood and teenage friends, the 'Richmond Road Gang,' many of whom were later lost during active service in World War II (Capstick and Clegg 2013). He uses the evocative and distinctly psychogeographical term *street-roving* to describe his loitering around Dalston in the 1930s. His narrative, with its constant return to places thronged with vivid associations from the past, exemplifies Bakhtin's concept of the chronotope (Greek, *chronos*—'time'; *topos*—'place'): 'Chronotopes are points in the geography of a community where time and space intersect and fuse. Time takes on flesh and becomes visible for human contemplation; likewise, space becomes charged and responsive to the movements of time and history and the enduring character of a people. . . . Chronotopes thus stand as monuments to the community itself, as symbols of it, as forces operating to shape its members' images of themselves' (1981, 84).

Here, for example, is Sid describing the process of remembering as a physical act of 'rewinding': 'When I look back over the years . . . I sit quietly sometimes. . . . I go right through the whole history of it, and everything goes back to the beginning. . . . It all runs back into a film, and it starts at the beginning with a baker's shop' (quoted in Bryce et al. 2010, vii).

The baker's shop and the lamppost outside it on the corner of his street are a constant theme in Sid's story:

> I often walk around those houses now, and there's a lamppost on the corner. . . . I often get up at night and go on to the corner, a few yards along near the baker's. . . . Sometimes I sit here and it gives me something to think about, going back over the different times, telling the story to myself over and over and over again. It seems to me like, for some particular reason, the past people are always trying to attract my attention. (ibid., viii–ix)

In Sid's narrative, time-space is noticeably different from linear time; the overall chronotopic organization is one that figures backward and forward, more often by way of allusion and free association than chronological order of events.

As Newland (2005) notes, chronotopes can function as metaphors that condense sociocultural history within a narrative form. Reflecting that as a child he spent a lot of time in hospital, Sid comments, for example, that he was 'in and out of hospital like, like . . . something that goes in and out a lot . . . a pawnbroker's' (Brown and Clegg 2007, 101). The narrative strands here are multiple and intertwined. Medical treatment wasn't free at the time, and it's possible that Sid's parents did have to pawn their possessions in order to pay for his mastoid operations. The hospital, he said just prior to this, is in City Road, which brings to mind the nursery rhyme 'Up and down the City Road / In and out of the Eagle / That's the way the money goes / Pop goes the weasel.' Putting something 'in pop' is slang for pawning it, and 'in hock' refers both to being in hospital and to putting an item in pawn. When Sid later refers to his brothers and sisters as the 'daily bakers, in life already' (quoted in Bryce et al. 2010, viii), he may mean that some of them literally worked in the bake house next door. On the other hand, the phrase is also reminiscent of the line from the Lord's Prayer, 'Give us this day our daily bread.' The imagery used here is overdetermined in the sense that Sigmund Freud (1900) used the term to refer to dream images: multilayered and incapable of determinate analysis.

Sid and his gang were 'hanging around the streets together' (Brown and Clegg 2007, 104) at much the same time as Breton and his contemporaries in Paris. The difference, of course, as has always been the case for the mass of the people, is that, for Sid and the Richmond Road Gang, their 'flânerie' was a matter of necessity, not an artistic or political gesture. Their homes were small and their families were large, so staying indoors was not an option. They walked for something to do and often, no doubt, in order to keep warm. Their 'street level gaze'—to borrow Coverley's (2010) phrase—is expressed in Sid's narrative through frequent reference to local landmarks they passed along the way: Canal Bridge, Mare Street, Hackney Town Hall, Carbie's Furniture Shop, Hackney Empire, the Wesleyan Church and the '(London) Fields.' In all, there are fifteen explicit references in just four pages of narrative to precise geographical locations that are possible to check against contemporary maps and archive photographs.

As a Northerner, I was not familiar with Dalston and had to transfer these locations onto a present-day map before I could chart out a walking route following Sid's narrative. The area in question was approximately one mile square, bordered by Dalston Lane on the north, Mare Street on the east, Regent's Canal on the south and Kingsland Highway to the west. It took four years from the initial inception of this idea to carry out the walk, but on two occasions, in March and June 2013, I walked the grid several times, taking photographs as I went. On the first visit, I walked from Regent's Canal Bridge at the southern border of the grid, up to Hackney Old Town Hall at the northern extreme. These are the landmarks mentioned first in Sid's account of his old stamping ground, and he describes his home as lying midway between them.

There were three different Hackney Town Hall buildings in Sid's lifetime. Hackney Old Town Hall at the top of Mare Street is now a gambling emporium owned by Coral's. The second building farther down the same street and adjacent to Hackney Empire was demolished in 1934 and replaced by the current one on the same site. When I was there in March 2013, it was shrouded in a sort of huge dustsheet, bearing a faint image of itself while it underwent further refurbishment, a literal palimpsest.

On the second visit, I spent time in the Hackney Archive looking at maps and photographs of the district from the 1920s and 1930s. Together with census data, they enabled me to identify the house Sid had lived in as 69 Middleton Road, on a junction with Holly Street. The area has undergone a degree of gentrification in recent years, and the house numbering has been altered. Number 69 is no longer on the corner where Sid describes it but farther down the street, and the houses on that side of the street have been replaced by low-rise villas. The houses on the opposite side of the street are still intact: narrow, three-storey terraces with a basement window, so it was still possible to see how Sid's house must once have looked. Records show that many houses in the area were demolished due to bombing and postwar slum-clearance projects. Prefabs came into use in the late 1940s and 1950s, followed by tower blocks erected in the 1960s, some of which were themselves demolished in subsequent decades. Currently new tower blocks are once again being built at the north end of Holly Street. Hackney Empire has an almost unchanged front elevation, but, from the side, an unpleasant new multiplex-style façade looks as though it has somehow forced itself up out of the earth, like a demolition in reverse.

Of other buildings Sid refers to, Hackney Road Children's Hospital closed down in 1998 and is currently derelict, although there are plans to convert it into flats. Like many other areas, Mare Street still has a noticeable profusion of pawnbrokers, cash converters and cash-for-gold shops, a part of the landscape of Sid's childhood that hasn't changed. Shop fronts are superficially different, but the architecture above ground-floor level is largely unchanged in the buildings that remain (see figure 13.1).

Many of the shops now sell kebabs and mobile phones rather than furniture, but there is still an independently owned fish shop (perhaps this has always been there, as the 'Fresh Fish' sign on the first-floor stucco suggests a long history). The planes that Sid describes as coming 'all the way from Germany to blow up the fish shop' did not prevail here, then. Elsewhere, however, there are many signs that buildings have been taken

Figure 13.1.   Shop front, Mare Street: surviving Victorian building with postwar infill

down by one or more storeys. The Wesleyan Church was completely demolished in 1949 due to bomb damage. Sid refers to it having taken a 'light bombing,' but I suspect this is his term for the *blitzkrieg* (or 'lightning war') rather than superficial damage. A 1993 survey found Mare

Street to be 'a nondescript mixture of low-rise factories, shops, and institutional buildings. . . . London Fields industrial area around London Lane appeared run down: nearly all the railway arches had been blocked up. . . . Victorian terraces were mixed with more prosperous industry in Ellingfort and Richmond Roads' (Baker 1995).

It is hard to say at what point, if any, Sid would have ceased to recognize his old haunts. What it does seem safe to say is that these changes in the external environment—demolitions, rebuildings, shifting skylines— have as much impact on the 'disorientation in time and space' held to characterize dementia as do any lesions in brain tissue. At the time of his death, Sid could still rely his own 'rewound' memory to find his way back to the lamppost on the corner outside 69 Middleton Street, where the 'past people,' many of them now long dead, were still waiting for him. In the outer world, though, his house no longer existed, and his address now belonged a different building altogether.

CONCLUSION

> I'd like to go back to London now
> and collect 20, or 30 or 40 people
> in a group and talk to them about it.
>   —Sid, quoted in Bryce et al. 2010, viii

Neurons may die and hemispheres shrink within an aging brain, but at the same time, in the external world, buildings are demolished, skylines fall and rise again, old slums are replaced with tower blocks and the tower blocks themselves are pulled down and replaced by something else. The vicissitudes of memory in dementia are not just a matter of individual pathology but also an ongoing negotiation between an internalized psychosocial landscape and the constantly shifting structure of the external world. In this, they are also the vicissitudes of postmodernity, with its many versions of reality and its deconstruction of the idea of time as linear progress. Thinking psychogeographically, dementia can be decentred from its assumed location within the individual brain, out into a shared social environment.

This chapter has attempted, among other things, to reclaim psychogeography for those for whom walking has been a socially and historically contingent act: of survival, protest or escape. The content is not driven by theory but instead attempts to use theory to understand the lived experience of dementia. I hope to have shown how psychogeographical concepts help to address some of these challenges.

BIBLIOGRAPHY

Baker, T. F. T., ed. 1995. 'Hackney: Mare Street and London Fields.' In *A History of the County of Middlesex*, vol. 10, 23–28. Accessed 3 March 2015. http://www.british-history.ac.uk/vch/middx/vol10/pp23-28.

Bakhtin, Mikhail. 1981. *The Dialogic Imagination: Four Essays*. Austin: University of Texas Press.

BBC TV. 1999. *A Life of Grime*. London: British Broadcasting Coorporation. Film.

Benjamin, Walter. 1938. 'The Paris of the Second Empire in Baudelaire.' In *Collected Works*, vol. 4, *1938–1940*, by Walter Benjamin, 3–92. Frankfurt: Suhrkamp.

———. 1999. 'Surrealism: The Last Snapshot of the European Intelligensia.' In *Walter Benjamin: Selected Writings*, vol. 2, *1927–1934*, edited by Michael W. Jennings, Howard Eiland, and Gary Smith, 207–21. Cambridge, MA: Harvard University Press.

———. 2006. *A Berlin Childhood around 1900*. Cambridge, MA: Harvard University Press.

Brown, Mark, and David Clegg. 2007. *Ancient Mysteries*. London: Trebus.

Bryce, Collette, Andrea Capstick, Gerald Cinamon, David Clegg, Paul E. H. Davis, Gillian Fairchild, David Greenberger, Ellen Hawley, and Sarah Hesketh. 2010. *Tell Mrs. Mill Her Husband Is Still Dead*. London: Trebus.

Bukowski, Charles. 1986. 'No Help for That.' In *You Get So Alone at Times That It Just Makes Sense*, by Charles Bukowski, 26. Santa Rosa, CA: Black Sparrow Press.

Capstick, Andrea. 2011. 'Travels with a Flipcam: Bringing the Community to People with Dementia through Visual Technology.' *Visual Studies* 26 (2): 142–47.

Capstick, Andrea, and John Chatwin. 2012. *Bay Tree Voices*. Bradford: University of Bradford. DVD.

Capstick, Andrea, John Chatwin, and Dennis Jubb. 2012. *Re-Walking the City: People with Dementia Remember*. Royal Geographical Society/International Society of Geographers Conference, University of Edinburgh.

Capstick, Andrea, and David Clegg. 2013. 'Behind the Stiff Upper Lip: War Narratives of Older Men with Dementia.' *Journal of War and Culture Studies* 6 (3): 239–54.

Chatwin, John, and Andrea Capstick. 2010. *Making Pictures at Armley Grange*. Bradford: University of Bradford. DVD.

Chaudhury, Habib. 2008. *Remembering Home: Rediscovering the Self in Dementia*. Baltimore: Johns Hopkins University Press.

Clark, Andrew, and Nick Emmel. 2010. 'Realities Toolkit #13: Using Walking Interviews.' ESRC National Centre for Research Methods. http://eprints.ncrm.ac.uk/1323/1/13-toolkit-walking-interviews.pdf.

Cohen, Margaret. 1993. *Profane Illumination: Walter Benjamin and the Paris of Surreal Revolution*. Berkeley: University of California Press.

Coverley, Merlin. 2010. *Psychogeography*. Harpenden: Pocket Essentials.

Debord, Guy. 1958. 'Theory of the Dérive.' In *Theory of the Dérive and Other Situationist Writings on the City*, edited by Libero Andreotti and Xavier Costa, 22–27. Barcelona: Museu d'Art Contemporani de Barcelona.

Debord, Guy, and Gil J. Wolman. [1956] 2006. 'A User's Guide to Détournement.' Translated by Ken Knabb. Bureau of Public Secrets. http://www.bopsecrets.org/SI/detourn.htm.

Freud, Sigmund. 1900. *The Interpretation of Dreams*. New York: Macmillan.

Hartnett, Michael. 1980. *Maiden Street Ballad*. London: Observer Press.

Jacoby, Russell. 1996. *Social Amnesia: A Critique of Contemporary Psychology*. London: Transaction.

Jones, Phil, Griff Bunce, James Evans, Hannah Gibbs, and Jane Ricketts Hein. 2008. 'Exploring Space and Place with Walking Interviews.' *Journal of Research Practice* 4 (2): Article D2. Accessed 18 March 2014. http://jrp.icaap.org/index.php/jrp/article/view/150/161.

Kusenbach, Margarethe. 2003. 'Street Phenomenology: The Go-Along as Ethnographic Research Tool.' *Ethnography* 4 (3): 455–85.

Mapes, Neil. 2010. 'It's a Walk in the Park: Exploring the Benefits of Green Exercise and Open Spaces for People Living with Dementia.' *Working with Older People* 14 (4): 25–31.

Newland, Paul. 2005. 'On an Eastern Arc: Reading Iain Sinclair's Interest in Christ Church, Spitalfields and Its Uncanny Territory through East End Discourse.' *Literary London: Interdisciplinary Studies in the Representation of London* 3 (2). Accessed 3 March 2015. www.literarylondon.org/london-journal/september2005/newland.html.

Serlin, David. 2006. 'Disabling the Flaneur.' *Journal of Visual Culture* 5 (2): 193–208.

Thomsen, Dorthe K., and Dorthe Berntsen. 2008. 'The Cultural Life Script and Life Story Chapters Contribute to the Reminiscence Bump.' *Memory* 16 (4): 420–35.

The Trebus Project. www.trebusprojects.org.

FOURTEEN

Psychogeography, Antipsychologies and the Question of Social Change

Alexander John Bridger[1]

Psychogeographical work doesn't get much mention in the discipline of psychology. Indeed, the 'high-status,' mainstream and funded psychology research focuses on the measurement of people's minds, attitudes and behaviours. However, in the past thirty years, psychologists have begun to conduct research that has shifted from the laboratory to fieldwork studies with the aim of using interviews and observations to study subjects' language and experiences in context. In terms of psychological studies about environments, much of that work has tended to be based in environmental psychology and social psychology, where researchers have attempted either to study the effects of environments on people's behaviours or to discern how people construct identities in places. While there is some value to that previous work, what I outline here is a quite different approach to studying environments that doesn't fit neatly into the existing mainstream paradigm of psychology. I explain why a psychogeographical approach in psychology is needed and how psychogeographical research should be entwined with political and activist practice to be part of a progressive agenda of radical social change. Clearly, these aims are in opposition to the mainstream scientific orientation of psychology research, but there are important reasons this needs to be done. Generally speaking, psychology work tends to be disconnected from social change except for instances where governments, the media and other corporations use psychology to back up their agendas and where, typically, psychological knowledge is used to uphold the status quo. In the introduction to this book, Tina Richardson discusses how it continues to be a challenge in academia to introduce literature-based psychogeography into academic arenas unless it is within literature-based courses. This is even more of a challenge in typically scientific and positivist enterprises, such as psychology. In this chapter, I present a distinctively radical, political orientation to psychology that draws on psychogeographical techniques to consider the spatialization of environments. This chapter outlines a rationale for why a psychogeographical analysis of environments in and against psychology is important, and I explain how such work can be done.

PSYCHOGEOGRAPHY 'IN,' 'AGAINST' AND 'WITH' PSYCHOLOGY

I argue against the mainstream environmental psychological notion that environments should simply be viewed as 'backdrops to social psychological processes' (Hodgetts et al. 2010, 287). Such an argument shuts out understandings of how individuals actually experience and make sense of their surroundings.

My second point is that social psychological research about environments has tended to overemphasize the study of identities in place (Dixon and Durrheim 2000).[2] Graham Hayes (2003) and I (see Bridger 2010) argue that mainstream psychological research has largely been disconnected from activist practice and has on the whole maintained an apolitical view of radical social change. Moreover, one Situationist argued for the importance of a 'language of lived experience, which, for me, merges with radical theory, the theory which penetrates the masses and becomes a material force' (Vaneigem 1967).

Indeed, many political theorists have argued that urban environments are enmeshed with such hegemonic discourses as 'capitalism, rationalism, modernization, the Puritan work ethic, and spectacle' (Sadler 1998, 96). It's also important to take into account how contemporary capitalist society is related to democracy as well as to call into question how everyday life is becoming increasingly consumerized (Žižek 2011). These arguments have implications for the data-collection methods that psychologists typically use. Indeed, some critical psychologists[3] have argued that methods should not be viewed as a path to absolute truth and knowledge (Curt 1994). Some critical psychologists also argue that 'methodolatry serves the purpose of enabling psychologists to cast themselves as the role of architects of legitimate knowledge about "the science of behaviour" which is then "presented as an antidote to armchair psychology"' (Rogers et al. 1995, 226).

Such psychologists as Hodgetts et al. (2010) have stated that walking can be used as a useful way to study environments. What is problematic about the majority of psychological research is the rather sedentary nature of interview and observational methods (Sheller and Urry 2006). Writers such as Mimi Sheller and John Urry (2006) and Jane Hein Ricketts, James Evans and Phil Jones (2008) argue that researchers should carry out mobile ethnographic research, while Steve Brown and Kevin Durrheim argue that knowledge is always 'constructed in and through mobile interactivity' (2009, 916). Therefore, I argue that the production of knowledge should be created via interaction with environments as well as with others.

My approach requires taking a cross-disciplinary standpoint in doing psychogeographical work and drawing on arguments from critical psychology, cultural studies, urban theory and geography.[4] Moreover, in documenting a walking-based methodology, it is useful to draw on data collection procedures such as 'go-along' methods, walking, driving, cycling and photo-voice methods.[5] It is therefore crucial to consider the importance and application of mobile-methods research in relation to psychogeographical psychology research.[6]

'SITUATIONISM' IN AND AGAINST PSYCHOLOGY

I want to begin by considering the following definition of *psychogeography*: 'Psychogeography could set for itself the study of the precise law and specific effects of the geographical environment, consciously organised or not, on the emotions and behaviours of individuals' (Debord 1955). A limitation of environmental and social psychological research is that environments are meant to simply affect people's behaviours and attitudes. However, that argument assumes that human beings are simply affected by the outside world and that we are just animalistic organisms that respond to external stimuli. This is quite a reductionist account of human behaviour, and what I argue here is for a socially, culturally and politically embedded notion of human behaviour and experience. The majority of psychological research uses quite conventional and traditional methods of data collection, such as physiological measures of bodily responses, laboratory observational studies and interviews. These methods tend to shut out alternative explanations of behaviour and experience through restrictive techniques that reduce phenomena to that which can only be directly observed and measured in a 'scientific' manner.[7] Moreover, Debord (1955) alludes to the idea of how environments affect us 'consciously, or not.' This suggests that there are conscious as well as unconscious dynamic processes at play in relation to how we experience environments. To extend this point further, psychogeographical techniques and concepts, such as the dérive, détournement and negation, involve ludic and playful strategies. These concepts can be related to the idea of how 'chance encounters and uncanny resonances could disrupt dominant ways of seeing and potentially reveal the marvellous buried within the everyday' (Pinder 2005, 4). Chance here is more important than the psychological criteria of control.[8] A key focus here should be on how consumerism is manifested in the 'physical-emotional environment' (Miles 2010, 8).

DÉTOURNEMENT AND NEGATION

The Situationists argued that capitalist environments should be not just interpreted but also questioned and negated. Their analysis of environments was inherently radical because they wanted to get rid of capitalist societies, as they envisioned a noncapitalist world: 'The spectacle is not a collection of images; it is a social relation between people that is mediated by images' (Debord 1967). These arguments are quite different from the approach of mainstream experimental social psychologists and environmental psychologists, who are not concerned with changing the order of things and instead take a micro-apolitical focus for investigating the psychological effects of environments on people's well-beings, identities and behaviours.[9] Moreover, such psychological explanations assume that we can find out how people really feel about being in environments, that we can find out what the 'real' effects are of environments on people's behaviours, and that the effects of environments exist in a strictly causal and mechanistic manner.

If we turn to critical psychology, this then enables us to consider how we position ourselves as subjects in relation to the physical layout of environments. Moreover, we can use discursive theory to question and challenge the ways in which we experience and make sense of environments. In towns and cities, there are 'preferred' and dominant ways of how we can see, move through and use built environments. However, while discursive theory is useful for deconstructing and challenging the taken-for-granted assumptions of built environments, it is necessary to draw on the Situationist concept of détournement to provide alternative, noncapitalist accounts.

THE DÉRIVE

A useful definition of this term is:

> Dérives involve playful constructive behaviour and awareness of psychogeographical effects; thus they are quite different from the classic notions of journey or stroll. In a dérive, one or more persons during a certain period drop their relations, their work and leisure activities and all other usual motives for movement and action, and let themselves be drawn by the attractions of the terrain and the encounters they find there. Chance is a less important factor in this activity than one might think: from a dérive point of view, cities have psychogeo-

graphical contours, with constant currents, fixed points and vortexes that strongly encourage and discourage entry into or exit from certain zones. (Debord 1958)

Dérives are not commonly used in psychological research, as they do not fit within the standard repertoire of experimental methods. I want to begin here with problematizing the use of experiments in psychological research. The current repertoire of psychological methods has tended to reinforce government and social policy rather than provide a vocal critique and attempt to politically change the world. Guy Debord's (1958) reference to 'playful constructive behaviour' is important here in order to enforce the importance of a practice, which is more anarchic, creative and ludic than the supposedly scientific and rigorous methods typically used by psychologists. David Pinder, a radical geographer, argues, 'Experimental arts and modes of exploration can play a vital role in the development of critical approaches to the geographies of cities, where they may challenge norms about how urban space is framed and represented, and where they may help to open up other possibilities' (2005, 385). The majority of mainstream environmental psychology and social psychology research serves to close down multiple interpretations of environments and does not enable a radical critique of environments, nor really engage with the 'arts,' 'critical approaches to geography' or various 'modes of exploration' (ibid.).[10] However, this also begs the question of whether psychology can and should be an experimental arts-based discipline rather than a hard science, or whether it can be both. Guy Debord's (1958) definition of *dérive*, as discussed previously, alludes to psychogeography as being both a science and an arts-based practice.[11] Indeed, Debord also explains how one should be 'drawn by the attractions of the terrain,' which also implies that it may be useful to draw on psychoanalytic principles in order to discern how one can free-associate one's experiences in environments.[12]

METHODS, REFLEXIVITY AND DOING RESEARCH

Before I present how I conduct psychogeographical research, it is important to lay out my reflective position. I'm a young white male of mainly British origin with some Greek heritage. I position myself as a critical social psychologist, which means that I take seriously the idea of reflexivity as well as my standpoint as ultra-left-wing Situationist and anarchic. I draw affiliation with other critical and radical psychologists, such as Babak Fozooni, Ian Parker and radical intellectual groups such as the Loiterers Resistance Movement and Precarias a la Deriva. Such a position is unusual for psychology academics to take, mainly because most mainstream psychologists aspire to be objective and politically neutral in their research. Most mainstream psychologists do not consider the relations of their personal views with their ontological standpoint as researchers. This means that, when I 'read' environments, these are the lenses used. Built environments affect each of us, regardless of whether we are academics, and so it is of vital importance to produce critical research that considers the various social roles that we hold and what type of knowledge that we present (Hollway 2007). There is not much research in psychology that considers subjectivity in relation to how it can be spatialized in places. Therefore, I think it is useful to draw on the work of Luis Carlos Sotelo:

> Through the lens of participation cartography, I modify Michel de Certeau's . . . idea that by walking, space is being practiced. Instead I suggest, that by walking, subjectivity-in-action-in space is being practiced. . . . Rather than seeing walking as a spatial practice, I see it as a subjective, environmental and unfolding practice or as a performance of self in spatio-temporal terms. (2010, 61)

PREPARATIONS FOR WALKING

In previous dérives that I have conducted, I have drawn on Abdelhafid Khatib's (1958) very useful account of a dérive that he conducted in the Les Halles district of Paris, France. I have drawn on that paper to inform questions in my psychogeographical research. The following reflective questions should be considered when doing dérives; the last question here is important to consider in terms of using Situationist work to determine what future noncapitalist environments could look like:

- What are your experiences, and would you usually visit that environment on a regular basis?
- Do you find that there are any recognizable or distinctive sites in the environment visited, and, if so, what effects does the environment have?
- How would you enter and exit the environment visited? It's useful at these times to indicate the exit and entrance points and if there are any main channels of movement.
- How do you feel in the particular environment? Note that your experience is not meant to be representative of anyone else's experiences. You need to account for your personal response in a politically situated and informed manner.
- Do you notice any distinct changes in atmosphere?
- What types of social encounters can be observed?
- What do you find agreeable and disagreeable about the environment visited?
- How should the environment be changed?

My dérive research has largely focused on the themes of consumerism, privatization, surveillance and social control (Bridger 2014). In terms of choosing somewhere to do a dérive, I have in the past conducted site-specific investigations of such places as Ground Zero in New York (Bridger 2009) and the Arndale Centre in Manchester, United Kingdom (Bridger 2014). I have done so in order to explore the capitalist regeneration that has taken place after terrorist attacks as well as to consider other themes, such as surveillance, privacy, consumerism and safety. I have also conducted dérives with psychology undergraduate students at the University of Huddersfield to introduce them to psychogeographical research (Bridger 2013).

However, one does not have to choose somewhere to drift, as it can be done anywhere. Guy Debord (1958) stated that dérives could be either specific studies in particular locations or those undertaken in random locations.

I like to use quite an unstructured approach to doing dérive research, as this enables more of a free-associative approach to exploring one's affective responses to environments as well as imagines what future environments could look like. Free association as a psychoanalytic concept can be brought to life in environments via simple psychogeographical tactics, such as dice walks and map-swap exercises. There are many other tactics that could be discussed here, but these two methods I use most often in my psychogeographical work. Both of these methods work against the typically rationalist and supposedly empirical methods of experimental psychologists, such as Likert scale questionnaires and physiological measures of heart rates and galvanic skin responses. Turning 'research' into a playful game can hopefully enable us to question our routinized behaviours and how we make sense of environments in order to think creatively about new possibilities for what our towns and cities could look like. Therefore, in order to do a dice walk, one would replace the numbers on a dice with directional markers. For example, the number 1 on a dice could be replaced with an instruction, such as 'turn left' or 'go straight on.' Then one would use this dice in a location of one's choice. The first time I tried this method was a few years ago in Huddersfield (Bridger 2013), where I started in the town centre by the Kingsgate Shopping Centre main entrance. I used a large foam dice and rolled it onto the streets to determine the direction that I took on the walk. Doing this exercise meant that I did go to parts of the town that I would not ordinarily go to. One consequence of that walk was that it alerted me to what could be considered as socially perceived 'safe' and 'less safe' areas of Huddersfield. That particular dérive led me to develop key areas of concern in developing a feminist approach to psychogeographical research, including 'representing which areas of urban environments that men and women use; whether men and women feel safe or vulnerable in particular places; reflecting upon men and women's political experiences of

Figure 14.1.   Cartographers writing strange codes on the University of Huddersfield campus

places; how men and women navigate through public and private environments; and how men and women think about and experience social environments' (Bridger 2014, 294).

Another dérive tactic is to use a map of a different town or city to get from one location to another location. For example, you could choose a route from home to work and then use a map of a different city in order to plot a route. So you would have to choose locations on a map to indicate where you are and where you intend to arrive. Using dice and maps is meant to cause disorientation in how one would usually navigate a path through a town or city that may be quite familiar. The aims are to disrupt our 'orderly' behaviours through a subversive engagement with environments in order to open us up to new experiences. This is where free association is meant to come into play, because it is when we are open to how we experience environments that we can see things with 'fresh eyes' and create new configurations of space and place.

We must consider how one should document the sort of psychogeographical practice that I have so far outlined in this chapter. When on a dérive, I often take photographs and brief descriptive notes based on where I walk and what seems to relate to themes and research questions, like consumerism, privacy, surveillance and capitalism. Photographs are also useful for remembering the places that one has encountered while on a dérive. Photographs can likewise evoke one's subjective experiences of environments and be helpful for reflecting on the research process (Waitt, Gill and Head 2009). After doing a dérive, it is also useful to create artistic and reflective maps. In one psychogeographical study of Manchester city centre (Bridger 2011), I created a map to represent how I had walked around the Arndale shopping centre. I wanted to deemphasize the consumerist focus of that space and foreground the importance of political conflict with reference to the Peterloo Massacre of 1819. That map was indebted to Debord and Jorn's (1957) Naked City map, which highlighted the movement of people between different working-class districts within Paris. I drew on their use of large black arrows to indicate the movement of people through inner-city Paris and used large black arrows in my map.[13]

In previous accounts of dérives that I have written, I used a combination of first-person narrative voice interspersed with academic arguments from critical psychology, political theory and cultural geography; photography; and poetry. I have found the psychogeographical work of Situationist Abdelhafid Khatib (1958) and the work of narrative critical psychologists Burnett, Cudworth and Tamboukou (2004) to be most useful in formulating my approach to writing dérive reports. For those who are interested in reading more about some of the psychogeographical reports that I have produced, consult Bridger 2009, 2010, 2011, 2013 and 2014.

CONCLUSIONS AND IMPLICATIONS

Having outlined my ambivalent position in psychology in terms of psychogeographical research, I now present the following core questions that should be considered in such work:

- How do environments make us feel?
- What do we need to rearrange and change in our environments?
- What should environments of the future look like?
- What can psychogeographical research change?
- To what extent can such strategies as the dérive and détournement be used to create new understandings of environments?

I do not believe that there are clear and fixed answers to these questions, nor should there be. If revolutionary social change is to be led by 'the people,' then it is not possible to map out how that will occur. Revolution cannot and should not be designed or planned by academics, artists or experts, as that presumes that they have some 'expert' knowledge that the masses do not have. Revolution is something that occurs spontaneously and should be led by people. One thing we can do collectively for the time being is to try to think imaginatively about what we want our environments to look like, how we want to 'feel' in those places and what should be done to enable those changes to take place. It is my hope that future environments will look very different from the current capitalist and consumerist environments in European and other Western and non-Western countries.

It is important to consider the question of whether this research is 'radical.' Sadie Plant argued that 'radical academics provided the appearance of revolutionary critique while similarly reproducing the specialisations of knowledge and the lucrative elitism of their roles' (1992, 76). I argue here that one way to address this issue is to do research that cuts across academic, activist and artistic boundaries in order to call into question the neoliberal order of things. Indeed, much of my psychogeography work in groups has not been with academics but with activists, artists and anyone else who takes an interest in the changing form of cities and with themes of gentrification, consumerism and local history. I've found it particularly useful and interesting to talk about these ideas and themes with people from all walks of life and have engaged with many psychogeographers, photographers, journalists and historians over the years. Nonetheless, future work in this area should aim to engage more fully with people who feel disengaged from recent social regeneration programmes in such areas as East Manchester, Huddersfield and Bradford.

Ian Parker (2007) argues that, in order to change society, one must work 'in and against' social systems, institutions and structures. Furthermore, McKenzie Wark (2011) argued that the ideas and practices of the Situationists should be used as a template for new types of social engagement as a means to take over and occupy environments. I agree with arguments provided by *Guardian* journalist Madeleine Bunting (2011), who argued that public environments should be sites for 'conviviality, learning and participation' instead of 'working, transport and shopping.' I argue that the questions and themes that the Situationists discussed in the late 1950s and early 1960s are still relevant today. There is clearly a range of issues and questions that we need to take seriously in terms of conducting politicized analyses of environments in order to map out a new, alternative and noncapitalist order of things.

NOTES

1. Over the years I've met people who have really inspired me and who have contributed to my radical and political approach to psychogeography and critical psychology. I'd like to thank the following individuals and groups: Ian Parker, Guy Debord, Geoff Bunn, Karl Marx, Rebecca Lawthom, Raoul Vaneigem, Babak Fozooni, Lisa Blackman, Melancholic Troglodytes, Erica Burman, Michel Foucault, Morag Rose, Anton Vagus, Tina Richardson, Manchester Area Psychogeographic, Phil Smith, the Loiterers Resistance Movement and Samantha Barnsley. I'd also like to thank my lovely cats: Oscar, Emily and Charlotte.

2. What I argue for is a focus on understanding people's everyday lived experiences of environments (Ingold 1993). However, I do not wish to take a simpler phenomenological or existential approach to assuming that people's experiences of environments are simply reflected in their language. Instead, I argue that experience is suffused through various social, cultural and political discourses and that such accounts need to be understood and interpreted in the contexts in which such accounts are produced.

3. Critical psychologists include Curt (1994) and Rogers, Stenner, Gleeson and Rogers (1995).

4. Critical psychologists include Burnett, Cudworth and Tamboukou (2004); Grup de Lesbianes Feminstes (2005); and Precarias a la Deriva (2005). Cultural studies theorists include Pinder (1996, 2000, 2005). Urban theorists include Joyce (2003) and Sadler (1998). Geographers include Harley (1988a, 1988b, 1992) and Thrift (2000).

5. Go-along methodologies include walking, driving and cycling (Kusenbach 2003) and photo-voice methods (Hodgetts, Chamberlain and Groot 2011).

6. See Bridger (2009, 2010, 2011, 2013, 2014); Chamberlain et al. (2011); Hodgetts, Chamberlain and Groot (2011); Radley et al. (2010); and Hodgetts, Chamberlain and Radley (2007).

7. The difficulty of introducing psychogeographical ideas into psychology puts one in quite a marginalized position compared to supposedly more credible research, where scientific psychologists aim to measure and quantify people's attitudes and behaviours in relation to situations, others and environments.

8. However, I don't claim that meanings of environments can simply be 'found' in everyday life. What I do argue is that we should try to understand how our interactions with environments and others can produce particular types of knowledges.

9. I am quite wary of these psychologized explanations of environments, as such explanations tend to focus solely on behaviour and cognitions as if these things can be found in people's heads and observed via their behaviours.

10. I think it is useful to connect with Foucault's ([1969] 2002) arguments on deconstructing dominant discourses of space in order to explore the conditions of possibility for how the order of things could be.

11. I think his vague definition of that concept is deliberate because it is actually quite difficult to say whether walking and observation should be scientific and rigorous or if they should be artistic and playful.

12. What I argue for is a complete politicization of the built environment by drawing on the Situationist concept of the dérive in relation to psychoanalytic and discursive concepts as already discussed.

13. My core argument is that maps do not have to be objective representations of environments. We can actually subvert what a map is meant to 'do' and use maps to represent our personal and political responses to environments as well as to depict what we think our environments should look like.

BIBLIOGRAPHY

Bridger, Alexander John. 2009. 'September 11th 2001 and the Aftermath: Extending Visual Methods in Psychology.' PhD diss., Manchester Metropolitan University, UK.

———. 2010. 'Walking as a Radicalised Critical Psychological Method? A Review of Academic, Artistic and Activist Contributions to the Study of Social Environments.' *Social and Personality Psychology Compass* 4 (2): 131–39.

———. 2011. 'Psychogeography and the Study of Social Environments: Extending Visual Methodological Research in Psychology.' In *Visual Methods in Psychology: Using and Interpreting Images in Qualitative Research*, edited by Paula Reavey, 284–95. Hove: Psychology Press.

———. 2013. 'Visualising Manchester: Exploring New Ways to Study Urban Environments with Reference to Situationist Theory, the Dérive and Qualitative Research.' *Qualitative Research in Psychology* 11: 78–97.

———. 2014. 'Psychogeography and Feminist Methodology.' *Feminism and Psychology* 23 (3): 285–98.

Brown, S., and K. Durrheim. 2009. 'Different Kinds of Knowing: Generating Interview Data through Mobile Interviewing.' *Qualitative Interviewing* 15 (5): 911–30.

Bunting, Madeleine. 2011. 'Occupy London Is a Nursery for the Mind: The Alternatives the Occupy London Protestors Are Looking for Can't Be Written Up in a Google Doc.' *Guardian*, 30 October. Accessed 10 November 2011. http://www.guardian.co.uk/commentisfree/2011/oct/30/occupy-london-nursery-mind.

Burnett, Judith, Erica Cudworth, and Maria Tamboukou. 2004. 'Women on Dérive: Autobiographical Explorations of Lived Spaces.' In *Geography and Gender Reconsidered*, edited by Women and Geography Study Group. London: Women and Geography Study Group and Institute of British Geographers. CD-ROM.

Chamberlain, Kerry, Trudie Cain, Joanna Sheridan, and Ann Dupuis. 2011. 'Pluralisms in Qualitative Research: From Multiple Methods to Integrated Methods.' *Qualitative Research in Psychology* 8 (2): 151–69.

Curt, Beryl. 1994. *Textuality and Techtonics: Troubling Social and Psychological Science.* Buckingham: Open University Press.

Debord, Guy. 1955. 'Introduction to a Critique of Urban Geography.' Translated by Ken Knabb. *Situationist International.* Accessed 19 January 2006. http://www.cddc.vt.edu/sionline/presitu/geography.html.

———. 1958. 'Theory of the Dérive.' Translated by Ken Knabb. *Situationist International.* Accessed 15 September 2004. http://www.cddc.vt.edu/sionline/si/theory.html.

———. 1967. 'The Society of the Spectacle.' Edited by K. Knabb. Bureau of Public Secrets. Accessed 26 February 2015. http://www.bopsecrets.org/SI/debord/1.htm.

Debord, Guy, and Asger Jorn. 1957. 'The Naked City Map.' In *The Situationist City*, by Simon Sadler, 60. London: MIT Press.

Dixon, John, and Kevin Durrheim. 2000. 'Displacing Place-Identity: A Discursive Approach to Locating Self and Other.' *British Journal of Social Psychology* 39: 27–44.

Foucault, Michel. [1969] 2002. *The Order of Things*. London: Taylor and Francis.

Grup de Lesbianes Feministes. 2005. 'Exploring New Ways of Insubmission in Social Representation.' *Annual Review of Critical Psychology* 1 (4): 107–14.

Harley, John Brian. 1988a. 'Deconstructing the Map.' *Cartographica* 26: 1–20.

———. 1988b. 'Maps, Knowledge and Power.' In *The Iconography of Landscape*, edited by Denis Cosgrove and Stephen Daniels, 277–312. Cambridge: Cambridge University Press.

———. 1992. 'Deconstructing the Map.' In *Writing Worlds: Discourse, Text and Metaphor in the Representation of Landscape*, edited by Trevor Barnes and James Duncan, 231–47. London: Routledge.

Hayes, Graham. 2003. 'Walking the Streets: Psychology and the Flâneur.' *Annual Review of Critical Psychology* 1 (3): 50–66.

Hein, Jane Ricketts, James Evans, and Phil Jones. 2008. 'Mobile Methodologies: Theory, Technology and Practice.' *Geography Compass* 2 (5): 1266–85.

Hodgetts, Darrin, Kerry Chamberlain, and Shiloh Groot. 2011. 'Reflections on the Visual in Community Research and Action.' In *Visual Methods in Psychology: Using and Interpreting Images in Qualitative Research*, edited by Paula Reavey, 299–313. Hove: Psychology Press.

Hodgetts, Darrin, Kerry Chamberlain, and Alan Radley. 2007. 'Considering Photographs Never Taken During a Photo-Production Project.' *Qualitative Research in Psychology* 4 (4): 263–80.

Hodgetts, Darrin, Ottile Stolte, Kerry Chamberlain, Alan Radley, Shiloh Groot, and Linda Waimarie Nikora. 2010. 'The Mobile Hermit and the City: Considering Links between Places, Objects, and Identities in Social Psychological Research on Homelessness.' *British Journal of Social Psychology* 49: 285–303.

Hollway, Wendy. 2007. 'Methods and Knowledge in Social Psychology.' In *Social Psychology Matters*, edited by Wendy Hollway, Helen Lucey, Ann Phoenix, and Gail Lewis, 59–91. Milton Keynes: Open University Press.

Ingold, Tim. 1993. 'The Temporality of the Landscape.' *World Archaeology* 25 (2): 152–74.

Joyce, Patrick. 2003. *The Rule of Freedom: Liberalism and the Modern City*. London: Verso.

Khatib, Abdelhafid. 1958. 'Attempt at a Psychogeographical Description of Les Halles.' *Situationist International*. Accessed 22 September 2004. http://www.cddc.vt.edu/sionline/si/leshalles.html.

Kusenbach, Margarethe. 2003. 'Street Phenomenology: The Go-Along as Ethnographic Research Tool.' *Ethnography* 4 (3): 455–85.

Miles, Stephen. 2010. *Spaces for Consumption*. Thousand Oaks, CA: Sage.

Parker, Ian. 2007. *Revolution in Psychology: From Alienation to Emancipation*. London: Pluto Press.

Pinder, David. 1996. 'Subverting Cartography: The Situationists and Maps of the City.' *Environment and Planning A* 28: 405–27.

———. 2000. 'Old Paris Is No More: Geographies of Spectacle and Anti-Spectacle.' *Antipode* 32 (4): 357–86.

———. 2005. *Visions of the City: Utopianism, Power and Politics in Twentieth Century Urbanism*. Edinburgh: Edinburgh University Press.

Plant, Sadie. 1992. *The Most Radical Gesture: The Situationist International in a Post-Modern Age*. London: Routledge.

Precarias a la Deriva. 2005. 'Housewives, Maids, Cleaning Ladies and Caregivers in General: Care in the Communication Continuum.' *Annual Review of Critical Psychology* 1 (4): 188–98.

Radley, Alan, Kerry Chamberlain, Darrin Hodgetts, Otille Stolte, and Shiloh Groot. 2010. 'From Means to Occasion: Walking in the Life of Homeless People.' *Visual Studies* 25 (1): 36–45.

Rogers, R. Stainton, Paul Stenner, Kate Gleeson, and Wendy Stainton Rogers. 1995. *Social Psychology: A Critical Agenda*. London: Polity Press.

Sadler, Simon. 1998. *The Situationist City*. Cambridge, MA: MIT Press.

Sheller, Mimi, and John Urry. 2006. 'The New Mobilities Paradigm.' *Environment and Planning A* 38 (2): 207–26.

Sotelo, Luis Carlos. 2010. 'Looking Backwards to Walk Forward: Walking Collective Memory and the Site of Intercultural in Site-Specific Performance.' *Performance Research* 15 (4): 59–69.

Thrift, Nigel. 2000. 'Still Life in Nearly Present Time: The Object of Nature.' *Body and Society* 6: 34–57.

Vaneigem, Raoul. 1967. *The Revolution of Everyday Life*. Translated by John Fullerton and Paul Sieveking. Nothingness: The Library. Accessed 22 September 2004. http://library.nothingness.org/articles/SI/ed/pub_contents/5.

Waitt, Gordon, Nicholas Gill, and Lesley Head. 2009. 'Walking Practice and Suburban Nature-Talk.' *Social and Cultural Geography* 10 (1): 41–60.

Wark, McKenzie. 2011. *The Beach beneath the Street: The Everyday Life and Glorious Times of the Situationist International*. London: Verso.

Žižek, Slavoj. 2011. 'Democracy Is the Enemy.' *London Review of Books* Blog. Accessed 11 May 2013. http://lrb.co.uk/blog/2011/10/28/slavoj-zizek/democracy-is-the-enemy.

Conclusion

The New Psychogeography

Tina Richardson

RESURGENCE AND REVIVAL

In an interview in *Fortean Times* in 2002, Iain Sinclair was asked what his involvement was in the revival of psychogeography during the 1990s. He replied, 'In a classic sense I don't think I had anything to do with it. But the whole term has been dusted down and reinvented and re-used by people like Stewart Home and the London Psychogeographical Association' (cited in Pilkington and Baker 2002, 3). Of this period in psychogeography, Sinclair explained that 'there was a kind of strategy to this rebranding, I was quite happy to run with it as a franchise, as a way of talking about doing the things I'd always done and providing a useful description that could be discussed in public. It became a bit of a monster on the back of that' (ibid.). He went on to explain that, by the time he was using the term, it was 'more like a psychotic geographer . . . a raging bull journey against the energies of the city' (ibid.).

At this point of writing, in the second decade of the twenty-first century and well over ten years after Sinclair's comments, what has psychogeography become? And, is the current resurgence just a continuation of the one Sinclair mentions (the one of the London Psychogeographical Association), or has it morphed into something else?[1] James D. Sidaway says of human geography and its related fields that 'increasing attention is being dedicated to the social relations of emotion and action under the label of "affect"' (2009, 1092). If there is a current focus on the affective response to space, then this could be connected to what is called *placiality* (Casey 2013). Postmodern space has become so complex in its palimpsest form that our reaction to it has reached a kind of critical mass whereby we feel compelled to attempt to articulate our response to the terrain. This is also reflected in cultural theory on space and place of the late twentieth century (such as that of Lefebvre 1991 and Bachelard 1994), as discussed by Stephen Hardy in 'Placiality: The Renewal of the Significance of Place in Modern Cultural Theory' (2000). In 1984, Michel Foucault stated, 'The present epoch will perhaps be above all the epoch of space' (2001, 237), but of today's epoch we can confidently say that it is one of 'place.' The concept of place is now finding its way into popular and everyday vocabulary. In December 2014, a BBC Radio 4 programme entitled *Sense of Place* was broadcast. It included an interview with Joanne Parker (see Tillotson 2014), who, on the concept of place, said, '[O]ne person's place is very much another person's space. . . . [L]andscape is first and foremost a way of creating belongingness and tying us together.'

Writing at the same time as Sidaway, Bonnett says, 'British psychogeography should be understood as a site of struggle over the politics of loss within radical imagination' (2009, 46). Our desire not only to explore the social history of a particular space but also to express it in a personal and affective way that responds to the aesthetics of that place as it is for us is one that comes about through description via our imaginations, an individual expression that is different for everyone—in other words, a psychogeographically articulated response. Bonnett (2013) says a 'much broader group of people are now interested and involved in psychogeography, many of whom have no interest in the Situationists. It may be argued that this is a form of depolitization or that psychogeography has outgrown the limited and exclusionary world of the revolutionary avant-garde.' If this is the case, then the sharing of psychogeographical accounts from whatever perspective (activist or otherwise) has been enabled through contemporary technology, with websites, blogs and social networking, and aided by new 'geo apps.'

Global positioning systems (GPS) and geographic information systems (GIS) have granted individuals access to data and aided them in creating representations of space and place in a totally different way, as the hobby of geocaching attests to. (Geocaching involves individuals locating secreted packages, with clues to their locations loaded online, via GPS.) Even navigating the Internet itself has been compared to exploring urban space (see 'Psychogeography, *Détournement*, Cyberspace' by Amy J. Elias [2010]).[2] Often appearing under the umbrella of neogeography, the use of the Internet and mobile technologies opens up space for groups and individuals and enables them to readily share the products of their walks. For example, OpenStreetMap is open-source software by the OpenStreetMap Foundation and a collaboration by its contributors, providing free geographical data and mapping. Anyone can contribute by signing up online. The data of routes walked can be picked up using GPS software on a smartphone and then made into maps and freely shared.[3]

This digital and satellite way of creating maps enables a synthesis with the older peripatetic method of simply talking and writing about walks. It allows psychogeographers to include more tools for tracking their walks, presenting their information and making it available for others to access. These maps and forms of data collection show the infinite possibility of cartographies and ways for walkers to present personal and qualitative information. They offer a large degree of control of the mapping process to the user and cartographer. The open-source software that is often used for these types of collaborations to a large extent disengages the data from capitalist production and, hence, provides more freedom of expression, production and distribution. This enables their use in explorations of space, creating mapping-oriented art for pleasure or for a variety of community-based projects.

The current resurgence in walking has coincided with a renewed interest in cartography encouraged by the availability of digital tools. While these tools are often used by nonspecialists in community and arts-based projects, the contemporary psychogeographer is at once embracing and critical of the new technology, preferring to use it as one tool among many for creating, recording and producing output from the dérive.

In *The View from the Train: Cities and Other Landscapes*, Keiller says that the current revival in the United Kingdom is very much Situationist-oriented and connected to the desire to explore the urban landscape with such tools as the dérive (2013, 133). While this seems to counter what Bonnet says, this may have more to do with a matter of perspective. Both seem to be occurring, separately and simultaneously. The objectives for walking are overdetermined. Some groups and individuals are interested in the process and practice of the dérive-type walk and are not politically oriented. Others are attempting an activist pursuit on differing scales. And some, even though they are not overtly interventionist, nevertheless will be intervening in the space as a side effect of what their other intentions might be.

The wish to explore one's town or city also extends to organized walks that probably would not come under the rubric of psychogeography but nevertheless express a flourishing of a generalized interest in the urban: 'Urban walking is now promoted as a leisure pursuit, with posses of rambling groups herded on to sanctioned routes and heritage trails that double as cycle highways' (Rogers 2013, 79). If the current revival is a separate one from that which occurred in the 1990s, then we might look to the economic crisis beginning in 2008 as having at least some degree of responsibility in fuelling interest in urban space as one of the areas affected by neoliberal policy. Political crises spur an interest in economic change on the street level, as can be seen in the early 1990s (see the Poll Tax Riots circa 1990). The recent loss of public houses and local suburban libraries are just two examples of how our urban locale is directly affected by 'austerity.' Both examples have generated the forming of pressure groups to challenge government policy. Also, many vacant lots lie in a transitional state on the edges of towns and cities, awaiting development. These brownfield sites are often explored under the umbrella of 'edgelands,' which are 'characterised by rubbish tips and warehouses, superstores and derelict industrial plant, office parks and gypsy encampments, golf courses, allotments and fragmented, frequently scruffy, farmland' (Shoard 2002, 117). This 'rurban fringe' (Coleman 1976) is both liminal and interstitial and is a measure of the financial value of space. Rather like a barometer, it fluctuates to reflect the economic status of a town or city.

There is also now more public engagement with regard to the gentrification of the high street than there was just ten years ago. In towns and cities, gentrification highlights a shift in a demographic to that of a wealthier resident and to more expensive retail outlets. Signifying a migration of richer individuals in and poorer individuals out of a particular region, it often results in local people being unable to buy property in areas where they may have grown up and also have existing family. On a sociopolitical level, gentrification ties class and consumption together, and urban walkers from the activist strand of psychogeography might explore this under the rubric of the spectacle.

The physical layout of the land, while having always been of interest to psychogeographers and geographers alike, appears to be reflected in a recent interest in cartography (digital or otherwise) by people who might be unconnected to either of these fields. For example, Katherine Harmon's *You Are Here: Personal Geographies and Other Maps of the Imagination* (2003) is a book full of beautiful maps through the ages and would interest anyone inside or outside the field, as would her other book *The Map as Art: Contemporary Artists Explore Cartography* (2010). Karen O'Rourke says in *Walking and Mapping: Artists as Cartographers*, 'Today the convergence of global networks, online databases, and new tools for location-based mapping coincides with a renewed interest in walking as an art form' (2013, xvii). And Bonnett's *Off the Map: Lost Spaces, Invisible Cities, Forgotten Islands, Feral Places and What They Tell Us about the World* (2014), while written by a geographer, is readily accessible to anyone interested in marginal, hidden and overlooked spaces.

Phil Baker explains that it is the cognitive-type maps that are the ones that appeal to psychogeographers: 'Psychogeography is not interested in "objective" panoptical mapping, but only in the private cognitive maps of our customized cities' (2003, 324). This is also expressed by psychogeographer Roy Bayfield when he says, 'Walking the territory redraws the map' (2009). The paths taken by critical urban walkers—whether psychogeographers, artists or performance practitioners—become a re-reading and rewriting of the landscape, forming what could be called 'temporary autonomous zones' (Bey 2011), spaces that can be momentarily diverted from their intended use. The creation of temporary autonomous zones is an underlying theme within contemporary psychogeography, and whether you are walking as a single psychogeographer or in a group carrying out participatory interventions, the territory is momentarily de- and reterritorialized.

THE PSYCHOGEOGRAPHICAL TURN

Attempting to define something as 'new' that has not appeared out of a distinct break from the past is beset with problems. In academic theory, the tendency is to use the word *turn* (*linguistic turn, spatial turn* and so on). I would prefer to describe the current movement in psychogeography as more like a gentle bend in the road. I see the motifs under discussion here as representing leanings rather than seeing them as a clearly defined set of criteria about what something is and what something is not. This is not a radical break. There are qualities of contemporary urban walking that are Situationist in the same way that there are similarities with the 1990s resurgence of psychogeography. An epoch of any kind does not end one day and the next day begin with a whole new set of different or opposing themes, as can be seen when discussing modernity 'versus' postmodernity within the framework of cultural epochs. They bleed into each other, but they also contain distinctions that respond to their cultural (politico-social) moment in time.

It could be argued that not enough time has lapsed to look at how and why today's psychogeography is different from that of the 1990s. A lack of critical distance might mean it is not possible to state what today's urban walking is in concrete terms. Labelling it in any way could be foolhardy. However, starting a dialogue about the changes that are taking place is important in a book about contemporary psychogeography. I also appreciate that attempts to define it can be thought to go against what psychogeography represents (labelling, constricting, limiting). Nevertheless, many of my own discussions in recent years with those in and out of the field and those I have read in journal articles or online blogs demonstrate that there is a general consensus that a revival is taking place. If this is the case, we need to consider what form this psychogeography might take and why, not least because we should think about how it can be used productively in a changing historical, political and cultural milieu.

While psychogeography groups are not new, whether activist or arts-based, there has been an effort directed toward community projects in the twenty-first century. In Britain, both Dougald Hine and John Rogers have used psychogeography in relation to urban planning. While a visiting fellow in higher education policy at the University of Lincoln, Hine worked on the Scarcity and Creativity in the Built Environment (SCIBE) project. SCIBE looks at how design affects the built environment and the various actors who inhabit it. Part of Hine's work with SCIBE included a dérive in Bow in East London, which was inspired by the Situationists. Rogers's project—Remapping High Wycombe (2005–2006)—was carried out with Cathy Rogers (his sister and an artist). They remapped the area before it became changed forever by the Wycombe Regeneration Project and produced both a hard-copy and an online booklet based on their work. Each project recognizes the changing environment and acknowledges its effects on the individuals who are living and working there. These types of psychogeographical projects are organized, strategic, critical and collaborative and represent how groups can work with public agencies (such as town planners and architects) and other stakeholders in the urban environment.

In the United States, Christina Ray—cofounder of Psy-Geo-Conflux and the Conflux Festival in New York (a psychogeography arts-based annual festival)—uses site- and street-based performance strategies to explore the built environment. She employs social networking, digital media and product design in order to work with businesses and other organizations in this field. Using psychogeography in tactical ways can often involve what at one time may have been seen as 'sleeping with the enemy' (as it would have been for the Situationists). However, in these instances, psychogeography can be seen as forming a bridge between what might be viewed as dialectically opposing groups: an urban community versus town planners or property developers. Also, arts-based collectives, inspired by groups like Conflux, are doing street-level work as a form of intervention that reclaims the city for its citizens. On a much smaller scale to Conflux, in the United Kingdom, psychogeography groups such as the Leeds Psychogeography Group and the Loiterers Resistance Movement in Manchester organize walks as a way of showing how the city can be rewritten by those participating, whether they are psychogeographers, artists or interested local people who are not related to either of these fields. Also, the German group of artists called the Urbe-Berlin project in 2012 carried out psychogeographical investigations in Mexico using both analogue and digital methods to explore the history of space through acoustics. This represents the collaborative nature that psychogeography can take in its most cross-cultural form.

David Pinder discussed the rise of urban exploration in the work of artists and practitioners. The themes he explored were centred around 'rights to the city' and 'writing the city.' He says, 'Part of its appeal has been the way it apparently renounces the centred, the panoptic and the hierarchical. It provides a means of engaging with urban spaces and experiences in ways that move beyond specialized arenas, whether those of art or academic institutions' (2005, 402).

THE MATTER OF POSITIONS

The idea of rewriting and remapping urban space has taken hold at a time when communicating with each other has never been easier (aided by the Internet and social networking). This has coincided with a geopolitical moment when people are aware they have a stake in a city that is diminishing before their eyes. The differing groups and alternative strategies that come under the umbrella of psychogeography today, more than at any other time, are making available psychogeographical tools to fellow urbanites in order to help them in expressing their subjective response to living and working in and moving about the city. Psychogeography-related events and projects—even if they are not overtly activist or even described as psychogeography—enable a re/connection with a material space that is always potentially under threat of being renegotiated into private or prohibited space.

This connection to the concrete space of our towns and cities reflects a desire to offer a material and archaeological critique that excavates the signs contained in the terrain that might be contrary to the dominant discourse (something that could be placed within the term *schizocartography*). It often involves an exploration of the social history of a space that may exist below the surface and might not be obvious on a cursory viewing. The study of material culture helps reveal social boundaries—and the very 'matter' under critique by psychogeographers is urban space itself. The current resurgence in psychogeography ties in to the recent 'material turn' mooted by Dan Hicks and Mary C. Beaudry (2010). The archaeological angle I am suggesting does not necessarily involve the process of physical excavation that may be implied by the term. However, it does involve the research and, often, archival exploration required to reveal historical signs of the past hidden in space and also the necessary physical enactment of placing one's body in the terrain in order to read the signs therein.

The issue of matter ties in well with the concept of the dialectical in regard to phenomenon. While viewing urban space through the window of your house or from a coffee shop in town, you can be forgiven for seeing such binaries as inside/outside, mind/matter and natural/man-made. But a conscious form of walking brings these oppositions into a different focus whereby they become constructs that are overridden through one's very movement through the space itself (you only have to pull back on a Google satellite map to see how scale makes the concept of inside/outside irrelevant in urban space). And believing you can walk through the city distinguishing the natural from the man-made in any clearly definable way is a fruitless task, if not an interesting one to attempt as a psychogeographical exercise. As the urban walker, you become part of the very landscape you are scrutinizing. You are the biological material connecting to the concrete matter of urban space. Also, the physical process of perambulation, of touching the ground with your feet and moving through space, makes the action itself a material one. The somatic response to the act of walking forms a feedback loop and creates a relationship to the space that can engage the walker in powerful ways. Rebecca Solnit summarizes it thus: '[T]he body and mind can work together, so that thinking becomes almost a physical, rhythmic act' and 'each walk moves through space like a thread through fabric, sewing it together into a continuous experience' (2002, xv). The actual act of walking deconstructs any concept of oppositions and is described by Solnit in an intertextual way similar to how Roland Barthes describes 'the Text' of a specific type of literary writing, it being open and heterogeneous—woven: 'The plural of the Text depends, that is, not on the ambiguity of its contents but on what might be called the *stereographic plurality* of its weave of signifiers (etymologically, the text is a tissue, a woven fabric)' (1977, 159). What makes for a particularly interesting reference to the woven fabric by Barthes is that he continues the passage by using walking to explain the Text further: 'The reader of the Text may be compared to someone at a loose end (someone slackened off from any imaginary); this passable empty subject strolls . . . on the side of a valley' and 'what he perceives is multiple, irreducible, coming from a disconnected, heterogeneous variety of substances and perspectives' (ibid.).

What these quotes of Barthes and Solnit demonstrate are that the psychogeographical experience is immersive, processual and nondialectical. Today's urban walking is not about 'the gaze.' The walker is both the subject and the object, is seen and seeing. Even though it can be scopophilic, as a contemporary psychogeographer, it is incumbent on one to consider scenarios when this might be problematic. Having carried out some psychogeographical work in the Holbeck area of Leeds, which involved walking around the terraced houses of local working-class people and taking photos, I found it important to question one's place in this setting, especially from the perspective of someone who would be considered middle class. I wrote up this account in the blog post 'The Scopophilic Psychogeographer and the Other-as-Exhibition.' Included is a full paragraph because it seems to be a subject that does not appear much in psychogeographical writings:

> My problem is not new in the field of ethnography (not that that is my field) or in any field when one is observing another group where there may be issues relating to power in regards to representation in sociopolitical life. This has a long history in relation to the postcolonial other, so there is much written about it, especially in cultural theory. My own concern is with regards to my own practice, that of psychogeography. . . . What troubles me is that while psychogeography is a psychological response to urban space that takes in all the senses, being a psychogeographer can be a very scopophilic pursuit (the love of looking). And while this isn't an issue most of the time, in certain situations it does feel like it is. I don't mean that I am a scientist observing another culture in an anthropological sense, but that I am in someone else's space, observing it, photographing it, and commenting upon it. And there are more than just ethics involved in the process of observing 'ethnoscapes' (Arjun Appadurai). (Richardson 2012)

While I did not photograph people in Holbeck, I did take photos of discarded items and decaying urban decor, which were later presented in a blog available for everyone on the Internet to view. Even though this is not on the same level as the invasion of space that occurred in Victorian times, when Henry Mayhew's photos were misused by the bourgeoisie, it is a serious consideration for psychogeographers when doing research. It is important that the very act of walking and carrying out research does not situate the other as subaltern. And while it might be difficult to find a satisfactory solution to this problem, articulating the concerns as part of the practice one is carrying out goes some way toward raising it as an issue. Part of what makes up the qualities of the new psychogeography is that it is neither touristic nor colonial.

It is also in this way that urban walking theory today promotes other psychogeographies and challenges the historical stereotype of the masculine walker whose aim is to dominate the space around him. Many contributions in this volume attest to the variety of feminist psychogeographies that are prevalent today. When picturing the singular walker in urban space, we could be excused for seeing it as a man. In 'The Solitary Stroller and the City' in *Wanderlust*, Solnit describes this classical character by invoking the poems of Joseph Addison ('Trivia, or the Art of Walking the Streets of London,' 1716) and Dr. Johnson ('London,' 1738). She goes on to say that at this time '[f]ew women other than prostitutes were free to wander the streets and that wandering the street was often enough to cause a woman to be considered a prostitute' (2002, 181).

We need to take into consideration that both the character of the urban walker and those representing this character through literary works were historically generally men. However, the turn of the twentieth century brings us what could be the first modernist fictional female psychogeographer in the character of Miriam, the protagonist of Dorothy Miller Richardson's *The Tunnel* (1919). Writing in a stream-of-consciousness style like that of Virginia Woolf, Richardson depicts Miriam walking the streets of London as a way of adjusting to her internal journey. Eventually, for Miriam, the two spaces—urban and psychological—become inextricably linked: 'She would be again soon . . . not a woman . . . a Londoner' (Richardson 1919, 284). Also, in regard to the strong literary background of psychogeography, I would suggest that today it is becoming something other than singularly literary. And it has been the intention of this book to bring the literary field and the academic one together in a shared space. While writing is an established method for representing urban walking, today the multiple forms of representation that are now available make for a new psychogeography that might be described as post-Sinclairian.[4]

There is a label that is often used within psychogeography to describe the British psychogeographers located in Greater London: 'The London Psychogeographers.' While this is not a derogatory term directed at them, it is not helpful even if it does represent how psychogeography sees itself. There is an implication that there are the London psychogeographers—then everyone else.[5] The rest of us are unlabelled: Are we 'the other' of psychogeography that this hierarchy/binary implies? Nevertheless, quite probably aided by the advent of blogging, other psycho/geographical concentrations are now well represented in the United Kingdom. This is one of the qualities of contemporary psychogeography: Psychogeography is becoming less London-centric, and at the same time, and perhaps because of this, there is also a move away from the pathos attached to some of the more nostalgic London-based psychogeographical accounts.

MINDFUL WALKING

It is apparent from the contents of this volume that psychogeography (especially that of the Situationists) has been and continues to be critically assessed. It is also the case that ethnographic walking practices are not an uncommon subject of study in academia, although they are not necessarily classified as psychogeography, and they have not been included here because they are well represented elsewhere. However, this volume demonstrates that psychogeography can be rigorous when applied methodologically, and it can also be aligned with relevant theories in order to be used to explore urban space by those inside and outside academia. The chapters included represent the diversity of psychogeographical writings, from the perspective of not only the voices expressed from within psychogeography but also those that are being represented through the texts themselves. The new psychogeography is, first and foremost, one of heterogeneity. It is not exclusive, closed, snobbish or protectionist.

I appreciate that the term *the new psychogeography* might be problematic for a number of reasons, the academicization of psychogeography being one of them. Because we are located in academia, what is the solution (also, is this a 'text book' on psychogeography)? However, I believe that the work represented here that is not by academics, along with the fact that most of the academics writing in this book are actually practitioners themselves, attests to the objective behind the book as endeavouring to raise the profile of psychogeography within academia, introducing the work of literary psychogeographers to a new audience and opening up discussions on psychogeography, especially with its detractors. As for the possible fetishization of psychogeography in describing it as 'new,' a discussion of this concept could make for a whole thesis in and of itself. However, a mooted label that describes the currents in the stream of a field that is already quite likely undervalued would be difficult to describe as fetishist. Also, the new psychogeography is certainly not displaced in the context of this book, nor does it propose any form of sublimation in regard to decontextualizing the theory from the practice itself. In fact, one of its main intentions is to encourage people to participate.

Perhaps the most engaging thing about psychogeography, or even urban walking in its broadest sense, is that anyone can do it. Because most British residents live in urban space, 82.4 percent as of the 2011 census (Department for Environment, Food and Rural Affairs 2013, 1), all we have to do is open the door and step into it.[6]

Even if one does not carry out the walk in any critical way, simply thinking about the physical act of walking, and the somatic sensation of thoughtfully connecting oneself with the ground, turns the walk into something entirely different from a regular stroll. This form of mindful walking can be adopted in any moment that one might walk in the normal course of the day or week. In order to turn your walk into something that is more psychogeographical, you do not have to adopt the activist strategies of the UrbExers or even the Situationists. You can start by just asking yourself how a particular piece of urban decor got to be placed where it is or why the pavement-to-road ratio might be the size it is. Your walk has then become a form of critical psychogeography. When you set out on a walk with this approach, there is also a sense of anticipation of the possibilities that may appear as the fruit of the labour of your walk: 'These sites, come upon by accident, prick our imagination, provoke reverie' (Sinclair 2009, 5). And you do not have to be an academic, a theorist, a researcher or a writer to be a psychogeographer. You are not even required to have your own blog. Call it psychogeography. Don't call it psychogeography. Walk. Don't walk. Either way, the 'franchise' endures.

NOTES

1. An online article in June 2014 on *The Quietus*, '"A Living Memory": Iain Sinclair on Life at 70,' describes the term *psychogeography* as having 'threatened to become an albatross around his neck' (Burrows 2014).

2. The flexibility of psychogeography enables it to be extended into many fields, such as tourism, as can be seen in Charles McIntyre's book *Tourism and Retail: The Psychogeography of Liminal Consumption* (2012).

3. For those who are interested in technology and its uses in psychogeography, the geographer and psychogeographer Tim Waters provides examples of his own work in this field on his blog at www.thinkwhere.wordpress.com.

4. This is not a slur on Sinclair or his works (see the introduction to this book) but based on a conversation he and I had. When inviting him to contribute to this volume, he said he felt that psychogeography was moving on and he did not have too much more to add to it in a theoretical sense. He felt a new group of psychogeographers should 'pick up the mantle.'

5. I had a discussion with a London-based psychogeographer friend whose blog and Twitter title were named after the area he lived in. He then moved to the south coast, so his online name became irrelevant to his practice and had to be changed.

6. I appreciate that this does not necessarily apply to individuals who cannot walk or are less able to. However, the very ground of urban space is easier to walk on, and often to access, than rural space. So wheelchairs and buggies (the pram type and the ones for the elderly) are better equipped to cope with urban rather than rural space. As part of a psychogeography collaboration I undertook on the British seaside (Reading

the Arcades/Reading the Promenades), I borrowed a mobility scooter and carried out a psychogeographical expedition on the promenade of Hunstanton in Norfolk so as to appreciate my fieldwork from this alternative perspective.

BIBLIOGRAPHY

Bachelard, Gaston. 1994. *The Poetics of Space: The Classic Look at How We Experience Intimate Places*. Translated by Maria Jolas. Boston: Beacon Press.

Baker, Phil. 2003. 'Secret City: Psychogeography and the End of London.' In *London: From Punk to Blair*, edited by Joe and Andrew Gibson Kerr, 323–33. London: Reaktion Books.

Barthes, Roland. 1977. *Image Music Text*. Translated by Stephen Heath. London: Fontana Press.

Bayfield, Roy. 2009. 'Destination: Argleton! Visiting an Imaginary Place.' Walking Home to 50. Accessed 12 August 2014. https://walkinghometo50.wordpress.com/2009/02/22/destination-argleton-visiting-an-imaginary-place.

Bey, Hakim. 2011. *TAZ: The Temporary Autonomous Zone, Ontological Anarchy, Poetic Terrorism*. New York: Autonomedia.

Bonnett, Alastair. 2009. 'The Dilemmas of Radical Nostalgia in British Psychogeography.' *Theory, Culture and Society* 26 (1): 45–70.

———. 2013. 'Psychogeography.' Oxford Bibliographies Online: Geography. Accessed 27 February 2015. http://www.oxfordbibliographies.com/view/document/obo-9780199874002/obo-9780199874002-0020.xml.

———. 2014. *Off the Map: Lost Spaces, Invisible Cities, Forgotten Islands, Feral Places and What They Tell Us about the World*. London: Aurum Press.

Burrows, Tim. 2014. '"A Living Memory": Iain Sinclair on Life at 70.' *The Quietus*. Accessed 13 August 2014. http://thequietus.com/articles/15457-iain-sinclair-interview-2.

Casey, Edward S. 2013. *The Fate of Place: A Philosophical History*. Berkeley: University of California Press.

Coleman, Alice. 1976. 'Is Planning Really Necessary?' *Geographical Journal* 142 (3): 411–30.

Department for Environment, Food and Rural Affairs. 2013. 'Rural Population and Migration.' Gov.uk. Accessed 20 August 2014. https://www.gov.uk/government/publications/rural-population-and-migration.

Elias, Amy J. 2010. 'Psychogeography, *Détournement*, Cyberspace.' *New Literary History* 41 (4): 821–45.

Foucault, Michel. 2001. 'Of Other Spaces.' In *The Visual Culture Reader*, edited by Nicholas Mirzoeff, 237–44. London: Routledge.

Hardy, Stephen. 2000. 'Placiality: The Renewal of the Significance of Place in Modern Cultural Theory.' *Brno Studies in English* 26 (25): 1211–1791.

Harmon, Katherine. 2003. *You Are Here: Personal Geographies and Other Maps of the Imagination*. New York: Princeton Architectural Press.

———. 2010. *The Map as Art: Contemporary Artists Explore Cartography*. New York: Princeton Architectural Press.

Hicks, Dan, and Mary C. Beaudry. 2010. *The Oxford Handbook of Material Culture Studies*. Oxford: Oxford University Press.

Keiller, Patrick. 2013. *The View from the Train: Cities and Other Landscapes*. London: Verso, 2013.

Lefebvre, Henri. 1991. *The Production of Space*. Translated by Donald Nicholson-Smith. Oxford: Blackwell.

McIntyre, Charles. 2012. *Tourism and Retail: The Psychogeography of Liminal Consumption*. London: Routledge.

O'Rourke, Karen. 2013. *Walking and Mapping: Artists as Cartographers*. Cambridge: MIT Press.

Pilkington, Mark, and Phil Baker. 2002. 'City Brain.' *Fortean Times*. Accessed 21 August 2014. http://www.forteantimes.com/features/interviews/37/iain_sinclair.html.

Pinder, David. 2005. 'Arts of Urban Exploration.' *Cultural Geographies* 12: 383–411.

Richardson, Dorothy Miller. 1919. *The Tunnel*. London: Forgotten Books.

Richardson, Tina. 2012. 'The Scopophilic Psychogeographer and the Other-as-Exhibition.' Particulations. Accessed 21 August 2014. http://particulations.blogspot.co.uk/2012/07/the-scopophilic-psychogeographer-and.html.

Rogers, John. 2013. 'Rambling: Escape the Grid.' *The New Statesman*, 79.

Shoard, Marion. 2002. 'Edgelands.' In *Remaking the Landscape: The Changing Face of Britain*, edited by Jennifer Jenkins, 117–46. London: Profile Books.

Sidaway, James D. 2009. 'Shadows on the Path: Negotiating Geopolitics on an Urban Section of Britain's South West Coast Path.' *Environment and Planning D* 27: 1091–1116.

Sinclair, Iain. 2009. 'A World You Never Knew Existed.' *Secret Britain*, April, 4–6.

Solnit, Rebecca. 2002. *Wanderlust: A History of Walking*. London: Verso.

Tillotson, Simon, prod. 2014. 'Sense of Place.' BBC Radio 4. http://www.bbc.co.uk/programmes/b04vk6kr.

Index

About the Contributors

Roy Bayfield is director of corporate communications at Edge Hill University, where his responsibilities range from marketing the institution to animating its arts and culture activities. His psychogeographical exploration of the nonexistent Google-town of 'Argleton' has received international media exposure. Bayfield's book *Bypass Pilgrim* (2010) deals with the lived experience of the 'unhealthy body' in the context of walking.

Luke Bennett is a senior lecturer in the Department of the Natural and Built Environment at Sheffield Hallam University. Formerly a solicitor, Bennett now teaches built-environment law and researches professional and enthusiast engagements with urban ruins and wastelands. He has written a great deal about amateur bunker hunters and blogs about being a lawyer trapped inside the body of a psychogeographer at http://lukebennett13.wordpress.com.

Alastair Bonnett is a professor of social geography in the School of Geography, Politics and Sociology, Newcastle University. His most recent book is *The Geography of Nostalgia: Local and Global Perspectives on the Power of Loss* (2015).

Alexander John Bridger is a senior lecturer in psychology and counseling at the University of Huddersfield. He has written and spoken about psychogeography in various arenas, including academic journals, blogs, conferences and other public events. He continues to be involved in various psychogeography groups and activities in the North of England and has recently become interested in ludic war gaming.

Andrea Capstick leads the MSc dementia studies programme at the University of Bradford and has research interests in the use of creative and participatory methods with people with dementia. Her recent study on participatory filmmaking in long-term social care was supported by a grant from the National Institute for Health Research School for Social Care Research.

Christopher Collier is a PhD candidate at the School of Philosophy and Art History, University of Essex, examining psychogeography's reemergence in the United Kingdom during the 1990s, particularly in relation to activist practices. While he has published on the topic in a number of books and journals, his research also occasionally leads him in what might be described as more 'psychogeographical' directions.

Merlin Coverley is the author five books: *London Writing* (2005), *Psychogeography* (2006), *Occult London* (2008), *Utopia* (2010) and *The Art of Wandering: The Writer as Walker* (2012). He lives in London.

Victoria Henshaw worked in town planning before returning to academia, where she was a lecturer in urban design and planning in the Department of Town and Regional Planning at the University of Sheffield. Her psychogeographical specialism was in the area of sensory perception. Henshaw's chapter is published posthumously following her untimely death in 2014.

Ian Marchant is a lecturer, writer, performer and broadcaster. In addition to two novels, he has written three travel memoirs: *Parallel Lines* (2004), *The Longest Crawl* (2007) and *Something of the Night* (2013). Marchant came to the attention of Britain's psychogeographical community after he made and broadcast 'Walking with Attitude' for BBC Radio 3.

Gareth E. Rees is the author of *Marshland* (2013). His essays and fiction appear in *Mount London: Ascents In the Vertical City* (2014), *Acquired for Development By: A Hackney Anthology* (2012) and the spoken-word album *A Dream Life of Hackney Marshes* (2013). He currently runs the website Unofficial Britain (http://www.unofficialbritain.com).

Tina Richardson is an academic, writer/editor and lecturer in psychogeography and urban aesthetics. Her background is in the field of urban cultural studies. She has had a number of articles published, for example, in *Spaces and Flows* and *disClosure*. In 2013 she self-published her first book, *Concrete, Crows and Calluses*. Tina is well known in urban walking circles for developing her own psychogeographical method and practice called schizocartography.

Morag Rose is researching her PhD on feminist psychogeographies at the University of Sheffield Department of Town and Regional Planning. She also curates monthly dérives, exhibitions, events and campaigns with the Loiterers Resistance Movement in Manchester.

Phil Smith (Crab Man, Mytho) is a performer, writer and researcher. His books include *On Walking* (2014), *Enchanted Things* (2014), *Counter-Tourism* (2012), *A Sardine Street Box of Tricks* (with Simon Persighetti; 2010) and *Mythogeography* (2010), and he has contributed to *Walking, Writing and*

Performance (2009). He is a member of Wrights & Sites and associate professor (reader) at Plymouth University.

Phil Wood describes himself as an urban therapist. He works on a freelance basis with towns and cities around the world, helping them find deep or hidden resources with which to negotiate the challenges of change. He is the author of *The Intercultural City: Planning for Diversity Advantage* (with Charles Landry; 2007). More on him and his work can be found at www.philwood.eu.

Printed in Great Britain
by Amazon